# enVision Mathematics

## Common Core

### Volume 2 Topics 8–16

## Authors

**Randall I. Charles**
Professor Emeritus
Department of Mathematics
San Jose State University
San Jose, California

**Jennifer Bay-Williams**
Professor of Mathematics
Education
College of Education and Human
Development
University of Louisville
Louisville, Kentucky

**Robert Q. Berry, III**
Professor of Mathematics
Education
Department of Curriculum,
Instruction and Special Education
University of Virginia
Charlottesville, Virginia

**Janet H. Caldwell**
Professor Emerita
Department of Mathematics
Rowan University
Glassboro, New Jersey

**Zachary Champagne**
Assistant in Research
Florida Center for Research in
Science, Technology, Engineering,
and Mathematics (FCR-STEM)
Jacksonville, Florida

**Juanita Copley**
Professor Emerita
College of Education
University of Houston
Houston, Texas

**Warren Crown**
Professor Emeritus of Mathematics
Education
Graduate School of Education
Rutgers University
New Brunswick, New Jersey

**Francis (Skip) Fennell**
Professor Emeritus of
Education and Graduate and
Professional Studies
McDaniel College
Westminster, Maryland

**Karen Karp**
Professor of Mathematics Education
School of Education
Johns Hopkins University
Baltimore, Maryland

**Stuart J. Murphy**
Visual Learning Specialist
Boston, Massachusetts

**Jane F. Schielack**
Professor Emerita
Department of Mathematics
Texas A&M University
College Station, Texas

**Jennifer M. Suh**
Associate Professor for
Mathematics Education
George Mason University
Fairfax, Virginia

**Jonathan A. Wray**
Mathematics Supervisor
Howard County Public Schools
Ellicott City, Maryland

## SAVVAS

LEARNING COMPANY

## Mathematicians

**Roger Howe**
Professor of Mathematics
Yale University
New Haven, Connecticut

**Gary Lippman**
Professor of Mathematics and
Computer Science
California State University, East Bay
Hayward, California

## ELL Consultants

**Janice R. Corona**
Independent Education Consultant
Dallas, Texas

**Jim Cummins**
Professor
The University of Toronto
Toronto, Canada

## Reviewers

**Katina Arnold**
Teacher
Liberty Public School District
Kansas City, Missouri

**Christy Bennett**
Elementary Math and Science
Specialist
DeSoto County Schools
Hernando, Mississippi

**Shauna Bostick**
Elementary Math Specialist
Lee County School District
Tupelo, Mississippi

**Samantha Brant**
Teacher
Platte County School District
Platte City, Missouri

**Jamie Clark**
Elementary Math Coach
Allegany County Public Schools
Cumberland, Maryland

**Shauna Gardner**
Math and Science Instructional Coach
DeSoto County Schools
Hernando, Mississippi

**Kathy Graham**
Educational Consultant
Twin Falls, Idaho

**Andrea Hamilton**
K-5 Math Specialist
Lake Forest School District
Felton, Delaware

**Susan Hankins**
Instructional Coach
Tupelo Public School District
Tupelo, Mississippi

**Barb Jamison**
Teacher
Excelsior Springs School District
Excelsior Springs, Missouri

**Pam Jones**
Elementary Math Coach
Lake Region School District
Bridgton, Maine

**Sherri Kane**
Secondary Mathematics
Curriculum Specialist
Lee's Summit R7 School District
Lee's Summit, Missouri

**Jessica Leonard**
ESOL Teacher
Volusia County Schools
DeLand, Florida

**Jill K. Milton**
Elementary Math Coordinator
Norwood Public Schools
Norwood, Massachusetts

**Jamie Pickett**
Teacher
Platte County School District
Kansas City, Missouri

**Mandy Schall**
Math Coach
Allegany County Public Schools
Cumberland, Maryland

**Marjorie Stevens**
Math Consultant
Utica Community Schools
Shelby Township, Michigan

**Shyree Stevenson**
ELL Teacher
Penns Grove-Carneys Point
Regional School District
Penns Grove, New Jersey

**Kayla Stone**
Teacher
Excelsior Springs School District
Excelsior Springs, Missouri

**Sara Sultan**
PD Academic Trainer, Math
Tucson Unified School District
Tucson, Arizona

**Angela Waltrup**
Elementary Math Content Specialist
Washington County Public Schools
Hagerstown, Maryland

ISBN-13:   978-0-13-495476-9
ISBN-10:     0-13-495476-9

9 2022

# Digital Resources

You'll be using these digital resources throughout the year!

## Go to SavvasRealize.com

 **Interactive Student Edition**
Access online or offline.

 **Interactive Additional Practice Workbook**
Access online or offline.

 **Videos**
Watch Math Practices Animations, Another Look Videos, and clips to support 3-Act Math.

**Math Tools**
Explore math with digital tools.

 **Glossary**
Read and listen in English and Spanish.

 **Visual Learning**
Interact with visual learning animations.

 **Activity**
Solve a problem and share your thinking.

 **Practice Buddy**
Do interactive practice online.

 **Games**
Play math games to help you learn.

 **Assessment**
Show what you've learned.

**SAVVAS realize™** Everything you need for math anytime, anywhere

# Contents

**Digital Resources at SavvasRealize.com**

And remember your Interactive Student Edition is available at SavvasRealize.com!

## TOPICS

Properties, such as the Commutative Property, can help you to add and subtract.

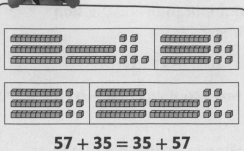

$$57 + 35 = 35 + 57$$

# TOPIC 8 Use Strategies and Properties to Add and Subtract

When you add by place value, you add the hundreds, the tens, and the ones.

$$
\begin{array}{r}
243 \\
+\ 179 \\
\hline
12 \\
110 \\
+\ 300 \\
\hline
422
\end{array}
$$

# TOPIC 9 Fluently Add and Subtract within 1,000

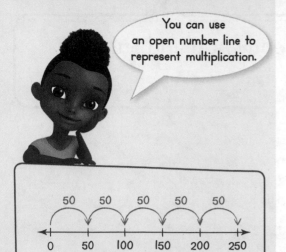

You can use an open number line to represent multiplication.

# TOPIC 10 Multiply by Multiples of 10

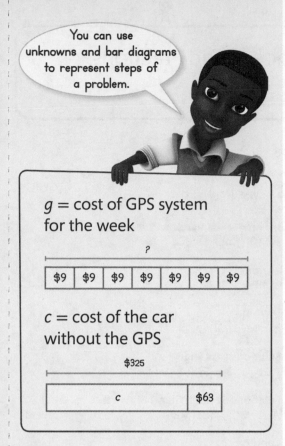

You can use unknowns and bar diagrams to represent steps of a problem.

$g$ = cost of GPS system for the week

| ? | | | | | | |
|---|---|---|---|---|---|---|
| $9 | $9 | $9 | $9 | $9 | $9 | $9 |

$c$ = cost of the car without the GPS

$325

| c | $63 |
|---|---|

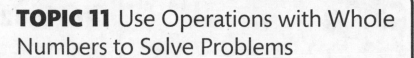

# TOPIC 11 Use Operations with Whole Numbers to Solve Problems

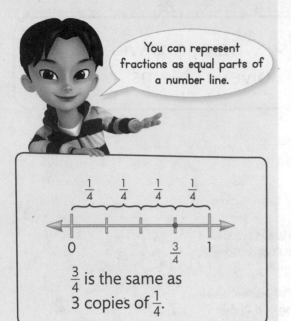

You can represent fractions as equal parts of a number line.

$\frac{1}{4}$  $\frac{1}{4}$  $\frac{1}{4}$  $\frac{1}{4}$

0        $\frac{3}{4}$    1

$\frac{3}{4}$ is the same as 3 copies of $\frac{1}{4}$.

# TOPIC 12 Understand Fractions as Numbers

You can use fraction strips to compare fractions.

$$\frac{5}{8} < \frac{5}{6}$$

# TOPIC 13 Fraction Equivalence and Comparison

You can use a number line to represent elapsed time.

# **TOPIC 14** Solve Time, Capacity, and Mass Problems

# Math Practices and Problem Solving Handbook

The **Math Practices and Problem Solving Handbook** is available at SavvasRealize.com.

**Math Practices**

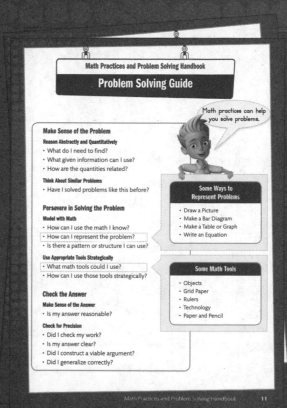

**Problem Solving Guide**
**Problem Solving Recording Sheet**
**Bar Diagrams**

A quadrilateral is a polygon with four sides. These are different quadrilaterals.

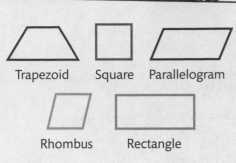

Trapezoid   Square   Parallelogram

Rhombus   Rectangle

# TOPIC 15 Attributes of Two-Dimensional Shapes

You can find the perimeter of a shape by adding the lengths of its sides.

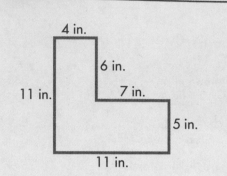

4 + 6 + 7 + 5 + 11 + 11 = 44

The perimeter of the shape is 44 inches.

# TOPIC 16 Solve Perimeter Problems

# Grade 3 Common Core Standards

Dear Families,

The standards on the following pages describe the math that students will learn this year.

## DOMAIN 3.OA
## OPERATIONS AND ALGEBRAIC THINKING

### MAJOR CLUSTER 3.OA.A
**Represent and solve problems involving multiplication and division.**

**3.OA.A.1** Interpret products of whole numbers, e.g., interpret $5 \times 7$ as the total number of objects in 5 groups of 7 objects each. *For example, describe a context in which a total number of objects can be expressed as $5 \times 7$.*

**3.OA.A.2** Interpret whole-number quotients of whole numbers, e.g., interpret $56 \div 8$ as the number of objects in each share when 56 objects are partitioned equally into 8 shares, or as a number of shares when 56 objects are partitioned into equal shares of 8 objects each. *For example, describe a context in which a number of shares or a number of groups can be expressed as $56 \div 8$.*

**3.OA.A.3** Use multiplication and division within 100 to solve word problems in situations involving equal groups, arrays, and measurement quantities, e.g., by using drawings and equations with a symbol for the unknown number to represent the problem.

**3.OA.A.4** Determine the unknown whole number in a multiplication or division equation relating three whole numbers. *For example, determine the unknown number that makes the equation true in each of the equations $8 \times ? = 48$, $5 = \square \div 3$, $6 \times 6 = ?$.*

---

### MAJOR CLUSTER 3.OA.B
**Understand properties of multiplication and the relationship between multiplication and division.**

**3.OA.B.5** Apply properties of operations as strategies to multiply and divide.[1] *Examples: If $6 \times 4 = 24$ is known, then $4 \times 6 = 24$ is also known. (Commutative property of multiplication.) $3 \times 5 \times 2$ can be found by $3 \times 5 = 15$, then $15 \times 2 = 30$, or by $5 \times 2 = 10$, then $3 \times 10 = 30$. (Associative property of multiplication.) Knowing that $8 \times 5 = 40$ and $8 \times 2 = 16$, one can find $8 \times 7$ as $8 \times (5 + 2) = (8 \times 5) + (8 \times 2) = 40 + 16 = 56$. (Distributive property.)*

**3.OA.B.6** Understand division as an unknown-factor problem. *For example, find $32 \div 8$ by finding the number that makes 32 when multiplied by 8.*

---

[1]Students need not use formal terms for these properties.

# Common Core Standards

## MAJOR CLUSTER 3.OA.C
**Multiply and divide within 100.**

**3.OA.C.7** Fluently multiply and divide within 100, using strategies such as the relationship between multiplication and division (e.g., knowing that $8 \times 5 = 40$, one knows $40 \div 5 = 8$) or properties of operations. By the end of Grade 3, know from memory all products of two one-digit numbers.

## MAJOR CLUSTER 3.OA.D
**Solve problems involving the four operations, and identify and explain patterns in arithmetic.**

**3.OA.D.8** Solve two-step word problems using the four operations. Represent these problems using equations with a letter standing for the unknown quantity. Assess the reasonableness of answers using mental computation and estimation strategies including rounding.[2]

**3.OA.D.9** Identify arithmetic patterns (including patterns in the addition table or multiplication table), and explain them using properties of operations. *For example, observe that 4 times a number is always even, and explain why 4 times a number can be decomposed into two equal addends.*

## DOMAIN 3.NBT
## NUMBER AND OPERATIONS IN BASE TEN

### ADDITIONAL CLUSTER 3.NBT.A
**Use place value understanding and properties of operations to perform multi-digit arithmetic.[3]**

**3.NBT.A.1** Use place value understanding to round whole numbers to the nearest 10 or 100.

**3.NBT.A.2** Fluently add and subtract within 1000 using strategies and algorithms based on place value, properties of operations, and/or the relationship between addition and subtraction.

**3.NBT.A.3** Multiply one-digit whole numbers by multiples of 10 in the range 10–90 (e.g., $9 \times 80$, $5 \times 60$) using strategies based on place value and properties of operations.

## DOMAIN 3.NF
## NUMBER AND OPERATIONS–FRACTIONS[4]

### MAJOR CLUSTER 3.NF.A
**Develop understanding of fractions as numbers.**

**3.NF.A.1** Understand a fraction $\frac{1}{b}$ as the quantity formed by 1 part when a whole is partitioned into $b$ equal parts; understand a fraction $\frac{a}{b}$ as the quantity formed by $a$ parts of size $\frac{1}{b}$.

**3.NF.A.2** Understand a fraction as a number on the number line; represent fractions on a number line diagram.

**3.NF.A.2a** Represent a fraction $\frac{1}{b}$ on a number line diagram by defining the interval from 0 to 1 as the whole and partitioning it into $b$ equal parts. Recognize that each part has size $\frac{1}{b}$ and that the endpoint of the part based at 0 locates the number $\frac{1}{b}$ on the number line.

**3.NF.A.2b** Represent a fraction $\frac{a}{b}$ on a number line diagram by marking off $a$ lengths $\frac{1}{b}$ from 0. Recognize that the resulting interval has size $\frac{a}{b}$ and that its endpoint locates the number $\frac{a}{b}$ on the number line.

**3.NF.A.3** Explain equivalence of fractions in special cases, and compare fractions by reasoning about their size.

**3.NF.A.3a** Understand two fractions as equivalent (equal) if they are the same size, or the same point on a number line.

**3.NF.A.3b** Recognize and generate simple equivalent fractions, (e.g., $\frac{1}{2} = \frac{2}{4}$, $\frac{4}{6} = \frac{2}{3}$). Explain why the fractions are equivalent, e.g., by using a visual fraction model.

**3.NF.A.3c** Express whole numbers as fractions, and recognize fractions that are equivalent to whole numbers. *Examples: Express 3 in the form $3 = \frac{3}{1}$; recognize that $\frac{6}{1} = 6$; locate $\frac{4}{4}$ and 1 at the same point of a number line diagram.*

**3.NF.A.3d** Compare two fractions with the same numerator or the same denominator by reasoning about their size. Recognize that comparisons are valid only when the two fractions refer to the same whole. Record the results of comparisons with the symbols >, =, or <, and justify the conclusions, e.g., by using a visual fraction model.

---

[2]This standard is limited to problems posed with whole numbers and having whole-number answers; students should know how to perform operations in the conventional order when there are no parentheses to specify a particular order (Order of Operations).

[3]A range of algorithms may be used.

[4]Grade 3 expectations in this domain are limited to fractions with denominators 2, 3, 4, 6, and 8.

# Common Core Standards

## DOMAIN 3.MD
## MEASUREMENT AND DATA

### MAJOR CLUSTER 3.MD.A
**Solve problems involving measurements and estimation of intervals of time, liquid volumes, and masses of objects.**

**3.MD.A.1** Tell and write time to the nearest minute and measure time intervals in minutes. Solve word problems involving addition and subtraction of time intervals in minutes, e.g., by representing the problem on a number line diagram.

**3.MD.A.2** Measure and estimate liquid volumes and masses of objects using standard units of grams (g), kilograms (kg), and liters (l).[5] Add, subtract, multiply, or divide to solve one-step word problems involving masses or volumes that are given in the same units, e.g., by using drawings (such as a beaker with a measurement scale) to represent the problem.[6]

### SUPPORTING CLUSTER 3.MD.B
**Represent and interpret data.**

**3.MD.B.3** Draw a scaled picture graph and a scaled bar graph to represent a data set with several categories. Solve one- and two-step "how many more" and "how many less" problems using information presented in scaled bar graphs. *For example, draw a bar graph in which each square in the bar graph might represent 5 pets.*

**3.MD.B.4** Generate measurement data by measuring lengths using rulers marked with halves and fourths of an inch. Show the data by making a line plot, where the horizontal scale is marked off in appropriate units—whole numbers, halves, or quarters.

### MAJOR CLUSTER 3.MD.C
**Geometric measurement: understand concepts of area and relate area to multiplication and to addition.**

**3.MD.C.5** Recognize area as an attribute of plane figures and understand concepts of area measurement.

**3.MD.C.5a** A square with side length 1 unit, called "a unit square," is said to have "one square unit" of area, and can be used to measure area.

**3.MD.C.5b** A plane figure which can be covered without gaps or overlaps by $n$ unit squares is said to have an area of $n$ square units.

**3.MD.C.6** Measure areas by counting unit squares (square cm, square m, square in, square ft, and improvised units).

**3.MD.C.7** Relate area to the operations of multiplication and addition.

**3.MD.C.7a** Find the area of a rectangle with whole-number side lengths by tiling it, and show that the area is the same as would be found by multiplying the side lengths.

**3.MD.C.7b** Multiply side lengths to find areas of rectangles with whole-number side lengths in the context of solving real world and mathematical problems, and represent whole-number products as rectangular areas in mathematical reasoning.

**3.MD.C.7c** Use tiling to show in a concrete case that the area of a rectangle with whole-number side lengths $a$ and $b + c$ is the sum of $a \times b$ and $a \times c$. Use area models to represent the distributive property in mathematical reasoning.

**3.MD.C.7d** Recognize area as additive. Find areas of rectilinear figures by decomposing them into non-overlapping rectangles and adding the areas of the non-overlapping parts, applying this technique to solve real world problems.

### ADDITIONAL CLUSTER 3.MD.D
**Geometric measurement: recognize perimeter as an attribute of plane figures and distinguish between linear and area measures.**

**3.MD.D.8** Solve real world and mathematical problems involving perimeters of polygons, including finding the perimeter given the side lengths, finding an unknown side length, and exhibiting rectangles with the same perimeter and different areas or with the same area and different perimeters.

[5]Excludes compound units such as $cm^3$ and finding the geometric volume of a container.

[6]Excludes multiplicative comparison problems (problems involving notions of "times as much").

# Common Core Standards

## DOMAIN 3.G
## GEOMETRY

### SUPPORTING CLUSTER 3.G.A
**Reason with shapes and their attributes.**

**3.G.A.1** Understand that shapes in different categories (e.g., rhombuses, rectangles, and others) may share attributes (e.g., having four sides), and that the shared attributes can define a larger category (e.g., quadrilaterals). Recognize rhombuses, rectangles, and squares as examples of quadrilaterals, and draw examples of quadrilaterals that do not belong to any of these subcategories.

**3.G.A.2** Partition shapes into parts with equal areas. Express the area of each part as a unit fraction of the whole. *For example, partition a shape into 4 parts with equal area, and describe the area of each part as $\frac{1}{4}$ of the area of the shape.*

## MATHEMATICAL PRACTICES

**MP.1** Make sense of problems and persevere in solving them.

**MP.2** Reason abstractly and quantitatively.

**MP.3** Construct viable arguments and critique the reasoning of others.

**MP.4** Model with mathematics.

**MP.5** Use appropriate tools strategically.

**MP.6** Attend to precision.

**MP.7** Look for and make use of structure.

**MP.8** Look for and express regularity in repeated reasoning.

# Use Strategies and Properties to Add and Subtract

**Essential Question:** How can sums and differences be estimated and found mentally?

**Digital Resources**

Interactive Student Edition  Activity  Visual Learning  Video  Practice

Assessment  Games  Tools  Glossary

The fur of an arctic fox changes color during the year.

In the winter, an arctic fox has white fur. During the summer, it can have gray or brown fur.

Where something lives can affect its traits. Here's a project on plant and animal traits and the environment.

## enVision STEM Project: Traits and the Environment

**Do Research** Use the Internet or other sources to find out how the environment can influence plants or animals. Describe a trait in an animal or plant that can change due to the environment.

**Journal: Write a Report** Include what you found. Also in your report:

- Make a table that includes the plant or animal, the trait, and changes in the environment. Record any related data about the environment, such as temperature or rainfall.

- Include information about why the trait is useful.

- Write and solve addition problems using your data. Use estimation to check for reasonableness.

Name _____

# Review What You Know

**Vocabulary**

Choose the best term from the box.
Write it on the blank.

| |
|---|
| • difference • number line |
| • equation • sum |

1. The amount that is left after you subtract is the *differ.* _____.

2. A line that shows numbers in order from left to right is a(n) _____.

3. The total when you add is the _____.

4. Both sides of a(n) _____ are equal.

## Addition and Subtraction Strategies

Find the sum or difference. Show your work.

**5.** 32 + 58

**6.** 27 + 46

**7.** 73 − 52

**8.** 63 + 16

**9.** 88 − 28

**10.** 76 − 49

## Numerical Expressions

**11.** Atif puts 45 rocks in a display box. He has 54 rocks in all.
Which expression can be used to find how many rocks
are not in the display box?

ⓐ 45 + 54     ⓑ 45 + 45     ⓒ 54 − 45     ⓓ 54 − 54

## Counting Money

**12.** Tony has the coins shown at the right. Does he have
enough money to buy a toy car that costs 86¢? Explain.

Name_____

**PROJECT 8A**

### How much citrus is grown in Florida?

**Project:** Plan a Citrus Grove

**PROJECT 8B**

### Would you like to travel across the country?

**Project:** Create and Perform Skits

## PROJECT 8C

### How can you add and subtract large numbers without a calculator?

**Project:** Make a Mental Math Game

## PROJECT 8D

### How many people live in our country?

**Project:** Design a Class Census and Give an Estimation Test

Name_____

Activity

**Solve & Share**

Olivia arranges cups of buttons on three trays. She records the number of buttons on each cup. Which tray has the most buttons? Use place-value blocks or drawings to help solve the problem.

**I can ...**
use place value and properties to understand addition.

© **Content Standards** 3.NBT.A.2 Also 3.OA.D.8
**Mathematical Practices** MP.1, MP.7

Are you making the same calculations more than once? How can you use structure to help solve the problem?

**Tray A**

**Tray B**

**Tray C**

**Look Back!** Olivia pours all the buttons on Tray A into a bowl. She then divides the buttons equally into 8 cups. How many buttons are in each cup? Explain.

**Essential Question**

# What Are Some Properties of Addition?

**A**

*You can use properties of addition to join groups.*

Parentheses show what to do first.

**Associative (Grouping) Property of Addition:** You can group addends in any way and the sum will be the same.

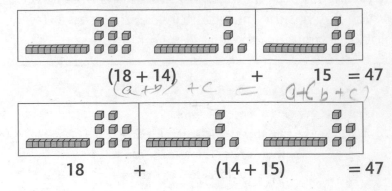

$$(18 + 14) + 15 = 47$$
$$(a + b) + c = a + (b + c)$$

$$18 + (14 + 15) = 47$$

$$(18 + 14) + 15 = 18 + (14 + 15)$$

**B** **Commutative (Order) Property of Addition:** You can add numbers in any order and the sum will be the same.

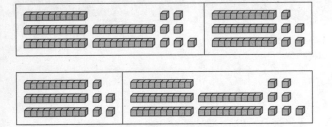

$$57 + 35 = 35 + 57$$
$$a + b = b + c$$

**C** **Identity (Zero) Property of Addition:** The sum of zero and any number is that same number.

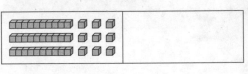

$$39 + 0 = 39$$

**Convince Me!** **Use Structure** Pick one of the properties above. Explain how you can use a number line to show an example of that property.

Name_____

## Solve & Share

Shade three sums that are next to each other on the addition table. Add the first and third sums you shaded. Find a pattern using that total and the second sum you shaded. How are the total and the second sum related? Is this true for other sets of three sums next to each other?

**I can ...**
find and explain addition patterns.

© **Content Standard** 3.OA.D.9
**Mathematical Practices** MP.7, MP.8

| + | 10 | 11 | 12 | 13 | 14 | 15 | 16 | 17 | 18 | 19 |
|----|----|----|----|----|----|----|----|----|----|----|
| 20 | 30 | 31 | 32 | 33 | 34 | 35 | 36 | 37 | 38 | 39 |
| 21 | 31 | 32 | 33 | 34 | 35 | 36 | 37 | 38 | 39 | 40 |
| 22 | 32 | 33 | 34 | 35 | 36 | 37 | 38 | 39 | 40 | 41 |
| 23 | 33 | 34 | 35 | 36 | 37 | 38 | 39 | 40 | 41 | 42 |
| 24 | 34 | 35 | 36 | 37 | 38 | 39 | 40 | 41 | 42 | 43 |
| 25 | 35 | 36 | 37 | 38 | 39 | 40 | 41 | 42 | 43 | 44 |
| 26 | 36 | 37 | 38 | 39 | 40 | 41 | 42 | 43 | 44 | 45 |
| 27 | 37 | 38 | 39 | 40 | 41 | 42 | 43 | 44 | 45 | 46 |
| 28 | 38 | 39 | 40 | 41 | 42 | 43 | 44 | 45 | 46 | 47 |
| 29 | 39 | 40 | 41 | 42 | 43 | 44 | 45 | 46 | 47 | 48 |

These are addends.

These are sums.

You can look for relationships in the addition table. The numbers in the shaded column and shaded row are addends. The other numbers are the sums.

**Look Back!** Explain how you can test to see if the relationship among the three sums that are next to each other is a pattern.

**Essential Question** **How Can You Find Addition Patterns?**

**A**

Helen found the sum of the purple numbers in the red square. Then she found the sum of the green numbers. The sums form a pattern. Find the sums and describe the pattern.

You can use a variety of strategies to find the sums!

| +  | 30 | 31 | 32 | 33 | 34 | 35 | 36 | 37 | 38 | 39 |
|----|----|----|----|----|----|----|----|----|----|----|
| 10 | 40 | 41 | 42 | 43 | **44** | 45 | **46** | 47 | 48 | 49 |
| 11 | 41 | 42 | 43 | 44 | 45 | 46 | 47 | 48 | 49 | 50 |
| 12 | 42 | 43 | 44 | 45 | **46** | 47 | **48** | 49 | 50 | 51 |
| 13 | 43 | 44 | 45 | 46 | 47 | 48 | 49 | 50 | 51 | 52 |
| 14 | 44 | 45 | 46 | 47 | 48 | 49 | 50 | 51 | 52 | 53 |
| 15 | 45 | 46 | 47 | 48 | 49 | 50 | 51 | 52 | 53 | 54 |
| 16 | 46 | 47 | 48 | 49 | 50 | 51 | 52 | 53 | 54 | 55 |
| 17 | 47 | 48 | 49 | 50 | 51 | 52 | 53 | 54 | 55 | 56 |
| 18 | 48 | 49 | 50 | 51 | 52 | 53 | 54 | 55 | 56 | 57 |
| 19 | 49 | 50 | 51 | 52 | 53 | 54 | 55 | 56 | 57 | 58 |

**B** Use the Associative Property.

$$44 + 48 = 44 + (2 + 46)$$
$$= (44 + 2) + 46$$
$$= 46 + 46$$

$$44 + 48 = 46 + 46$$

The sum of the purple numbers is equal to the sum of the green numbers. That's a pattern!

**C** Use mental math.

$$44 + 48 = (44 + 2) + (48 - 2)$$
$$= 46 + 46$$

$$44 + 48 = 46 + 46$$

**D** Use the Commutative and Associative Properties.

$$44 + 48 = (10 + 34) + (12 + 36)$$
$$46 + 46 = (12 + 34) + (10 + 36)$$

Use the properties to rearrange the addends.

$$(10 + 34) + (12 + 36) =$$
$$(10 + 34) + (12 + 36)$$

The sum of the purple numbers is 92.
The sum of the green numbers is 92.

The sums are double the middle number in the red square. That is another pattern.

**Convince Me! Generalize** The red square above is 3 squares tall by 3 squares wide. Sebastian says there are other size squares in the addition table that have patterns. Describe a different-size square and its patterns.

Name _____

# ☆ Guided Practice

## Do You Understand?

**1.** Are the sums of any two sets of diagonal corner numbers in a 3-by-3 square in a standard addition table always equal? Explain.

## Do You Know How?

**2.** Look at the addition table in Box A on the previous page. Why do the numbers going down to the right on the diagonal increase by 2? Explain.

# Independent Practice ☆

In **3** and **4**, use the table at the right.

**3.** Look at the sums that are shaded the same color. Describe a pattern shown by these pairs of sums. Explain why this pattern is true.

| +  | 20 | 21 | 22 | 23 | 24 | 25 | 26 | 27 |
|----|----|----|----|----|----|----|----|----|
| 20 | 40 | 41 | 42 | 43 | 44 | 45 | 46 | 47 |
| 21 | 41 | 42 | 43 | 44 | 45 | 46 | 47 | 48 |
| 22 | 42 | 43 | 44 | 45 | 46 | 47 | 48 | 49 |
| 23 | 43 | 44 | 45 | 46 | 47 | 48 | 49 | 50 |
| 24 | 44 | 45 | 46 | 47 | 48 | 49 | 50 | 51 |
| 25 | 45 | 46 | 47 | 48 | 49 | 50 | 51 | 52 |
| 26 | 46 | 47 | 48 | 49 | 50 | 51 | 52 | 53 |
| 27 | 47 | 48 | 49 | 50 | 51 | 52 | 53 | 54 |

**4.** Find other pairs of sums with a similar pattern. Shade them on the table. Explain why you chose those sums.

In **5** and **6**, use the table at the right.

**5.** Shade the table to show a pattern you see. Describe your pattern.

| +  | 20 | 21 | 22 | 23 | 24 | 25 | 26 | 27 |
|----|----|----|----|----|----|----|----|----|
| 44 | 64 | 65 | 66 | 67 | 68 | 69 | 70 | 71 |
| 45 | 65 | 66 | 67 | 68 | 69 | 70 | 71 | 72 |
| 46 | 66 | 67 | 68 | 69 | 70 | 71 | 72 | 73 |
| 47 | 67 | 68 | 69 | 70 | 71 | 72 | 73 | 74 |
| 48 | 68 | 69 | 70 | 71 | 72 | 73 | 74 | 75 |
| 49 | 69 | 70 | 71 | 72 | 73 | 74 | 75 | 76 |

**6.** Explain why your pattern is true.

# Problem Solving

**7. Look for Relationships** Greg drew a rectangle on the addition table at the right. He colored the corners. Find the sum of the green corners. Find the sum of the orange corners. What pattern do you notice?

| + | 36 | 37 | 38 | 39 | 40 | 41 | 42 |
|---|----|----|----|----|----|----|----|
| 22 | 58 | 59 | 60 | 61 | 62 | 63 | 64 |
| 23 | 59 | 60 | 61 | 62 | 63 | 64 | 65 |
| 24 | 60 | 61 | 62 | 63 | 64 | 65 | 66 |
| 25 | 61 | 62 | 63 | 64 | 65 | 66 | 67 |
| 26 | 62 | 63 | 64 | 65 | 66 | 67 | 68 |
| 27 | 63 | 64 | 65 | 66 | 67 | 68 | 69 |
| 28 | 64 | 65 | 66 | 67 | 68 | 69 | 70 |

**8.** Draw another rectangle on the addition table. See if Greg's pattern is true for this rectangle.

**9.** Explain why Greg's pattern works.

**10.** Which multiplication fact does the number line show? Write a related division fact.

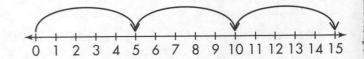

**11. Higher Order Thinking** Pierre made an addition table. He skip counted by 3 for the addends. Find and describe a pattern in Pierre's table.

| + | 20 | 23 | 26 | 29 | 32 | 35 | 38 |
|---|----|----|----|----|----|----|----|
| 10 | 30 | 33 | 36 | 39 | 42 | 45 | 48 |
| 13 | 33 | 36 | 39 | 42 | 45 | 48 | 51 |
| 16 | 36 | 39 | 42 | 45 | 48 | 51 | 54 |
| 19 | 39 | 42 | 45 | 48 | 51 | 54 | 57 |
| 22 | 42 | 45 | 48 | 51 | 54 | 57 | 60 |
| 25 | 45 | 48 | 51 | 54 | 57 | 60 | 63 |
| 28 | 48 | 51 | 54 | 57 | 60 | 63 | 66 |

## ✓ Assessment Practice

**12.** Look at the shaded cells in the addition table below.

| + | 10 | 13 | 16 | 19 | 22 | 25 | 28 |
|---|----|----|----|----|----|----|----|
| 0 | 10 | 13 | 16 | 19 | 22 | 25 | 28 |
| 10 | 20 | 23 | 26 | 29 | 32 | 35 | 38 |
| 20 | 30 | 33 | 36 | 39 | 42 | 45 | 48 |
| 30 | 40 | 43 | 46 | 49 | 52 | 55 | 58 |
| 40 | 50 | 53 | 56 | 59 | 62 | 65 | 68 |
| 50 | 60 | 63 | 66 | 69 | 72 | 75 | 78 |
| 60 | 70 | 73 | 76 | 79 | 82 | 85 | 88 |

Which pattern and property of operations are shown in the shaded cells?

Ⓐ Each orange sum is equal to zero plus the other addend; The Identity Property of Addition

Ⓑ Each green sum is 10 greater than one of its addends; The Identity Property of Addition

Ⓒ Each green sum is ten greater than the sum before; The Associative Property of Addition

Ⓓ There are no patterns or properties.

Name _____

## Solve & Share

A school store sold 436 pencils last week and 7 packages that each had 4 pencils today. Use mental math to find how many pencils were sold in all. Explain how you found your answer.

**I can ...**
use mental math to add.

Content Standards 3.NBT.A.2 Also 3.OA.C.7, 3.OA.D.8
Mathematical Practices MP.3, MP.4, MP.7

You can use structure by examining the quantities in the problem.

**Look Back!** What is another way you can find the sum of 436 pencils plus 7 packages of 4 pencils each using mental math?

 **Essential Question**

# How Can You Add with Mental Math?

**A**

Dr. Gomez recorded the number of Northern Right Whales, Atlantic Spotted Dolphins, and Western Atlantic Harbor Seals she saw off the coast of Florida in two different years. How many whales did Dr. Gomez see during the two years?

| DATA | Marine Animals Seen | | |
|------|--------|--------|--------|
| | **Animal** | **Year 1** | **Year 2** |
| | Whales | 325 | 114 |
| | Dolphins | 228 | 171 |
| | Seals | 434 | 212 |

You can use an open number line, mental math strategies, and properties of operations to solve this problem.

**B** **One Way**

Find $325 + 114$. Use the adding on strategy.

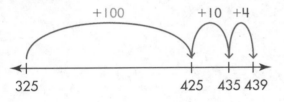

+100     +10   +4

325        425   435 439

Start at 325. Break apart 114.

Add 100 to 325.
Add 10 to 425.
Add 4 to 435.

$325 + 114 = 439$

Dr. Gomez saw 439 whales.

**C** **Another Way**

Find $325 + 114$. Use the make ten strategy.

Break apart 114.
$114 = 5 + 100 + 9$

Add 5 to 325 to make ten.
$325 + 5 = 330$

Then, add 100.
$330 + 100 = 430$

Break 114 apart to find a number that makes a ten when added to 325.

Finally, add 9.
$430 + 9 = 439$

$325 + 114 = 439$

Dr. Gomez saw 439 whales.

**Convince Me!** **Model with Math** Show two ways to find the total number of dolphins seen.

# ☆Guided Practice

## Do You Understand?

**1.** Compare the One Way and Another Way on the previous page. How are they the same? How are they different?

**2.** Use mental math to find how many animals Dr. Gomez saw during Year 2. Show your work.

## Do You Know How?

**3.** Use the make ten strategy to add 738 + 126.

$126 = 2 + 24 + 100$

$738 + \underline{\hspace{1cm}} = 740$

$740 + \underline{\hspace{1cm}} = 764$

$764 + \underline{\hspace{1cm}} = 864$

So, $738 + 126 = \underline{\hspace{1cm}}$.

**4.** Use the adding on strategy to add 325 + 212.

$212 = 200 + 10 + 2$

$325 + 200 = \underline{\hspace{1cm}}$

$525 + 10 = \underline{\hspace{1cm}}$

$\underline{\hspace{1cm}} + 2 = 537$

So, $325 + 212 = \underline{\hspace{1cm}}$.

# ☆Independent Practice ☆

In **5–12**, find each sum using mental math or an open number line.

**5.** 252 + 44

**6.** 236 + 243

**7.** 651 + 150

**8.** 378 + 542

**9.** 473 + 198

**10.** 319 + 339

**11.** 208 + 511

**12.** 523 + 169

# Problem Solving

**13. Higher Order Thinking** Maxine earns $8 each hour that she works as a cashier. She starts with $233. Today she cashiers for 6 hours. How much does she have at the end of the day? Explain how you found your answer.

**14.** Lauren sorted the 4 solids into 2 groups. Use mathematical terms to explain how she sorted the solids.

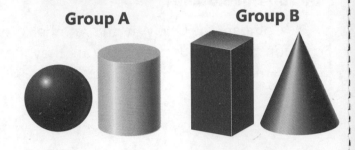

Group A          Group B

**15.** The Rodriguez family drives 229 miles on Friday and 172 miles on Saturday. Explain how you can use the adding on strategy to find the total number of miles the Rodriguez family drives.

**16. Critique Reasoning** Bill added 438 + 107. He recorded his reasoning below. Critique Bill's reasoning. Are there any errors? If so, explain the errors.

Find 438 + 107.
I'll think of 7 as 2 + 5.
438 + 2 = 440
440 + 7 = 447
447 + 100 = 547
So, 438 + 107 is 547.

## ✓ Assessment Practice

**17.** Find 153 + 121. Break apart 121 by place value, and then use the adding on strategy. Select numbers to complete the equations.

| 0 | 1 | 2 | 3 | 4 | 5 | 6 | 7 | 8 | 9 |

153 + ☐☐☐ = ☐☐☐

253 + ☐☐ = 273

273 + ☐ = ☐☐☐

**18.** Find 123 + 176. Break apart 176 by place value, and then use the adding on strategy. Select numbers to complete the equations.

| 0 | 1 | 2 | 3 | 4 | 5 | 6 | 7 | 8 | 9 |

123 + ☐☐☐ = ☐☐☐

223 + ☐☐ = 293

293 + ☐ = ☐☐☐

Name_____

Activity

☆ Solve & Share ☆

Peyton wants to buy one item that costs $425 and another item that costs $210. If she gets the discount shown on the sign below, what is the sale price? Explain how you can use mental math to find your answer.

**I can ...**
use mental math to subtract.

© **Content Standards** 3.NBT.A.2 Also 3.OA.D.8
**Mathematical Practices** MP.3, MP.4

**DISCOUNT:**
**$170 off**
total cost of items

Even when you use mental math, you can still show your work! You can construct arguments using mental math.

**Look Back!** What is another way you can use mental math to solve the problem?

# How Can You Subtract with Mental Math?

**A**

A store is having a sale on jackets. A jacket is on sale for $197 less than the original price. What is the sale price?

$352 — $197 off!

You can use mental math and the relationship between addition and subtraction to solve this problem.

The difference is the answer when subtracting two numbers.

---

**B** ## One Way

### Count Back on the Number Line
Find $352 - 197$.

To subtract 197 on an open number line, you can subtract 200, and then add 3.

$352 - 200 = 152$
$152 + 3 = 155$

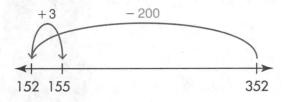

$+3$    $-200$

152 155      352

So, $352 - 197 = 155$.
The sale price is $155.

**C** ## Another Way

### Count Up on the Number Line
Find $352 - 197$.

To find $352 - 197$, you can think addition:
$197 + ? = 352$

$197 + 3 = 200$
$200 + 100 = 300$
$300 + 52 = 352$

Addition and subtraction are inverse operations.

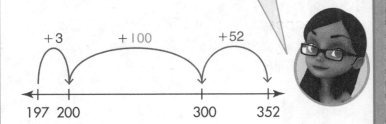

$+3$    $+100$    $+52$

197 200     300    352

$3 + 100 + 52 = 155$
$197 + 155 = 352$, so $352 - 197 = 155$.

The sale price is $155.

---

**Convince Me!** **Construct Arguments** Which of the two ways above would you use to solve $762 - 252$? Explain.

## Another Example!

You can make a simpler problem to find $352 - 197$.

Add 3 to both numbers.

$352 + 3 = 355$ and $197 + 3 = 200$.

Then you have $355 - 200$.

So, $355 - 200 = 155$ and $352 - 197 = 155$.

*If you get stuck using one strategy, another strategy may be easier!*

## ☆ Guided Practice

### Do You Understand?

1. In the One Way example on the previous page, why do you add 3 to 152 instead of subtracting 3 from 152?

2. Suppose a computer costs $573. If you buy it today, it costs $498. What is the discount? Show your work.

### Do You Know How?

In **3-6**, solve using mental math.

3. $846 - 18$
$848 - 20 = $ _____

4. $534 - 99$
$535 - 100 = $ _____

5. $873 - 216$
$877 - 220 = $ _____

6. $782 - 347$
$785 - 350 = $ _____

7. Find $400 - 138$ using the make ten strategy.

$138 + $ _____ $= 140$

$140 + $ _____ $= 200$

$200 + $ _____ $= 400$

_____ $+$ _____ $+$ _____ $=$ _____

## ☆ Independent Practice ☆

In **8-15**, use an open number line or the think addition strategy to find each difference.

8. $128 - 19$

9. $887 - 18$

10. $339 - 117$

11. $468 - 224$

12. $784 - 515$

13. $354 - 297$

14. $853 - 339$

15. $638 - 372$

# Problem Solving

**16.** Sarah has $350. How much money will she have after buying the computer at the sale price?

$299 SALE! Take $58 off the original price.

**17. Model with Math** Jessica has an array with 9 columns. There are 36 counters in the array. How many rows does her array have? Show how to represent the problem and find the answer.

**18.** Of the students at Paul's school, 270 are girls and 298 are boys. There are 354 students at Alice's school. How many more students are there at Paul's school than at Alice's school?

**19. Higher Order Thinking** To find 357 − 216, Tom added 4 to each number and then subtracted. Saul added 3 to each number and then subtracted. Will both ways work to find the correct answer? Explain.

---

✅ **Assessment Practice**

**20.** Use the relationship between addition and subtraction to find 233 − 112. Select numbers from the box to complete the work on the open number line and the equations.

> 0   1   2   3   4   5

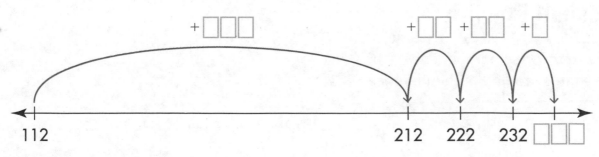

$+\boxed{\phantom{0}}\boxed{\phantom{0}}\boxed{\phantom{0}}$   $+\boxed{\phantom{0}}\boxed{\phantom{0}}$  $+\boxed{\phantom{0}}\boxed{\phantom{0}}$  $+\boxed{\phantom{0}}$

112                    212   222   232   $\boxed{\phantom{0}}\boxed{\phantom{0}}\boxed{\phantom{0}}$

$100 + \boxed{\phantom{0}}\boxed{\phantom{0}} + \boxed{\phantom{0}}\boxed{\phantom{0}} + \boxed{\phantom{0}} = \boxed{\phantom{0}}\boxed{\phantom{0}}\boxed{\phantom{0}}$

$233 - 112 = \boxed{\phantom{0}}\boxed{\phantom{0}}\boxed{\phantom{0}}$

Name_____

## Solve & Share

Think about ways to find numbers that tell *about* how much or *about* how many. Derek has 277 stickers. What number can you use to describe *about* how many stickers Derek has? Explain how you decided.

**I can ...**
use place value and a number line to round whole numbers.

© **Content Standards** 3.NBT.A.1 Also 3.OA.D.8
**Mathematical Practices** MP.1, MP.3, MP.6

Think about whether you need to be precise.

**Look Back!** Derek gets 3 more packages of 10 stickers. About how many stickers does Derek have now?

Essential Question **How Can You Round Numbers?**

**A**

About how many rocks does Tito have? Round 394 to the nearest ten.

Place value is the value of the place a digit has in a number. Think about the place value of the digits in 394.

When you round to the nearest ten, you are finding the closest multiple of ten for a given number.

Donna 350 rocks

Carl 345 rocks

Tito 394 rocks

**B** You can use place-value understanding and a number line to round to the nearest ten.

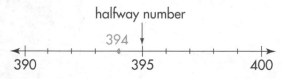

halfway number

394

390    395    400

394 is closer to 390 than 400, so 394 rounds to 390.

Tito has about 390 rocks.

**C** About how many rocks does Donna have? Round 350 to the nearest hundred.

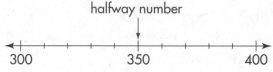

halfway number

300    350    400

If a number is halfway between, round to the greater number.

350 is halfway between 300 and 400, so 350 rounds to 400.

Donna has about 400 rocks.

**Convince Me!** **Make Sense and Persevere** Susan says, "I am thinking of a number that has a four in the hundreds place and a two in the ones place. When you round it to the nearest hundred, it is 500." What number could Susan be thinking of? What other numbers could be Susan's number?

**306**    **Topic 8** | Lesson 8-5

## Another Example

About how many rocks does Carl have? Round 345 to the nearest ten and hundred.

**Round to the nearest ten.**

345 is halfway between 340 and 350, so 345 rounds to 350.

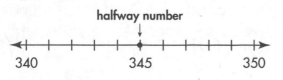

340        345        350

**Round to the nearest hundred.**

345 is closer to 300 than 400, so 345 rounds to 300.

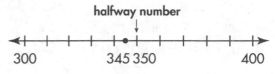

300     345 350        400

# ☆ Guided Practice

## Do You Understand?

1. What number is halfway between 200 and 300?  250

2. Sheri rounds 678 to 680. What place does she round to?  tens

3. Tito adds one more rock to his  collection on the previous page. About how many rocks does he have now, rounded to the nearest ten? Rounded to the nearest hundred? Explain.

   +400          h400

## Do You Know How?

In **4–6**, round to the nearest ten.

4.

517

510        515        520

520

5. 149  150          6. 732  730

In **7–9**, round to the nearest hundred.

7.

640

600        650        700
600

8. 305  700          9. 166  200

# ☆ Independent Practice ☆

In **10–12**, round to the nearest ten.

10. 88  90          11. 531  530          12. 855
                                              860

In **13–15**, round to the nearest hundred.

13. 428  400          14. 699          15. 750  800
                          700

# Problem Solving

**16.** The Leaning Tower of Pisa in Italy has 294 steps. To the nearest ten, about how many steps are there? To the nearest hundred, about how many steps are there?

290

**17. Critique Reasoning** Zoe says 247 rounded to the nearest hundred is 300 because 247 rounds to 250 and 250 rounds to 300. Is Zoe correct? Explain.

no

**18.** Use the number line to show a number that rounds to 200 when it is rounded to the nearest ten.

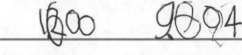 250        200

**19.** Name the least number of coins you can use to show $0.47. What are the coins?

1 quarter 2 dime 2 penny

**20.** Suppose you are rounding to the nearest hundred. What is the greatest number that rounds to 600? What is the least number that rounds to 600?

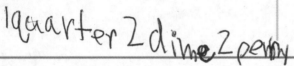 9894

**21. Higher Order Thinking** A 3-digit number has the digits 2, 5, and 7. To the nearest hundred, it rounds to 800. What is the number? Show how you found the answer.

752

**22.** Emil says, "I am thinking of a number that is greater than 142, rounds to 100 when rounded to the nearest hundred, and has a 5 in the ones place." What is Emil's number?

 145

What else can you try if you get stuck?

---

### ✓ Assessment Practice

**23.** Select all the numbers that will equal $100 when rounded to the nearest hundred.

- ☐ $10
- ☑ $89
- ☑ $91
- ☑ $110
- ☐ $150

**24.** Select all the numbers that will equal 70 when rounded to the nearest ten.

- ☐ 62
- ☑ 72
- ☑ 73
- ☐ 75
- ☐ 83

Name_____

☆ ☆
**Solve & Share**

Look at the table below. Is the mass of a female and male sun bear together more or less than the mass of one female black bear? Without finding an exact answer, explain how you can decide.

**I can ...**
use what I know about addition and place value to estimate sums.

© **Content Standards** 3.NBT.A.2 Also 3.NBT.A.1, 3.MD.A.2
**Mathematical Practices** MP.2, MP.6

You can use symbols, numbers, and words to be precise in your explanation.

DATA

| Type of Bear | Mass | |
| --- | --- | --- |
| | **Female** | **Male** |
| Sun bear | 38 kilograms | 43 kilograms |
| Black bear | 105 kilograms | 156 kilograms |

**Look Back!** Why is an exact answer not needed to solve the problem?

Essential Question **How Can You Estimate Sums?**

**A**

*Do the two pandas together weigh more than 500 pounds?*

*Estimate 255 + 329.*

Female
255 pounds

Male
329 pounds

You can estimate to find about how much the two pandas weigh.

---

**B** **One Way**

Round to the nearest hundred.

255 →300
+ 329 →300
          600

255 + 329 is about 600.
600 > 500

The pandas together weigh more than 500 pounds.

---

**C** **Another Way**

Use compatible numbers.

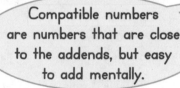

Compatible numbers are numbers that are close to the addends, but easy to add mentally.

255 →250
+ 329 →325
          575

255 + 329 is about 575 and 575 > 500.
The total weight is more than 500 pounds.

---

**Convince Me!** **Be Precise** Sandy said, "Just look at the numbers. 200 and 300 is 500. The pandas weigh over 500 pounds because one panda weighs 255 pounds and the other weighs 329 pounds." What do you think she means? Use numbers, words, or symbols to explain.

---

## Another Example!

Suppose one panda ate 166 pounds of bamboo in a week and another ate 158 pounds. About how many pounds of bamboo did the two pandas eat?

You can estimate 166 + 158 by rounding to the nearest ten.

$$166 \rightarrow 170$$
$$\underline{+\ 158 \rightarrow 160}$$
$$330$$

The pandas ate about 330 pounds of bamboo in a week.

# ☆ Guided Practice

## Do You Understand?

1. Two addends are rounded to greater numbers. Is the estimate greater than or less than the actual sum?

2. Mary and Todd estimate 143 + 286. They have different answers. Can they both be correct? Explain why or why not.

## Do You Know How?

Round to the nearest ten to estimate.

3. 218 + 466     ____ + ____ = ____

4. 108 + 223     ____ + ____ = ____

Round to the nearest hundred to estimate.

5. 514 + 258     ____ + ____ = ____

6. 198 + 426     ____ + ____ = ____

# ☆ Independent Practice ☆

In **7–10**, round to the nearest ten to estimate.

7. 138 + 435       8. 563 + 289       9. 644 + 172       10. 376 + 295

In **11–14**, round to the nearest hundred to estimate.

11. 403 + 179      12. 462 + 251      13. 274 + 443      14. 539 + 399

In **15–18**, use compatible numbers to estimate.

15. 175 + 126      16. 167 + 27       17. 108 + 379      18. 145 + 394

# Problem Solving

Use the table to answer **19** and **20**.

**19.** Ms. Tyler drove from Albany to Boston, and then from Boston to Baltimore. To the nearest ten miles, about how many miles did she drive in all?

**20.** Ms. Tyler drove from Boston to New York City and back again. To the nearest hundred miles, about how many miles did she drive?

| Distance from Boston, MA | |
|---|---|
| **City** | **Miles Away** |
| Albany, NY | 166 |
| Baltimore, MD | 407 |
| Philadelphia, PA | 313 |
| New York, NY | 211 |
| Norfolk, VA | 577 |

**21. Reasoning** Jen has $236. Dan has $289. Do Jen and Dan have more than $600 in all? Estimate to solve. Explain.

**22.** Ralph has 75¢. How much more money does he need to buy a pencil for 90¢? Complete the diagram.

90¢

| 75¢ | |
|---|---|

Money Ralph has    Money needed

**23. Higher Order Thinking** Susan drove 247 miles on Wednesday morning. Then she drove 119 miles on Wednesday afternoon. On Thursday, Susan drove 326 miles. About how far did Susan drive in all? Explain the method you used to estimate.

Remember that you learned different estimation strategies.

## Assessment Practice

**24.** Round to the nearest 10 to estimate the sums.

| | Estimate |
|---|---|
| 273 + 616 is about | |
| 542 + 338 is about | |
| 435 + 441 is about | |

**25.** Round to the nearest 100 to estimate the sums.

| | Estimate |
|---|---|
| 173 + 139 is about | |
| 155 + 177 is about | |
| 289 + 18 is about | |

Name _____

# Lesson 8-7
## Estimate Differences

**I can ...**
use what I know about subtraction and place value to estimate differences.

**Content Standards** 3.NBT.A.2 Also 3.OA.C.7, 3.OA.D.8
**Mathematical Practices** MP.1, MP.4

**Solve & Share**

Sara collected 220 cans on Monday, 80 cans on Tuesday, and 7 cartons with 8 cans each on Wednesday to recycle. Pierre collected 112 cans. About how many more cans did Sara collect than Pierre?

You can make sense and persevere. What is a good strategy for solving this problem?

**Look Back!** Which strategy gives an estimate that is closest to the exact answer? How did you decide?

**Essential Question** # How Can You Estimate Differences?

**A**

*All of the tickets for a concert were sold. So far, 126 people have arrived at the concert. About how many people who have tickets have not arrived?*

*Estimate 493 – 126 by rounding.*

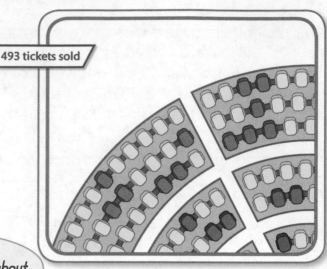

493 tickets sold

You can estimate to find *about* how many.

**B** **One Way**

Round each number to the nearest hundred and subtract.

$$
\begin{array}{r}
493 \rightarrow 500 \\
-126 \rightarrow 100 \\
\hline
400
\end{array}
$$

About 400 people have not yet arrived.

**C** **Another Way**

Round each number to the nearest ten and subtract.

$$
\begin{array}{r}
493 \rightarrow 490 \\
-126 \rightarrow 130 \\
\hline
360
\end{array}
$$

About 360 people have not yet arrived.

**Convince Me!** **Model with Math** Suppose 179 people have arrived at the concert. Estimate how many people have not arrived.

**Another Example!**
You can use compatible numbers to estimate differences.

Estimate 372 − 149.

$$\begin{array}{r} 372 \rightarrow 375 \\ -\ 149 \rightarrow 150 \\ \hline 225 \end{array}$$

375 and 150 are compatible numbers for 372 and 149.

 **Guided Practice**

## Do You Understand?

1. Does rounding to the nearest ten or nearest hundred give an estimate closer to the exact answer for 295 − 153?

2. A theater sells 408 tickets. Two hundred seventy-three people arrive. About how many more people are expected to arrive? Use compatible numbers. Show your work.

## Do You Know How?

In **3–6**, estimate. Use rounding or compatible numbers. Tell how you made each estimate.

**3.** 321 − 182        **4.** 655 − 189

**5.** 763 − 471        **6.** 816 − 297

## Independent Practice

In **7–10**, round to the nearest hundred to estimate.

**7.** 286 − 189    **8.** 461 − 216    **9.** 891 − 686    **10.** 724 − 175

In **11–14**, round to the nearest ten to estimate.

**11.** 766 − 492    **12.** 649 − 487    **13.** 241 − 117    **14.** 994 − 679

In **15–18**, use compatible numbers to estimate.

**15.** 760 − 265    **16.** 355 − 177    **17.** 481 − 105    **18.** 794 − 556

# Problem Solving

**19.** The Grand Concert Hall sold 100 more tickets on Sunday than on Friday. On what day did it sell about 150 tickets more than it sold on Sunday?

*Saturday*

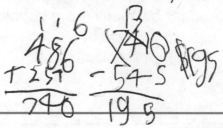

**Grand Concert Hall**

| Day | Number of Tickets Sold |
| --- | --- |
| Wednesday | 506 |
| Thursday | 323 |
| Friday | 251 |
| Saturday | 427 |
| Sunday | ? |

Use estimation strategies to help find your answers.

**20. Model with Math** Find the total number of tickets sold on Thursday and Friday. Explain what math you used.

$$323$$
$$+251$$
$$\overline{574}$$

*574*

**21. Algebra** Anna and Joe write reports for their science class. Anna's report is 827 words long. Joe's report is 679 words long. Round each report length to the nearest ten and estimate how many more words Anna's report is. Then write an equation that shows exactly how many more words Anna's report is.

*134*

**22. Higher Order Thinking** One week Mrs. Runyan earned $486, and the next week she earned $254. If Mrs. Runyan's goal was to earn $545, by about how much did she exceed her goal? Show how you used estimation to find your answer.

$$486$$
$$+254$$
$$\overline{740}$$

$$740$$
$$-545$$
$$\overline{195}$$

**23.** About how many inches longer was a *Brachiosaurus* than a *Tyrannosaurus rex*?

$$972$$
$$-468$$
$$\overline{504\ in}$$

*Tyrannosaurus rex* 468 inches

*Brachiosaurus* 972 inches

✓ **Assessment Practice**

**24.** Estimate 753 − 221 by rounding each number to the nearest ten.

- (A) 540
- (B) 530
- (C) 520
- (D) 510

**25.** Estimate 812 − 369 by rounding each number to the nearest hundred.

- (A) 500
- (B) 400
- (C) 300
- (D) 200

Name_____

**Solve & Share**

A pond has 458 rosy red minnows, 212 white cloud minnows, and 277 goldfish. How many more minnows than goldfish live in the pond?

Activity

**I can ...**
apply the math I know to solve problems.

© **Mathematical Practices** MP.4 Also MP.3 MP.5
**Content Standards** 3.NBT.A.2 Also 3.OA.D.8

## Thinking Habits

*Be a good thinker!*
*These questions can help you.*

- How can I use math I know to help solve this problem?

- How can I use pictures, objects, or an equation to represent the problem?

- How can I use numbers, words, and symbols to solve the problem?

**Look Back!** **Model with Math** Explain what math you used to solve this problem.

**Essential Question** **How Can You Model with Math?**

**A**

David has $583 to spend on soccer uniforms. He buys this soccer jersey and 2 soccer shorts. How much money does David spend?

Shorts $35

Jersey $109

**What math do I need to use to solve the problem?**

I need to show what I know and then choose the needed operations.

**B** **How can I model with math?**

**I can**

- apply math I know to solve the problem.

- use a bar diagram and equations to represent the problem.

- use an unknown to represent the number I am trying to find.

**C**

Here's my thinking...

I will use a bar diagram and an equation.

The hidden question is: How much does David spend on shorts?

**? for both shorts**

| 35 | 35 |
|----|----|

$35 + $35 = ?
$35 + $35 = $70. The shorts cost $70.

So I need to find the total including the jersey.

**? total**

| 70 | 109 |
|----|-----|

$70 + $109 = ?
$70 + $109 = $179. David spends $179.

**Convince Me!** **Model with Math** How does the bar diagram help you model with math?

# ☆ Guided Practice

**Model with Math**

Harris's office building has 126 windows. Morgan's bank has 146 windows. Devon's bank has 110 windows. How many more windows do the banks have altogether than the office building?

*One way you can model with math is by using bar diagrams to represent each step of a two-step problem.*

**1.** What is the hidden question you need to answer before you can solve the problem?

**2.** Solve the problem. Complete the bar diagrams. Show the equations you used.

? windows in banks

| | |
|---|---|
| _____ | _____ |

banks
| |
|---|
| _____ |

office
| | |
|---|---|
| _____ | ? more |

# Independent Practice ☆

**Model with Math**

Regina's bakery made 304 pies in January. Her bakery made 34 fewer pies in February. How many pies did her bakery make in both months?

**3.** What is the hidden question you need to answer before you can solve the problem?

**4.** Solve the problem. Complete the bar diagrams. Show the equations you used.

**5.** How would your equations change if the bakery made 34 more pies in February than in January?

# Problem Solving

**Skyscraper Heights**

The Empire State Building in New York is 159 meters taller than the Republic Plaza in Denver. The John Hancock Building in Chicago is 122 meters taller than the Republic Plaza. The Empire State Building is 712 miles away from the Hancock Building. The Hancock Building is 920 miles away from the Republic Plaza. Manuel wants to know how tall the Hancock Building is. Answer Exercises **6–9** to solve the problem.

Empire State Building
381 meters

6. **Critique Reasoning** Tom said to solve the problem, you should add 159 to the height of the Empire State Building. Do you agree? Explain why or why not.

7. **Model with Math** What is the hidden question you need to solve in this problem? How can you represent the hidden question?

8. **Model with Math** Solve the problem. Show the equations you used.

9. **Use Appropriate Tools** Which tool would you use to represent and explain how to solve the problem: counters, cubes, or place-value blocks? Explain.

Model with math means you apply math you have learned to solve problems.

**Find a Match**

Work with a partner. Point to a clue. Read the clue. Look below the clues to find a match. Write the clue letter in the box next to the match. Find a match for every clue. Once you find the matches, write the fact families for each of the facts.

**I can ...**
multiply and divide within 100.

© **Content Standard** 3.OA.C.7
**Mathematical Practices** MP.3, MP.6, MP.7, MP.8

**Clues**

**A** The missing number is 9.

**E** The missing number is 7.

**B** The missing number is 10.

**F** The missing number is 4.

**C** The missing number is 3.

**G** The missing number is 8.

**D** The missing number is 6.

**H** The missing number is 5.

| e | C | B | D |
|---|---|---|---|
| $42 \div 7 = 6$ | $24 \div 8 = 3$ | $10 \div 5 = 2$ | $18 \div 3 = 4$ |

| H | H | f | A |
|---|---|---|---|
| $5\overline{)30}$ (6) | $8 \div 2 = 4$ | $40 \div 4 = 10$ | $7\overline{)63}$ (4) |

# TOPIC 8 · Vocabulary Review

Glossary

## Word List

- Associative Property of Addition
- Commutative Property of Addition
- compatible numbers
- estimate
- Identity Property of Addition
- inverse operations
- mental math
- place value
- round

## Understand Vocabulary

Circle the property of addition shown in the following examples.

**1.** $17 + 14 = 14 + 17$

Associative Property    Commutative Property    Identity Property

**2.** $93 + 0 = 93$

Associative Property    Commutative Property    Identity Property

**3.** $8 + (5 + 9) = (8 + 5) + 9$

Associative Property    Commutative Property    Identity Property

**4.** $65 + 0 = 0 + 65$

Associative Property    Commutative Property    Identity Property

Choose the best term from the box. Write it in the blank.

**5.** You _____ when you use the nearest multiple of ten or hundred.

**6.** Addition and subtraction are _____.

**7.** _____ is the value given to the place a digit has in a number.

**8.** Numbers that are easy to compute mentally are _____.

**9.** You do not need pencil and paper when using _____.

## Use Vocabulary in Writing

**10.** Jim found that $123 + 284$ is about 400. Explain what Jim did. Use at least 3 terms from the Word List in your answer.

**Reteaching**

**Set A** pages 289–292

You can use properties of addition to help solve addition problems.

The Commutative Property of Addition

$12 + \boxed{\phantom{0}} = 15 + 12$

$12 + 15 = 15 + 12$

You can order addends in any way, and the sum will be the same.

The Associative Property of Addition

$3 + (7 + 8) = (3 + \boxed{\phantom{0}}) + 8$

$3 + (7 + 8) = (3 + 7) + 8$

You can group addends in any way, and the sum will be the same.

The Identity Property of Addition

$30 + \boxed{\phantom{0}} = 30$

$30 + 0 = 30$

The sum of any number and zero is that same number.

**Remember** that both sides of the equal sign must have the same value.

In **1–6**, write each missing number.

1. $18 + \underline{\phantom{000}} = 18$

2. $14 + (16 + 15) = (\underline{\phantom{000}} + 16) + 15$

3. $\underline{\phantom{000}} + 13 = 13 + 17$

4. $28 + (\underline{\phantom{000}} + 22) = 28 + (22 + 25)$

5. $62 + 21 + 0 = 62 + \underline{\phantom{000}}$

6. $\underline{\phantom{000}} + (26 + 78) = (31 + 26) + 78$

7. Use 78 and 34 to write an equation that shows the Commutative Property of Addition.

**Set B** pages 293–296

You can find patterns using an addition table.

| +  | 4  | 5  | 6  | 7  |
|----|----|----|----|----|
| 3  | 7  | 8  | 9  | 10 |
| 4  | 8  | 9  | 10 | 11 |
| 5  | 9  | 10 | 11 | 12 |
| 6  | 10 | 11 | 12 | 13 |
| 7  | 11 | 12 | 13 | 14 |
| 8  | 12 | 13 | 14 | 15 |

The green sums increase by 2 down the column and are even numbers.

The yellow sums increase by 2 down the column and are odd numbers.

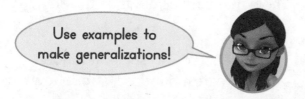

Use examples to make generalizations!

**Remember** that properties can help you understand patterns.

| +  | 0  | 1  | 2  | 3  | 4  | 5  | 6  | 7  |
|----|----|----|----|----|----|----|----|----|
| 0  | 0  | 1  | 2  | 3  | 4  | 5  | 6  | 7  |
| 1  | 1  | 2  | 3  | 4  | 5  | 6  | 7  | 8  |
| 2  | 2  | 3  | 4  | 5  | 6  | 7  | 8  | 9  |
| 3  | 3  | 4  | 5  | 6  | 7  | 8  | 9  | 10 |
| 4  | 4  | 5  | 6  | 7  | 8  | 9  | 10 | 11 |
| 5  | 5  | 6  | 7  | 8  | 9  | 10 | 11 | 12 |

1. Find the doubles-plus-2 facts. What pattern do you notice about the sums?

2. Explain why your pattern works.

## Set C | pages 297–300

Use mental math to find 374 + 238.

Break apart 238: 200 + 30 + 8.

Add hundreds, tens, and ones.
374 + 200 = 574
574 + 30 = 604
604 + 8 = 612

So, 374 + 238 = 612.

**Remember** that you can break apart addends when finding sums mentally.

**1.** 302 + 56          **2.** 463 + 418

**3.** 222 + 725          **4.** 689 + 115

## Set D | pages 301–304

Think addition to find 400 − 168.

Count on.

168 + 2 = 170
170 + 30 = 200
200 + 200 = 400
2 + 30 + 200 = 232

So, 400 − 168 = 232.

**Remember** that you can count on when subtracting mentally.

**1.** 523 − 163          **2.** 847 − 372

**3.** 768 − 259          **4.** 282 − 125

## Set E | pages 305–308

You can use a number line to round.

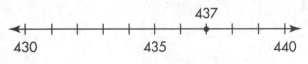

Nearest ten: 437 rounds to 440.

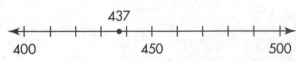

Nearest hundred: 437 rounds to 400.

Think about place value when you round.

**Remember** that if a number is halfway between, round to the greater number.

**1.** Round 374 to the nearest ten and the nearest hundred.

**2.** Round 848 to the nearest ten and the nearest hundred.

**3.** Mark's family traveled 565 miles. Rounded to the nearest ten, about how many miles did they travel?

**4.** Sara collected 345 shells. Rounded to the nearest hundred, about how many shells did she collect?

Name _____

**Set F** pages 309–312

Estimate 478 + 112.

Round each addend to the nearest ten.

$$
\begin{array}{r}
478 \rightarrow 480 \\
+\ 112 \rightarrow 110 \\
\hline
590
\end{array}
$$

Round each addend to the nearest hundred.

$$
\begin{array}{r}
478 \rightarrow 500 \\
+\ 112 \rightarrow 100 \\
\hline
600
\end{array}
$$

Use compatible numbers.

$$
\begin{array}{r}
478 \rightarrow 475 \\
+\ 112 \rightarrow 110 \\
\hline
585
\end{array}
$$

**Remember** that compatible numbers are numbers close to the actual numbers and are easier to add mentally.

Round to the nearest hundred.

**1.** 367 + 319  **2.** 737 + 127

Round to the nearest ten.

**3.** 298 + 542  **4.** 459 + 85

Use compatible numbers.

**5.** 372 + 173  **6.** 208 + 164

**7.** Will rounding to the nearest ten or the nearest hundred give a closer estimate of 314 + 247? Explain your answer.

**Set G** pages 313–316

Estimate 486 − 177.

Round each number to the nearest hundred.

$$
\begin{array}{r}
486 \rightarrow 500 \\
-\ 177 \rightarrow 200 \\
\hline
300
\end{array}
$$

Round each number to the nearest ten.

$$
\begin{array}{r}
486 \rightarrow 490 \\
-\ 177 \rightarrow 180 \\
\hline
310
\end{array}
$$

Use compatible numbers.

$$
\begin{array}{r}
486 \rightarrow 475 \\
-\ 177 \rightarrow 175 \\
\hline
300
\end{array}
$$

**Remember** that an estimate is close to the actual answer.

Round to the nearest hundred.

**1.** 527 − 341  **2.** 872 − 184

Round to the nearest ten.

**3.** 387 − 298  **4.** 659 − 271

Use compatible numbers.

**5.** 472 − 228  **6.** 911 − 347

**7.** Will rounding to the nearest ten or the nearest hundred give a closer estimate of 848 − 231? Explain your answer.

Think about these questions to help you **model with math**.

## Thinking Habits

- How can I use math I know to help solve this problem?

- How can I use pictures, objects, or an equation to represent the problem?

- How can I use numbers, words, and symbols to solve the problem?

**Remember** to apply the math you know to solve problems.

Elena has $265. She buys a jacket that costs $107 and a sweater that costs $69. How much money does Elena have left?

1. What is the hidden question you need to answer before you can solve the problem?

2. Solve the problem. Draw bar diagrams to represent the problem. Show the equations you used.

Toni read 131 pages on Monday, 56 pages on Tuesday, and some pages on Wednesday. She read 289 pages in all. How many pages did Toni read on Wednesday?

1. What is the hidden question you need to answer before you can solve the problem?

2. Solve the problem. Use equations to represent your work.

Name _____

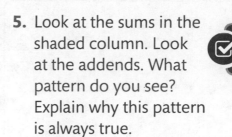

**1.** What is the sum of 243, 132, and 157?

[ ]

**2.** Find a reasonable estimate for the sum of 171 and 69. Select all that apply.

- [ ] 175 + 70 = 245
- [ ] 100 + 60 = 160
- [ ] 170 + 70 = 240
- [ ] 175 + 75 = 250
- [ ] 130 + 70 = 200

**3.** Subtract 382 − 148 mentally. Which of the following should you do first to find the difference?

Ⓐ Add 2 to 148 and add 2 to 382.

Ⓑ Add 2 to 148 and subtract 2 from to 382.

Ⓒ Subtract 8 from 148 and subtract 2 from 382.

Ⓓ Subtract 12 from 382 and add 12 to 148.

**4.** Estimate the difference of 765 and 333. Explain your estimate.

[ ]

**5.** Look at the sums in the shaded column. Look at the addends. What pattern do you see? Explain why this pattern is always true.

| + | 0 | 1 | 2 | 3 | 4 | 5 |
|---|---|---|---|---|---|----|
| 0 | 0 | 1 | 2 | 3 | 4 | 5 |
| 1 | 1 | 2 | 3 | 4 | 5 | 6 |
| 2 | 2 | 3 | 4 | 5 | 6 | 7 |
| 3 | 3 | 4 | 5 | 6 | 7 | 8 |
| 4 | 4 | 5 | 6 | 7 | 8 | 9 |
| 5 | 5 | 6 | 7 | 8 | 9 | 10 |

[ ]

**6.** Use mental math to add 332 and 154. Which of these shows how to break apart the numbers into hundreds, tens, and ones?

Ⓐ Break 332 into 320 + 12. Break 154 into 125 + 29.

Ⓑ Break 332 into 100 + 230 + 2. Break 154 into 100 + 52 + 2.

Ⓒ Break 332 into 300 + 16 + 16. Break 154 into 100 + 27 + 27.

Ⓓ Break 332 into 300 + 30 + 2. Break 154 into 100 + 50 + 4.

**7.** Use mental math to find 634 − 528.

**8.** Select all the equations that are true.

☐ 32 + 56 + 10 = 10 + 56 + 32

☐ (49 + 28) + 5 = 49 + (28 + 5)

☐ 56 + 890 = 890 + 56

☐ 82 + 0 = 82

☐ 45 + 27 = 27 + 35

**9.** Look at the table.

| A | 168 |
| B | 153 |
| C | 161 |
| D | 179 |

Write the letters A, B, C, and D above the number line to show each number rounded to the nearest ten.

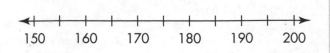

150   160   170   180   190   200

**10.** Use the subtraction work shown.

$$\begin{array}{r} 169 \\ -\ \ 57 \\ \hline 112 \end{array}$$

Which strategy shows a way to check the work using inverse operations?

Ⓐ  Subtract 57 from 169.

Ⓑ  Add 57 and 112.

Ⓒ  Add 112 and 169.

Ⓓ  Add 169 and 57.

**11.** Estimate the sum of 405 and 385 by rounding to the nearest hundred. Explain your estimate.

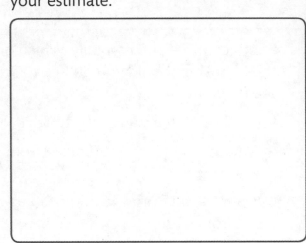

**12.** What addition equation can be used to check the answer for 456 − 342 = 114? Draw a bar diagram to show how the numbers in this problem are related.

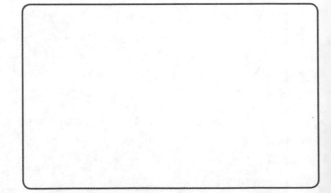

**13.** Find the sum of 350, 62, and 199.

**A.** Draw a bar diagram that represents the problem.

**B.** What is the first step you would do to solve this problem using mental math?

**14.** Subtract 341 − 97 mentally. First add 3 to 97 to get 100. What should the next step be? What is the difference?

Ⓐ Add 6 to 341. The difference is 247.

Ⓑ Add 200 to 100. The difference is 100.

Ⓒ Subtract 3 from 341. The difference is 238.

Ⓓ Add 3 to 341. The difference is 244.

**15.** Round each number on the left to the nearest hundred. Select the appropriate answer.

| | 400 | 500 | 600 | 700 |
|---|---|---|---|---|
| 668 | ❑ | ❑ | ❑ | ❑ |
| 404 | ❑ | ❑ | ❑ | ❑ |
| 649 | ❑ | ❑ | ❑ | ❑ |
| 489 | ❑ | ❑ | ❑ | ❑ |

**16.** Explain how to use mental math to find 620 − 278.

**17.** How can you check the answer for
693 − 231 = 462?

   Ⓐ  Subtract 639 − 300 = 339.

   Ⓑ  Subtract 462 − 231 = 231.

   Ⓒ  Add 693 + 231 = 924.

   Ⓓ  Add 462 + 231 = 693.

---

**18.** Consider the sum of 123, 201, and 387.

   **A.** Estimate the sum by rounding to the
nearest ten. Explain your estimate.

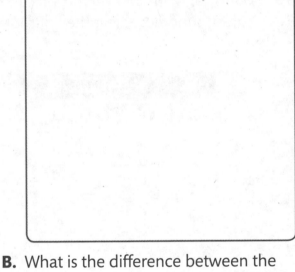

   **B.** What is the difference between the
exact sum of 123, 201, and 387 and
your estimate? Explain your answer.

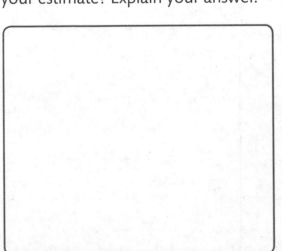

**19.** Consider the equation 360 = ____ + 84.

Use a bar diagram to represent the
equation. Then solve for the
unknown value.

Name_____

**Vacation Trip**
Mia is planning a vacation in Orlando, FL.
The **Mia's Route** table shows her route and the miles she will drive.

Use the **Mia's Route** table to answer Questions **1–3**.

1. Round each distance to the nearest ten to show about how many
   miles Mia will drive on each part of her trip.

   Memphis, TN, to Birmingham, AL:

   [                                    ]

   | Mia's Route | | |
   | --- | --- | --- |
   | **City 1** | **City 2** | **Miles** |
   | Memphis, TN | Birmingham, AL | 237 |
   | Birmingham, AL | Gainesville, FL | 422 |
   | Gainesville, FL | Orlando, FL | 183 |

   Birmingham, AL, to Gainesville, FL:

   [                                    ]

   Gainesville, FL, to Orlando, FL:

   [                                    ]

2. Use mental math to find the actual number of miles Mia will drive to
   reach Gainesville. Show your work.

   [                                    ]

3. Mia says, "Birmingham is 185 miles closer to Memphis than to Gainesville."
   Her brother says, "No, it is 175 miles closer." Use mental math to decide
   who is correct. Show your work.

   [                                    ]

Mia has to book a hotel and buy theme park tickets.
The **Hotel Prices** and **Theme Park Prices** tables show the total prices for Mia's stay. The **Mia's Options** list shows two plans that Mia can choose from.

4. Mia has $600 to spend on a hotel and tickets.

**Part A**

Which option does Mia have enough money for? Explain using estimation.

**Part B**

Create a new option for Mia. Fill out the table with a hotel and a theme park. Explain why Mia has enough money for this plan.

| Hotel Prices | |
|---|---|
| **Hotel** | **Price for Mia's Stay** |
| Hotel A | $362 |
| Hotel B | $233 |
| Hotel C | $313 |

| Theme Park Prices | |
|---|---|
| **Theme Park** | **Price for a Ticket** |
| Theme Park X | $331 |
| Theme Park Y | $275 |
| Theme Park Z | $302 |

| Mia's Options | | |
|---|---|---|
| **Option** | **Hotel** | **Theme Park** |
| 1 | A | Z |
| 2 | B | Y |
| 3 | | |

5. One theme park has a special offer. For each ticket Mia buys, she gets another ticket free. Shade the squares in the table at the right to show this pattern. Explain why the pattern is true.

| + | 0 | 1 | 2 | 3 | 4 | 5 |
|---|---|---|---|---|---|---|
| **0** | 0 | 1 | 2 | 3 | 4 | 5 |
| **1** | 1 | 2 | 3 | 4 | 5 | 6 |
| **2** | 2 | 3 | 4 | 5 | 6 | 7 |
| **3** | 3 | 4 | 5 | 6 | 7 | 8 |
| **4** | 4 | 5 | 6 | 7 | 8 | 9 |
| **5** | 5 | 6 | 7 | 8 | 9 | 10 |

# Fluently Add and Subtract within 1,000

**Essential Question:** What are procedures for adding and subtracting whole numbers?

Forest fires cause many changes within an environment.

A forest fire can be destructive. But it also helps a new forest start to grow.

My knowledge is growing! Here is a project on changing environments and populations.

## enVision STEM Project: Changing Environments

**Do Research** Forest fires destroy, but they also make room for new growth. Use the Internet or other sources to find information about forest fires. Describe the effect of forest fires on plant and animal populations.

**Journal: Write a Report** Include data with numbers for the population you researched. Also in your report:

• Choose a kind of animal or plant. Tell how a change in the environment can affect the number of animals or plants.

• Write and solve an addition and a subtraction problem using your data.

Name _____

# Review What You Know

## Vocabulary

Choose the best term from the box.
Write it on the blank.

- Associative Property of Addition
- Commutative Property of Addition
- compatible numbers
- inverse operations

1. _____
   are easy to add or subtract
   mentally.

2. According to the _____, the grouping of
   addends can be changed, and the sum will remain the same.

3. Addition and subtraction are _____.

## Rounding

Round each number to the nearest ten.

4. 57                5. 241               6. 495

Round each number to the nearest hundred.

7. 732               8. 81                9. 553

## Estimating Sums

Use compatible numbers to estimate each sum.

10. $27 + 12$                    11. $133 + 102$

12. $504 + 345$                  13. $52 + 870$

14. $293 + 278$                  15. $119 + 426$

## Estimating Differences

16. Tony and Kim play a video game. Tony scores 512 points. Kim scores
    768 points. About how many more points does Kim score than Tony?
    Which estimation method did you use?

17. Which number sentence shows the most reasonable estimate for $467 - 231$?

    Ⓐ $425 - 250 = 175$              Ⓒ $400 - 300 = 100$

    Ⓑ $500 - 200 = 300$              Ⓓ $470 - 230 = 240$

Name_____

### PROJECT 9A

**How do you know which is the tallest building?**

**Project:** Research the Heights of Tall Buildings

### PROJECT 9B

**How can you record what you bought over time?**

**Project:** Create an Addition Skit

### PROJECT 9C

**How long before the space shuttle launches?**

**Project:** Write a Report About Your Vacation

## Math Modeling

### Fun Raiser

▶ Video

Before watching the video, think:

When a school needs extra money for a field trip or a student club, it might hold a fundraiser to collect that money.

This check is SO BIG, we must have collected a ton of money!

John Doe  $ | 1,000,000 |

One Million Dollars _____ DOLLARS

**I can ...**

model with math to solve a problem that involves adding and subtracting.

© **Mathematical Practices** MP.4 Also MP.3, MP.5
**Content Standards** 3.NBT.A.2 Also 3.OA.D.8, 3.NBT.A.1

Activity

☆ Solve & Share ☆

There are 2 bins of oranges. One bin has 378 oranges. The other bin has 243 oranges. Find the sum of 378 + 243. Think about place value.

**I can ...**
use place value to break apart and add numbers.

© **Content Standards** 3.NBT.A.2 Also 3.OA.D.8
**Mathematical Practices** MP.3, MP.4, MP.7

You can use structure. You can break apart the problem to show each of the addends in expanded form.

**Look Back!** Adam has 9 bags of oranges with 8 oranges in each. He also has a bin with 325 oranges. How many oranges does Adam have in all? Think about how you can use place value or other tools to help solve the problem. Explain your solution, what tool you used, and why.

**Essential Question**

# How Can You Break Apart Addition Problems to Solve?

**A**

Margot counted 243 manatees one year and 179 manatees the next. How many manatees did Margot count all together?

| Hundreds | Tens | Ones |
|---|---|---|
| | | |

**B**

You can estimate and then use place value to add the numbers.

243 is about 200.  
179 is about 200.

$$200$$
$$+\ 200$$
$$400$$

The sum is about 400 manatees.

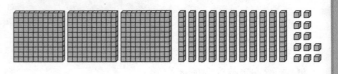

**C One Way**

Add each place value. Start with hundreds.

243  
+ 179

| 300 | 2 hundreds + 1 hundred |
| 110 | 4 tens + 7 tens |
| + 12 | 3 ones + 9 ones |

422

300, 110, and 12 are partial sums.

243 + 179 = 422 manatees

**D Another Way**

Add each place value. Start with ones.

243  
+ 179

12  
110  
+ 300

422

When you add by place value, you add the hundreds, the tens, and the ones.

243 + 179 = 422 manatees

422 is close to the estimate of 400. So, 422 is a reasonable sum.

**Convince Me! Critique Reasoning** Lexi used partial sums to complete the problem. Critique Lexi's reasoning. Is her work correct? Explain.

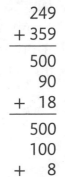

249  
+ 359

500  
90  
+ 18

500  
100  
+ 8

608

# ☆Guided Practice

## Do You Understand?

1. Suppose you were adding 527 + 405. What numbers would you combine when adding the tens? Why?

2. Find the error. Show how to find the correct answer.

   237
   + 285
   ──────
    12
    11
   + 400
   ──────
   423

## Do You Know How?

In **3**, estimate the sum. Use place-value blocks or drawings and partial sums to add.

3.   365
   + 422
   ──────

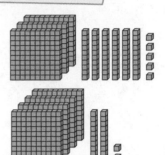

# Independent Practice ☆

**Leveled Practice** In **4–11**, estimate each sum. Use place-value blocks or drawings and partial sums to add.

4.   356
   + 123
   ──────

 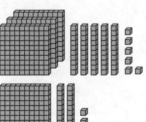

5.   550
   + 423
   ──────

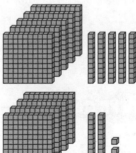 

6. 185 + 613

7. 730 + 168

8. 546 + 143

9. 362 + 524

10. 644 + 101

11. 463 + 315

# Problem Solving

12. **Model with Math** John read a book with 377 pages. Jess read a book with 210 pages. How many pages did John and Jess read? Use place-value blocks and partial sums to solve. Draw a model to represent the problem.

13. Explain how the solids shown in Group A and Group B could have been sorted.

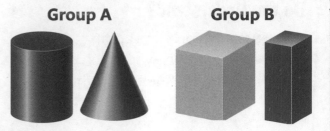

Group A          Group B

14. Henry believes the sum of 275 + 313 is 598. Is Henry correct? Use place-value blocks or drawings and partial sums in your explanation.

| ? | |
|---|---|
| 275 | 313 |

15. **Higher Order Thinking** A school cafeteria sold 255 lunches on Monday, 140 lunches on Tuesday, and 226 lunches on Wednesday. Did the cafeteria sell more lunches on Monday and Tuesday or on Tuesday and Wednesday? Use place-value blocks or drawings to solve.

## ☑ Assessment Practice

16. Which shows breaking 622 + 247 apart by place value to find the sum?

Ⓐ  600 + 200; 22 + 40; 2 + 7

Ⓑ  600 + 300; 20 + 40; 2 + 7

Ⓒ  600 + 200; 20 + 40; 2 + 7

Ⓓ  600 + 200; 20 + 47; 2 + 7

17. Break 331 + 516 apart by place value. Find the sum.

Ⓐ  848

Ⓑ  847

Ⓒ  748

Ⓓ  488

Name _____

☐ Activity

☆ ☆
**Solve & Share**

Suppose a bus travels 276 miles on Monday and 248 miles on Tuesday. How many miles does the bus travel?

**I can ...**
use different strategies to regroup when adding 3-digit numbers.

© **Content Standards** 3.NBT.A.2 Also 3.OA.D.8
**Mathematical Practices** MP.1, MP.4, MP.5

You can use appropriate tools, such as place-value blocks, to add larger numbers. What other strategies can you use to solve this problem?

**Look Back!** On Wednesday, the bus gets stuck in traffic. It travels 8 miles each hour for 8 hours. The bus needs to travel 600 miles total from Monday to Wednesday to make it to its destination. Does the bus make it to its destination? Why would it be a good idea to estimate first before you solve this problem?

Visual Learning  A-Z Glossary

 **Essential Question**

# How Can You Use Regrouping to Solve Addition Problems?

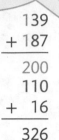 **Visual Learning Bridge**

**A**

*Jason's family drove from Ocala, Florida to Miami. They drove 139 miles in the morning and 187 miles in the afternoon. How far did Jason's family drive? Find 139 + 187.*

You know one way to record partial sums.

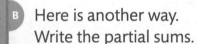
? miles

| 139 | 187 |

139 miles driven      187 miles driven

Estimate: 139 + 187 is about 100 + 200, or 300 miles.

```
  139
+ 187
-----
  200
  110
+  16
-----
  326
```

Jason's family drove 326 miles.

300 is close to 326, so the sum is reasonable.

**B** Here is another way. Write the partial sums.

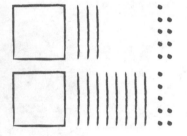

| Hundreds | Tens | Ones |
|----------|------|------|
| 1 | 3 | 9 |
| + 1 | 8 | 7 |
| 2 | 11 | 16 |

Regroup the ones.
16 ones = 1 ten + 6 ones

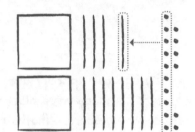

| Hundreds | Tens | Ones |
|----------|------|------|
| 1 | 3 | 9 |
| + 1 | 8 | 7 |
| 2 | 11 | ~~16~~ |
| 2 | 12 | 6 |

Regroup the tens.
12 tens = 1 hundred + 2 tens

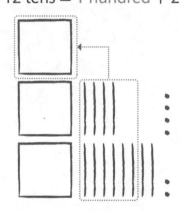

| Hundreds | Tens | Ones |
|----------|------|------|
| 1 | 3 | 9 |
| + 1 | 8 | 7 |
| 2 | 11 | ~~16~~ |
| 2 | ~~12~~ | 6 |
| 3 | 2 | 6 |

139 + 187 = 326
Jason's family drove 326 miles.

When you regroup, you name a whole number in a different way.

---

 **Convince Me!** **Model with Math** Show how to use place-value blocks to find 128 + 235 using regrouping.

---

**342** **Topic 9** | Lesson 9-2

Practice   Tools   Assessment

## Another Example!

Find 154 + 163.

| Hundreds | Tens | Ones |
|---|---|---|
| 1 | 5 | 4 |
| + 1 | 6 | 3 |
| 2 | ++ | 7 |
| 3 | 1 | 7 |

You can find partial sums. Then you can regroup place values to find the final sum.

Regroup the tens.
1 hundred + 1 ten = 11 tens

154 + 163 = 317

# Guided Practice

## Do You Understand?

**1.** When you add 3-digit numbers, how do you know if you need to regroup?

**2.** To add 546 + 327, would you need to regroup? Explain.

## Do You Know How?

In **3** and **4**, estimate by rounding. Then find each sum. Use place-value blocks or drawings to help.

**3.**   538
       + 429

**4.**   415
       + 198

# Independent Practice

In **5–12**, estimate and then find each sum.

**5.**   136
       + 252

**6.**   678
       + 129

**7.**   564
       + 283

**8.**   118
       + 335

**9.** 172 + 534

**10.** 324 + 508

**11.** 582 + 230

**12.** 207 + 238

# Problem Solving

In **13** and **14**, use the table at the right.

**13.** How many soup can labels did Grades 1 and 2 collect? Estimate by rounding to the nearest hundred. Then solve. Write an equation that represents the problem.

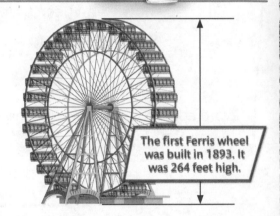

| DATA | Soup Can Labels Collected | |
|---|---|---|
| | **Grades** | **Number** |
| | Grade 1 | 385 |
| | Grade 2 | 294 |
| | Grade 3 | 479 |
| | Grade 4 | 564 |

**14. Make Sense and Persevere** Is your answer to Exercise 13 reasonable? Explain.

**15. Number Sense** The roller coaster Kingda Ka is 192 feet taller than the first Ferris wheel. Use the symbols < and > to compare the heights of the two rides in two different ways.

The first Ferris wheel was built in 1893. It was 264 feet high.

**16. Higher Order Thinking** Pete can run 178 yards in one minute. Sharon can run 119 more yards than Pete in one minute. How many yards can they both run in one minute?

**17.** Abi practiced her flute for 215 minutes last week and 178 minutes this week. How many minutes has Abi practiced?

## Assessment Practice

**18.** What is $126 + 229$?

Ⓐ 355
Ⓑ 345
Ⓒ 255
Ⓓ 245

**19.** What is the value of the unknown in $248 + \square = 521$?

Ⓐ 248
Ⓑ 263
Ⓒ 273
Ⓓ 283

Name _____

### Solve & Share

A pet store has 162 goldfish, 124 angelfish, and 6 bowls with 9 pufferfish in each. How many fish are there in all?

**I can ...**
add three or more numbers using what I know about adding 3-digit numbers.

© **Content Standards** 3.NBT.A.2 Also 3.OA.C.7, 3.OA.D.8
**Mathematical Practices** MP.2, MP.4, MP.8

You can generalize. Use what you know about adding two numbers to add three numbers.

**Look Back!** How can you decide if your answer is reasonable?

**How Can You Add More Than 2 Numbers?**

### A

*Different kinds of birds are for sale at a pet store. How many birds are for sale?*

*Find 137 + 155 + 18.*

*Round to the nearest ten to estimate:*
*140 + 160 + 20 = 320.*

Parrots 18

Canaries 137

Parakeets 155

? birds

| 137 | 155 | 18 |
|-----|-----|-----|

137 canaries · 155 parakeets · 18 parrots

A bar diagram can show 3 addends.

### B One Way

**Use partial sums.**

```
   137
   155
 +  18
 ─────
   200
    90
 +  20
 ─────
   310
```

In all, 310 birds are for sale.

### C Another Way

**Use column addition.**

| Hundreds | Tens | Ones |
|----------|------|------|
| 1 | 3 | 7 |
| 1 | 5 | 5 |
| + | 1 | 8 |
| 2 | 9 | ~~20~~ |
| 2 | ~~+~~+ | 0 |
| 3 | 1 | 0 |

The answer is reasonable because 310 is close to the estimate of 320.

In all, 310 birds are for sale.

**Convince Me! Model with Math** For the partial sums above, Billy said, "20 plus 90 is 110. 110 plus 200 equals 310." Is Billy correct? Use models, properties, or equations to represent and explain your thinking.

Name_____

# ☆ Guided Practice

## Do You Understand?

In **1** and **2**, look at the example on the previous page.

**1.** If you add the numbers in this order, do you get the same sum? Explain why or why not.

$$
\begin{array}{r}
155 \\
137 \\
+\ 18 \\
\hline
\end{array}
$$

**2.** Why is the 20 crossed out in the column addition problem?

## Do You Know How?

In **3** and **4**, estimate and then find each sum.

**3.**
$$
\begin{array}{r}
123 \\
168 \\
+\ 36 \\
\hline
\end{array}
$$

**4.**
$$
\begin{array}{r}
247 \\
362 \\
+\ 149 \\
\hline
\end{array}
$$

You can use partial sums or column addition to add.

# Independent Practice ☆

**Leveled Practice** In **5–15**, estimate and then find each sum.

**5.**
$$
\begin{array}{r}
64 \\
42 \\
+\ 88 \\
\hline
\end{array}
$$

**6.**
$$
\begin{array}{r}
354 \\
85 \\
+\ 72 \\
\hline
\end{array}
$$

**7.**
$$
\begin{array}{r}
307 \\
37 \\
+\ 234 \\
\hline
\end{array}
$$

**8.**
$$
\begin{array}{r}
714 \\
163 \\
+\ 99 \\
\hline
\end{array}
$$

**9.**
$$
\begin{array}{r}
602 \\
125 \\
+\ 231 \\
\hline
\end{array}
$$

**10.**
$$
\begin{array}{r}
246 \\
54 \\
233 \\
+\ 205 \\
\hline
\end{array}
$$

**11.**
$$
\begin{array}{r}
164 \\
68 \\
+\ 35 \\
\hline
\end{array}
$$

**12.**
$$
\begin{array}{r}
125 \\
35 \\
124 \\
+\ 239 \\
\hline
\end{array}
$$

**13.** 32 + 9 + 56 + 8

**14.** 481 + 78 + 42

**15.** 398 + 219 + 23 + 251

**16.** Use the picture at the right to find the height of President Washington's head carved in Mt. Rushmore. Write an equation to solve the problem.

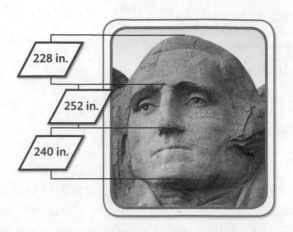

228 in.

252 in.

240 in.

**17. Algebra** Jada spends $74 on a hat, shoes, and shorts. If the hat costs $22 and the shoes cost $33, how much were the shorts? Write and solve an equation. Use an unknown to represent the cost of the shorts.

**18. Higher Order Thinking** Meg says 95 + 76 + 86 is greater than 300, but less than 400. Is Meg correct? Why or why not?

**19. Reasoning** Karin had cereal, a glass of milk, and a banana for breakfast. How many calories were in her meal? Round to the nearest ten to estimate and then solve. Write an equation that includes your solution.

Banana: 105 calories
Bowl of dry cereal: 110 calories
Glass of milk: 150 calories

## Assessment Practice

**20.** Use place value, partial sums, or properties of operations to find each sum.

| Equation | Sum |
|---|---|
| 25 + 120 + 175 = ? | |
| 26 + 241 + 324 = ? | |
| 242 + 163 + 312 = ? | |

**21.** Use place value, column addition, or properties of operations to find each sum.

| Equation | Sum |
|---|---|
| 125 + 250 + 125 = ? | |
| 31 + 32 + 337 = ? | |
| 154 + 239 + 574 = ? | |

Name _____

☆ Solve & Share ☆

Find the difference of 534 − 108. Think about how place value can help you subtract.

I can ...
use place value to solve simple problems when subtracting multi-digit numbers.

Content Standards 3.NBT.2 Also 3.OA.C.7, 3.OA.D.8
Mathematical Practices MP.6, MP.7

You can use structure. How could you use place value to help solve the problem?

**Look Back!** Jim had 388 marbles. He gave 8 marbles to each of 7 friends. How many marbles does Jim have left? How can place value help you to subtract 3-digit numbers?

**Essential Question**

# How Can You Use Partial Differences to Subtract?

**A**

*At the end of the fourth round of a game of Digit Derby, Marco's score was 462 points. During the fifth round of the game, Marco loses points. What is Marco's score at the end of the fifth round? Find 462 − 181.*

**End of Round 4**

Marco has 462 points.

Estimate first.
462 − 181 = ?
500 − 200 = 300

Place value can help you break a subtraction problem into smaller problems.

**End of Round 5**

Marco loses 181 points.

---

**B** ## What You Think

Use place value to subtract.
Count back by hundreds, tens, and ones.

181 = 100 + 80 + 1

Start at 462. Count back 100 to 362.
Count back 80 to 282.
Break apart 80 into 60 and 20.
Count back 1 to 281.

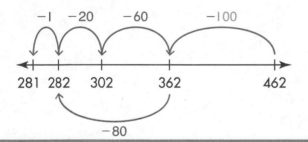

```
     −1   −20    −60        −100
    ↓    ↓     ↓         ↓
  ┼──┼──┼─────┼─────────┼──────→
 281 282  302     362          462
         ↖_____↗
              −80
```

---

**C** ## What You Write

```
   462
 − 100
   362
 −  60
   302
 −  20
   282
 −   1
   281
```

362, 302, and 282 are partial differences.

At the end of the fifth round, Marco's score is 281 points.

The score is close to the estimate. The difference is reasonable.

---

**Convince Me!** **Be Precise** Why was 80 broken into 60 and 20 in the computation above?

---

Name_____

# ☆ Guided Practice

## Do You Understand?

**1.** Why do you need to record the numbers you subtract at each step?

So you know whareyouca

**2.** Ana is trying to find 634 − 210. She decides to start by subtracting 10 from 634. Do you agree with Ana? Explain.

Yes

## Do You Know How?

In **3** and **4**, estimate and then use partial differences to subtract. Use open number lines to help.

**3.** Find 374 − 236.

374

**4.** Find 369 − 175.

369

# Independent Practice ☆

In **5–10**, estimate and then use partial differences to subtract. Use open number lines to help.

**5.** 738 − 523

738

**6.** 755 − 315

755

**7.** 336 − 217

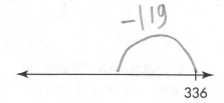
336

**8.** 455 − 182

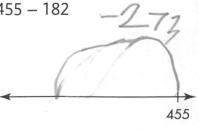
455

**9.** 865 − 506

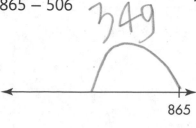
865

**10.** 794 − 355

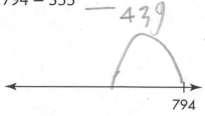
794

# Problem Solving

**11.** Don's book has 316 pages. He read 50 pages last week. He read another 71 pages this week. How many more pages does Don have left to read?

195

**12.** A-Z **Vocabulary** Explain why it is necessary to *regroup* when adding 172 + 264.

1 digit is over ten

**13.** **Use Structure** Beth had a necklace with 128 beads. The string broke, and she lost 49 beads. How many beads does Beth have left? Explain how you can break the problem into smaller problems to solve.

79

**14.** Write the time shown on the clock in two different ways.

9:15

9 qorter past 9

**15.** **Higher Order Thinking** Which weighs more, two Basset Hounds or one Great Dane? Show the difference in pounds between two Basset Hounds and a Great Dane. Draw bar diagrams to represent and help solve the problem.

Great Dane: 145 pounds

Basset Hound: 66 pounds

Great Dane

**16.** Which have a difference of 181? Use place value and partial differences to solve. Select all that apply.

- ▨ 428 − 247 = ?
- ☐ 562 − 381 = ?
- ☐ 498 − 307 = ?
- ☐ 875 − 696 = ?
- ▨ 946 − 765 = ?

**17.** Which have a difference of 237? Select all that apply.

- ▨ 877 − 640 = ?
- ☐ 412 − 176 = ?
- ▨ 652 − 415 = ?
- ☐ 700 − 459 = ?
- ☐ 802 − 565 = ?

Name_____

## Solve & Share

Last year, there were 347 houses for sale in Mill County and 289 houses for sale in Hunter County. Of the houses for sale in both counties, 162 were sold. How many houses were not sold? Solve this problem two different ways.

**I can ...**
use place-value reasoning to subtract 3-digit numbers.

Content Standards 3.NBT.A.2 Also 3.OA.D.8
Mathematical Practices MP.4, MP.5, MP.8

You can generalize when you subtract 3-digit numbers. Think about all the strategies you can use.

**Look Back!** How are your solution strategies alike and how are they different?

Essential Question

# How Can You Use Regrouping to Solve Subtraction Problems?

**A**

*Mike and Linda play a game. Linda has 528 points. Mike has 349 points. How many more points does Linda have than Mike? Find 528 − 349.*

MIKE 341    528 LINDA

Estimate:
528 − 349 = ?
530 − 350 = 180

**B** Draw place-value blocks to show 528.

**C** Subtract 9 ones.

```
  528
−   8   First subtract 8 ones.
  520
```

Regroup 1 ten as 10 ones.

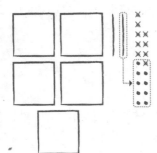

```
  520
−   1   Then,
  519   subtract 1 one.
```

Subtract 4 tens.

```
  519
−  10   First subtract 1 ten.
  509
```

Regroup 1 hundred as 10 tens.

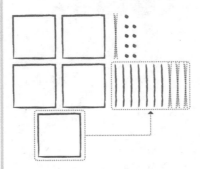

```
  509
−  30   Then, subtract 3 tens.
  479
```

 You can use place value to regroup when subtracting.

Subtract 3 hundreds.

```
  479
− 300   Subtract 3 hundreds.
  179
```

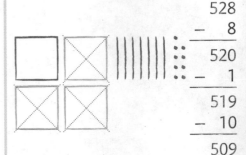

```
  528
−   8
  520
−   1
  519
−  10
  509
−  30
  479
− 300
  179
```

Linda has 179 more points.

179 is close to the estimate. The answer is reasonable.

---

**Convince Me!** **Use Appropriate Tools** How could you use a tool to find 326 − 143?

Name_____

# ☆ Guided Practice

## Do You Understand?

1. In the example on the previous page, explain how to decide if regrouping is necessary.

So it's posible

2. What strategies could you use to find 507 – 348?

497
– 348
159

## Do You Know How?

In **3** and **4**, estimate each difference and then use partial differences to subtract.

3.    374
    – 176
    198

4.    856
    – 219
    637

# Independent Practice ☆

In **5–12**, estimate each difference and then use partial differences to subtract.

5.    431
    – 145
    286

6.    276
    –  97
    179

7.    516
    – 402
    114

8.    526
    – 238
    288

9. 574 – 86

488

10. 629 – 453

176

11. 979 – 569

410

12. 764 – 237

527

# Problem Solving

**13.** At the end of their game, Lora had 426 points and Theo had 158 points. How many more points did Lora have than Theo?

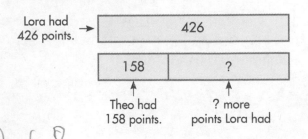

Lora had 426 points. → | 426 |

| 158 | ? |

↑ Theo had 158 points.    ↑ ? more points Lora had

268

**14. Model with Math** Zac and Malcolm each wrote short stories. Zac's story is 272 lines long. Malcolm's story is 145 lines longer than Zac's. How long is Malcolm's story? Explain how you can model with math to solve this problem.

$$\begin{array}{r} 272 \\ + 145 \\ \hline 417 \end{array}$$

**15.** The world's largest basket is 186 feet tall from the base to the top of the handles. What is the height of the handles?

83 ft

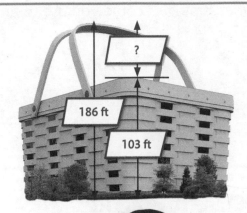

? 

186 ft

103 ft

**16. Higher Order Thinking** How many more swimmers signed up for the 1st session at Oak Pool than the 1st and 2nd sessions at Park Pool combined? Write an equation that represents the problem and includes the solution.

$$\begin{array}{r} 314 \\ + 179 \\ \hline 593 \end{array} \qquad \begin{array}{r} 763 \\ - 593 \\ \hline 170 \end{array}$$

### Swim Class Enrollment

| Pool | Number of Swimmers | |
| --- | --- | --- |
| | 1st session | 2nd session |
| Oak | 763 | 586 |
| Park | 314 | 179 |
| River | 256 | 163 |

DATA

---

✅ **Assessment Practice**

**17.** Which shows the estimate of 627 − 441 by rounding to the nearest ten, and then the correct difference?

ⓐ 200; 186    ©  190; 186

Ⓑ 200; 176    ⓓ 190; 176

**18.** Which shows the estimate of 901 − 512 by rounding to the nearest ten, and then the correct difference?

ⓐ 390; 389    © 400; 389

Ⓑ 390; 379    ⓓ 400; 379

Name _____

## Solve & Share

Rick is allowed to receive 1,000 text messages each month. How many more text messages can Rick receive this month? Solve any way you choose. Explain how you found the answer.

**I can ...**
use place-value reasoning to add and subtract 3-digit numbers.

© **Content Standards** 3.NBT.A.2 Also 3.OA.D.8
**Mathematical Practices** MP.2, MP.3, MP.5

> Rick's Text Messages
> Last week : 125
> This week : 213

Use reasoning. First think about the operations you should use.

**Look Back!** Is your answer reasonable? How can you check?

**Essential Question**

# How Can You Use Strategies to Add and Subtract?

**A**

*There are 136 fewer cell phone towers in Jurloe County than in Fraser County. How many cell phone towers are there in Jurloe County? Choose a strategy, and then solve.*

You can use addition or subtraction to solve.
$$402 = ? + 136$$
$$402 - 136 = ?$$
Addition and subtraction are inverse operations.

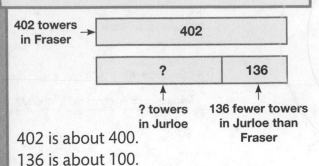

402 towers in Fraser → | 402 |

| ? | 136 |

? towers in Jurloe    136 fewer towers in Jurloe than Fraser

Fraser County has 402 cell phone towers.

402 is about 400.
136 is about 100.
The difference is about 300.

---

**B** **One Way**

Use the adding on strategy.

Find $402 = ? + 136$.

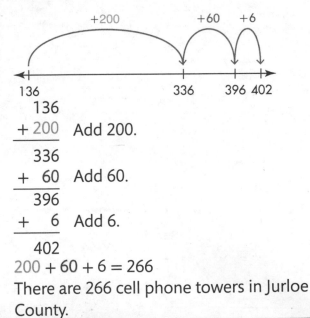

+200          +60    +6

136                336    396 402

$$\begin{array}{r} 136 \\ + \ 200 \quad \text{Add 200.} \\ \hline 336 \\ + \ \ 60 \quad \text{Add 60.} \\ \hline 396 \\ + \ \ \ 6 \quad \text{Add 6.} \\ \hline 402 \end{array}$$

$200 + 60 + 6 = 266$

There are 266 cell phone towers in Jurloe County.

---

**C** **Another Way**

Use partial differences to subtract.

The answer is reasonable because it is close to the estimate of 300.

Find $402 - 136 = ?$

$$\begin{array}{r} 402 \\ - \ 100 \quad \text{Subtract 100.} \\ \hline 302 \\ - \ \ 30 \quad \text{Subtract 30.} \\ \hline 272 \\ - \ \ \ 2 \quad \text{Subtract 2.} \\ \hline 270 \\ - \ \ \ 4 \quad \text{Subtract 4.} \\ \hline 266 \end{array}$$

There are 266 cell phone towers in Jurloe County.

---

**Convince Me!** **Use Appropriate Tools** Show how to use a tool (such as a number line or place-value blocks) to solve the problem above.

Name _____

## Another Example!

The Yellowstone River is 692 miles long. It is 51 miles shorter than the Kansas River. How long is the Kansas River? Choose a strategy, and then solve.
Find 692 + 51 = ?

You can use column addition to add.

Length of Kansas River → 

| ? |
|---|

| 692 | 51 |
|-----|----|

↑ 692 miles, length of Yellowstone River   ↑ 51 miles shorter than Kansas River

| Hundreds | Tens | Ones |
|----------|------|------|
| 6 | 9 | 2 |
| + | 5 | 1 |
| 6 | ̶1̶4 | 3 |
| 7 | 4 | 3 |

The Kansas River is 743 miles long.

## ☆ Guided Practice

### Do You Understand?

1. To subtract 507 − 348, how can you regroup the tens if there are 0 tens?

2. How is using partial sums to add like using place-value blocks and regrouping?

### Do You Know How?

In **3–6**, estimate and then find each sum or difference.

3.  816
   − 335

4.  163
   + 50

5.  900
   − 375

6.  508
   − 247

## ☆ Independent Practice ☆

In **7–14**, find each sum or difference. Then use estimation to check your answer.

7.  549
   − 167

8.  411
   − 238

9.  560
   + 144

10.  783
    + 68

11. 400 − 219

12. 904 − 703

13. 700 + 64

14. 807 + 38

# Problem Solving

**15.** How much more money does the Elm School Art Club need to raise? Complete the bar diagram and solve the problem.

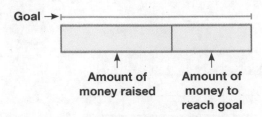

Goal →

Amount of money raised

Amount of money to reach goal

Elm School Art Club Fundraiser!

GOAL — $305

Raised $178

---

**16.** There were some ears of corn for sale at the farmers' market. Three hundred eighty-eight ears of corn were sold. At the end, there were 212 ears left. How many ears of corn were for sale at the start?

**17.** Dina was adding books to the library shelves. She put 117 nonfiction books on the shelves. Then there were 204 nonfiction books. How many nonfiction books were on the shelves before?

---

**18. Construct Arguments** The students at Cleveland School are collecting soda can tabs. The goal of each class is to collect 500 tabs. So far, the second graders have collected 315 tabs. The third graders have collected 190 more tabs than the second graders. Have the third graders reached their goal? Construct an argument to explain.

**19. Higher Order Thinking** Dylan had $405 in his savings account and spent $253. Brian had $380 in his savings account and spent $48 less than Dylan. Now who has more money in his savings account? How much more?

---

## ✓ Assessment Practice

**20.** Use a place-value strategy to find the value of the unknown in $426 + ? = 712$.

Ⓐ 186
Ⓑ 216
Ⓒ 284
Ⓓ 286

**21.** Use the relationship between addition and subtraction to find the value of the unknown in $? + 334 = 800$.

Ⓐ 434
Ⓑ 466
Ⓒ 534
Ⓓ 566

Name_____

**Solve & Share**

Use each of the digits 0, 1, 2, 3, 4, and 5 only once. Write the digits in the space below to make two 3-digit addends with the greatest sum. Write the sum of the two addends. How do you know you have made the greatest sum?

$$
\begin{array}{r}
5\ 3\ 0 \\
+\ 4\ 2\ 1 \\
\hline
9\ 5\ 1
\end{array}
$$

**I can ...**
construct math arguments using what I know about addition and subtraction.

Ⓒ **Mathematical Practices** MP.3 Also MP.1, MP.2
**Content Standards** 3.NBT.A.2 Also 3.OA.D.8

**Thinking Habits**

*Be a good thinker! These questions can help you.*

• How can I use numbers, objects, drawings, or actions to justify my argument?

• Am I using numbers and symbols correctly?

• Is my explanation clear and complete?

**Look Back!** **Construct Arguments** Make different 3-digit addends to find the least possible sum. What is the difference between the greatest possible sum and the least possible sum? Construct an argument to explain how you know that your answer is correct.

**Essential Question** ## How Can You Construct Arguments?

**A**

Nancy has $457 in her savings account and wants to have $500 by the end of the year. Christopher has $557 in his savings account and wants to have $600 by the end of the year. Who needs to save more money by the end of the year?

My conjecture: They both need to save the same amount.

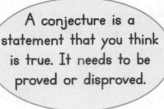

A conjecture is a statement that you think is true. It needs to be proved or disproved.

**How can I explain why my conjecture is correct?**

I need to construct an argument to justify my conjecture.

Here's my thinking...

**B** **How can I construct an argument?**

**I can**

- use numbers, objects, drawings, or actions correctly to explain my thinking.

- make sure my explanation is simple, complete, and easy to understand.

**C** I will use drawings and numbers to explain my thinking.

The distance from 457 to 500 on the number line is the same as the distance from 557 to 600.

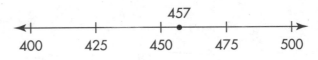

The number lines show that it takes the same amount of money to get from $457 to $500 as it takes to get from $557 to $600.

So, $500 - 457 = 600 - 557$. My conjecture is correct.

**Convince Me!** **Construct Arguments** Construct another math argument to justify the conjecture above.

# Guided Practice

**Construct Arguments**

Mr. Lee had $375 in the bank. Then he spent $242. Ms. Davis had $675 in the bank, and then spent $542. Who has more money left?
*Conjecture: They both have the same amount of money left.*

1. Draw a diagram to represent the math.

Diagrams can help you support an argument.

2. Use your diagram to justify the conjecture.

# Independent Practice

**Construct Arguments**

A Grade 2 class has made 165 paper cranes and wants to reach a total of 250.
A Grade 3 class has made 255 paper cranes and wants to reach a total of 350.
Which class has fewer paper cranes left to make to reach its goal?
*Conjecture: The Grade 2 class has to make fewer paper cranes to reach its goal.*

3. Draw a diagram at the right to represent the math.

4. Use your diagram to justify the conjecture.

5. Explain another way you could justify the conjecture.

# Problem Solving

## Band Practice

Some musicians set goals for the number of minutes they want to practice before a concert, which is 5 days away. They want to know who has to practice the least number of minutes to reach his or her goal.

| Student | Aria | Dexter | Yin | Sawyer |
|---|---|---|---|---|
| Minutes Practiced | 608 | 612 | 604 | 612 |
| Goal in Minutes | 700 | 650 | 625 | 675 |

6. **Make Sense and Persevere** How can you find the number of minutes Aria has to practice to reach her goal?

7. **Reasoning** So far Dexter and Sawyer have both practiced the same number of minutes. Do they need the same amount of practice time to reach their goals? Explain.

When you construct arguments, you explain why your work is right.

8. **Reasoning** Who has the least number of minutes left to practice to reach his or her goal?

9. **Construct Arguments** Construct a math argument to explain why your answer to Exercise **8** is correct.

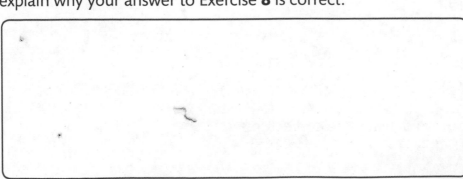

364    **Topic 9** | Lesson 9-7

Name_____

Point & Tally

Find a partner. Get paper and a pencil. Each partner chooses a different color: light blue or dark blue. Partner 1 and Partner 2 each point to a black number at the same time. Both partners add those numbers.

If the answer is on your color, you get a tally mark. Work until one partner has seven tally marks. While playing the game, partners can use subtraction to check their addition.

**I can ...**
add and subtract within 1,000.

Content Standard 3.NBT.A.2
Mathematical Practices MP.3, MP.6, MP.7, MP.8

**Partner 1**

| 400 |
| 120 |
| 233 |
| 275 |
| 412 |

| 812 | 591 | 520 |
| 687 | 758 | 824 |
| 800 | 240 | 353 |
| 675 | 508 | 532 |
| 645 | 770 | 633 |
| 395 | 550 | 478 |

**Partner 2**

| 358 |
| 275 |
| 412 |
| 400 |
| 120 |

**Tally Marks for Partner 1**

**Tally Marks for Partner 2**

A-Z
Glossary

**Word List**

- conjecture
- estimate
- inverse operations
- place value
- regroup
- round

## Understand Vocabulary

Draw a line to match each term to an example.

**1.** place value          515 + 141 is about 660.

**2.** estimate          305 + 299 = 604 and
           604 − 299 = 305

**3.** regroup          232 = 2 hundreds 3 tens 2 ones

**4.** inverse operations          47 = 3 tens 17 ones

Write *always*, *sometimes*, or *never*.

**5.** When *rounding* to the nearest ten, a number with a 5 in the ones digit
_____ rounds to the next ten.

**6.** A *conjecture* is _____ true.

**7.** A digit with a greater *place value* is _____
written to the right of a digit with a lesser place value.

**8.** A ten can _____ be *regrouped* as 10 hundreds.

## Use Vocabulary in Writing

**9.** Explain how to find 600 − 281, and then explain how to
check that the difference is correct. Use at least 2 terms
from the Word List in your explanation.

Name_____

### Set A | pages 337–340

Find the sum of 257 + 186.

You can break apart 257 + 186 by place value to solve.

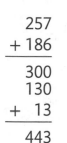

Break apart each number by place value and find the sum of the numbers in each place. Then add the sums.

```
   257
 + 186
   300
   130
 +  13
   443
```

So, 257 + 186 = 443.

**Reteaching**

**Remember** that you can use place value to add numbers by breaking large addition problems into smaller addition problems.

In **1–5**, use place-value blocks or drawings and partial sums to add.

**1.** 135 + 152   **2.** 650 + 138

**3.** 535 + 423   **4.** 475 + 264

**5.** Yvette took 137 photographs on Friday. She took 248 photographs on Saturday. How many did she take in all?

### Set B | pages 341–344

Find 235 + 187.

Estimate by rounding: 240 + 190 = 430.

Use place-value blocks to represent each number and find partial sums. Regroup to find the final sum.

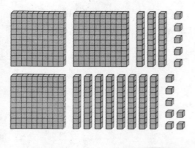

```
  235
+ 187
  422
```

The answer is reasonable because 422 is close to 430.

**Remember** that an estimate can help you check whether your answer is reasonable.

In **1–6**, estimate and find each sum.

**1.**   236
       + 217

**2.**   407
       + 436

**3.** 235 + 59   **4.** 584 + 326

**5.** 196 + 243   **6.** 465 + 357

Find 124 + 32 + 238.

Estimate by rounding:
120 + 30 + 240 = 390.

You can solve using partial sums.

```
    124
     32
  + 238
  -----
    300
     80
  +  14
  -----
    394
```

You can solve using column addition.

| Hundreds | Tens | Ones |
|----------|------|------|
| 1        | 2    | 4    |
|          | 3    | 2    |
| + 2      | 3    | 8    |
| 3        | 8    | 14   |
| 3        | 9    | 4    |

The answer is reasonable because 394 is close to 390.

So, 124 + 32 + 238 = 394.

**Remember** that adding three numbers is like adding two numbers.

In **1–7**, estimate and then use partial sums to add.

1.
```
    209
     48
  + 312
```

2.
```
    412
    273
  + 139
```

3. 146 + 86 + 53

4. 125 + 224 + 306

5. A flower shop has 124 tulips, 235 roses, and 85 carnations. How many flowers does the flower shop have?

6. Mike's Café sells 237 sandwiches on Friday. It sells 448 sandwiches on Saturday and 102 sandwiches on Sunday. How many sandwiches are sold on all 3 days?

7. Three planes leave an airport. Each plane has 239 seats. The first plane has 224 passengers. The second plane has 189 passengers. The third plane has 122 passengers. How many passengers are on all 3 planes?

**Set D** pages 349–352

Use place value to help find 548 − 263.

Subtract the hundreds. 548 − 200 = 348

Subtract the tens. 348 − 40 = 308
First subtract 4 tens.

Then subtract 2 308 − 20 = 288
more tens.

Subtract the ones. 288 − 3 = 285

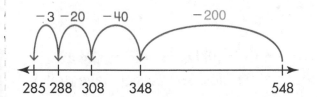

285  288  308      348                    548

So, 548 − 263 = 285.

**Remember** that place value can help you break a subtraction problem into smaller problems.

In **1–6**, find each difference. Estimate and then use place value and partial differences to subtract.

**1.** 489 − 253          **2.** 544 − 162

**3.** 856 − 328          **4.** 349 − 98

**5.** 873 − 184          **6.** 526 − 207

**Set E** pages 353–356

Find 416 − 243.
Estimate: 420 − 240 = 180.

Subtract 3 ones.
$$\begin{array}{r} 416 \\ -\ \ 3 \\ \hline 413 \end{array}$$

Subtract 1 ten.
$$\begin{array}{r} 413 \\ -\ \ 10 \\ \hline 403 \end{array}$$

Regroup 1 hundred as 10 tens.
Subtract 3 tens.
$$\begin{array}{r} 403 \\ -\ \ 30 \\ \hline 373 \end{array}$$

Subtract 2 hundreds.
$$\begin{array}{r} 373 \\ -\ 200 \\ \hline 173 \end{array}$$

The answer is reasonable because 173 is close to 180.

So, 416 − 243 = 173.

**Remember** to regroup if necessary.

In **1–8**, estimate each difference. Then find each difference.

**1.** $\begin{array}{r} 458 \\ -\ 176 \\ \hline \end{array}$     **2.** $\begin{array}{r} 236 \\ -\ 79 \\ \hline \end{array}$

**3.** $\begin{array}{r} 863 \\ -\ 526 \\ \hline \end{array}$     **4.** $\begin{array}{r} 748 \\ -\ 279 \\ \hline \end{array}$

**5.** 400 − 227          **6.** 306 − 198

**7.** 220 − 187          **8.** 657 − 122

Two hundred seventy-three people have finished a marathon. A total of 458 people entered the marathon. How many people are still running?

You can use a bar diagram and addition or subtraction to solve.

| 458 | |
|---|---|
| 273 | ? |

$273 + ? = 458$

$458 - 273 = ?$

Estimate:

$460 - 270 = 190$

Solve:

The solution, 185, is reasonable. It is close to the estimate.

$273 + \textbf{185} = 458$

$458 - 273 = \textbf{185}$

185 people are still running.

**Remember** to regroup when needed.

In **1** and **2**, estimate. Then solve.

1. Damian's conservation club wants to plant 640 seedlings. They have 172 seedlings that they still need to plant to meet their goal. How many seedlings have they planted so far?

2. The Smith family is driving to Dallas. The trip is 450 miles. So far, they have driven 315 miles. How many miles are left in the trip?

Think about these questions to help you **construct arguments**.

### Thinking Habits

- How can I use numbers, objects, drawings, or actions to justify my argument?

- Am I using numbers and symbols correctly?

- Is my explanation clear and complete?

**Remember** that a conjecture needs to be proved to be true.

Emma has $191. She spends $105. She donates $52 to charity. Can Emma save $30?

**Conjecture: Emma can save $30.**

1. Draw a diagram to represent the math.

2. Use your diagram to justify the conjecture.

Name_____

**1.** Find the sum of 337 and 285. Use place value and find the sums of the hundreds, tens, and ones.

| Hundreds | Tens | Ones |
|---|---|---|
|  |  |  |
|  |  |  |
| 2   3 | 5   7 | 3   8 |

**2.** An estimate of 431 − 249 using compatible numbers is 425 − 250 = 175. Would it be reasonable for the exact difference to be 182? Explain.

**3.** Which addends are broken apart correctly? Select all that apply.

☐ 320 + 148
$(300 + 100) + (20 + 40) + (20 + 8)$

☐ 270 + 341
$(2 + 70) + (3 + 4 + 1)$

☐ 318 + 393
$300 + (10 + 90) + (8 + 3)$

☐ 532 + 360
$(500 + 300) + (30 + 60) + 2$

☐ 526 + 230
$(500 + 200) + (20 + 30) + 6$

**4.** Find the sum of 176, 204, and 59.

Ⓐ 329

Ⓑ 339

Ⓒ 429

Ⓓ 439

**5.** What is 276 + 289?

Ⓐ 509

Ⓑ 537

Ⓒ 565

Ⓓ 593

**6.** Find 237 + 20. Then subtract the sum from 302.

**7.** Subtract 168 from 300.

Ⓐ 32

Ⓑ 122

Ⓒ 132

Ⓓ 142

**8. A.** Is 268 + 37 less than 346? Make a conjecture.

**B.** Construct an argument to prove your conjecture.

**9.** What is 825 − 647?

Ⓐ 78

Ⓑ 82

Ⓒ 128

Ⓓ 178

**10.** Find 335 + 108 + 12. Then subtract the sum from 600.

**11.** Find 283 + 45. Then subtract 139 from the sum. What is the difference?

Ⓐ 189

Ⓑ 328

Ⓒ 377

Ⓓ 467

**12.** Describe how to use place-value blocks to regroup to solve the subtraction problem below. What is the difference?

$$\begin{array}{r} 316 \\ - 226 \\ \hline \end{array}$$

**13.** Find the difference between 254 and 125.

**A.** If you need to regroup to find the difference, explain how to do it. If you do not need to regroup, explain why not.

**B.** Find the difference.

**14.** Put the steps in order to find 756 − 345.

| | Step 1 | Step 2 | Step 3 |
|---|---|---|---|
| Subtract 416 − 5 | ❑ | ❑ | ❑ |
| Subtract 756 − 300 | ❑ | ❑ | ❑ |
| Subtract 456 − 40 | ❑ | ❑ | ❑ |

**15.** What is the difference between 408 + 240 and 259?

**16.** Use place value to subtract 639 from 737. How many times do you have to regroup?

Ⓐ 3

Ⓑ 2

Ⓒ 1

Ⓓ 0

**17.** Subtract.

457 − 338

Ⓐ 109

Ⓑ 119

Ⓒ 121

Ⓓ 129

**18.** Subtract 246 from 332.

Name_____

## Video Arcade

Nita, Arif, and Sarah have been playing games at the video arcade.
The **Tickets Estimates** list below shows the number of tickets the
friends estimated they would win before they started playing.
The **Tickets Won** table shows the numbers of tickets each friend won.

**Tickets Estimates**

• Nita estimated she would win 165 tickets.
• Arif estimated he would win 150 tickets.
• Sarah estimated she would win 175 tickets.

The friends want to compare the tickets
they won to their estimates. Use the **Tickets
Estimates** list and **Tickets Won** table to
answer Questions **1** and **2**.

| | Tickets Won | |
|---|---|---|
| **Name** | **Tickets Won Playing Sports Games** | **Tickets Won Playing Action Games** |
| Nita | 96 | 112 |
| Arif | 94 | 91 |
| Sarah | 104 | 117 |

1. How many tickets did each of the friends
   win in all?

2. Show how many more tickets each friend won than his or her estimate.

3. Arif says if he won 24 more tickets, he would have won more tickets
   than Nita. Is he correct? Explain.

4. The three friends put all of their tickets together.
   How many tickets did they win in all?

Tickets can be used to buy prizes. The **Arcade Prizes** table shows how many tickets each prize costs.

Use the **Arcade Prizes** table to answer Question **5**.

5. Use the total number of tickets you found in Question **4**. The 3 friends will use this number of tickets to get 1 prize each and 1 more prize as a gift.

There are 2 rules the friends must follow.

• They cannot use more than their total number of tickets.
• After their purchases, they do not want more than 50 tickets remaining.

| Arcade Prizes | |
|---|---|
| **Prize** | **Cost (Tickets)** |
| Board Game | 138 |
| Stuffed Animal | 85 |
| Action Figures | 73 |
| Wristwatch | 170 |
| Calculator | 142 |
| Mystery Book | 92 |
| Video Game | 235 |
| Photo Album | 79 |

**Part A**

Arif starts a prize log to record the prizes they will get. In the table below, record some prizes the friends could choose, the cost of the prize, and show how many tickets they will have left.

| Prize | Cost (Tickets) | Number of Tickets Left |
|---|---|---|
| Wristwatch | 170 | _____ − 170 = 444 |
| | | |
| | | |
| | | |

**Part B**

If the friends made your choices from Part A, how many of their tickets would they use to get prizes? Explain how you found the answer.

# TOPIC 10

## Multiply by Multiples of 10

**Essential Question:** What strategies can be used for multiplying by multiples of 10?

**Digital Resources**

Interactive Student Edition · Activity · Visual Learning · Video · Practice

Assessment · Games · Tools · Glossary

The insect in this picture is hiding to avoid being eaten.

Animals that have a better camouflage color than others are more likely to survive.

It is like playing hide-and-seek! Here is a project on animal and plant characteristics and multiplication.

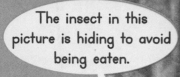 STEM Project: Animal and Plant Characteristics

**Do Research** Use the Internet or other sources to find information about how the characteristics of some plants and animals help them survive. Think about how characteristics can be different among members of the same species.

**Journal: Write a Report** Include what you found. Also in your report:

- Tell about an insect that uses camouflage.

- Describe an example of how a plant's thorns help it survive.

- Make up and solve multiplication problems about the animals or plants you research. Use multiples of 10.

Topic 10      377

# Review What You Know

## A-Z Vocabulary

Choose the best term from the box.
Write it on the blank.

| • factor | • multiplication |
| • equation | • Zero Property of Multiplication |

1. A number sentence where the value on the left and right of the equal sign (=) is the same is called a(n) _____.

2. The _____ states that any number multiplied by zero has a product of zero.

3. _____ is an operation that gives the total number that results when you join equal groups.

## Multiplication Table

Find the value that makes the equations true.
Use the multiplication table to help.

4. $21 \div 7 =$ ____

   $7 \times$ ____ $= 21$

5. $45 \div 5 =$ ____

   $5 \times$ ____ $= 45$

| × | 0 | 1 | 2 | 3 | 4 | 5 | 6 | 7 |
|---|---|---|---|---|---|---|---|---|
| 0 | 0 | 0 | 0 | 0 | 0 | 0 | 0 | 0 |
| 1 | 0 | 1 | 2 | 3 | 4 | 5 | 6 | 7 |
| 2 | 0 | 2 | 4 | 6 | 8 | 10 | 12 | 14 |
| 3 | 0 | 3 | 6 | 9 | 12 | 15 | 18 | 21 |
| 4 | 0 | 4 | 8 | 12 | 16 | 20 | 24 | 28 |
| 5 | 0 | 5 | 10 | 15 | 20 | 25 | 30 | 35 |
| 6 | 0 | 6 | 12 | 18 | 24 | 30 | 36 | 42 |
| 7 | 0 | 7 | 14 | 21 | 28 | 35 | 42 | 49 |
| 8 | 0 | 8 | 16 | 24 | 32 | 40 | 48 | 56 |
| 9 | 0 | 9 | 18 | 27 | 36 | 45 | 54 | 63 |

6. $48 \div 6 =$ ____

   $6 \times$ ____ $= 48$

7. $56 \div 8 =$ ____

   $8 \times$ ____ $= 56$

## Multiplication Properties

Find each product.

8. $3 \times 3 \times 2 =$ ____

9. $5 \times 1 \times 3 =$ ____

10. $4 \times 2 \times 4 =$ ____

11. $2 \times 2 \times 4 =$ ____

12. $4 \times 0 \times 2 =$ ____

13. $2 \times 5 \times 3 =$ ____

## Multiplication on the Number Line

14. Which equation does the number line show?

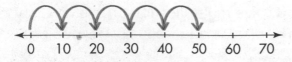

ⓐ  $1 \times 10 = 10$     ⓑ  $3 \times 10 \times 1 = 30$     ⓒ  $4 \times 5 = 20$     ⓓ  $5 \times 10 = 50$

Name_____

**PROJECT 10A**

## What do you need to do to plan a trip?

**Project:** Research the Distance Between Two Cities

**PROJECT 10B**

## How do stores make sure they have enough of an item to sell?

**Project:** Create Your Own Store

### PROJECT
### 10C

## How do trees help our environment?

**Project:** Design a Park and Sing a Song

### PROJECT
### 10D

## How many items can you fit in a box?

**Project:** Make a Product Game

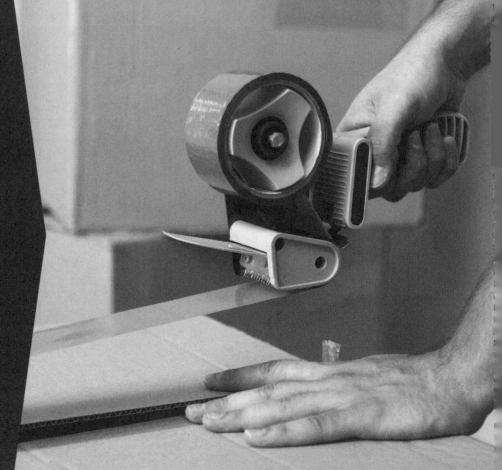

Name_____

☆ ☆
**Solve & Share**
Companies package their goods in a variety of ways. One company packages a case of water as 2 rows of 10 bottles. How many bottles are in the number of cases shown in the table below? Explain your thinking.

**I can ...**
use patterns to multiply by multiples of 10.

© **Content Standards** 3.NBT.A.3 Also 3.OA.D.8
**Mathematical Practices** MP.2, MP.5, MP.7

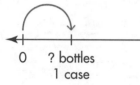

2 rows of 10 bottles = 1 case

0    ? bottles
     1 case

| Number of Cases | Number of Bottles |
|:---:|:---:|
| 1 | |
| 2 | |
| 3 | |
| 4 | |

You can use appropriate tools. Place-value blocks or a number line can help you apply the math you know.

**Look Back!** How can place-value patterns help you when multiplying by 20?

**Essential Question**

# How Can You Use Patterns to Multiply?

**A**

A half-century is a period of 50 years. Find the number of years in 5 half-centuries.

You can use place-value blocks or an open number line to multiply.

| Factor | Multiple of 10 | Product |
|--------|----------------|---------|
| 1 | 50 | 50 |
| 2 | 50 | |
| 3 | 50 | |
| 4 | 50 | |
| 5 | 50 | |

**B** **One Way**

Find 5 × 50. Use place-value blocks.

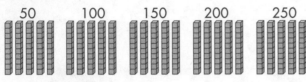

50    100    150    200    250

1 × 50 is 1 group of 5 tens =   5 tens or   50
2 × 50 is 2 groups of 5 tens = 10 tens or 100
3 × 50 is 3 groups of 5 tens = 15 tens or 150
4 × 50 is 4 groups of 5 tens = 20 tens or 200
5 × 50 is 5 groups of 5 tens = 25 tens or 250

You can skip count to find the number of years in 5 half-centuries.

There are 250 years in 5 half-centuries.

**C** **Another Way**

Find 5 × 50. Use an open number line.

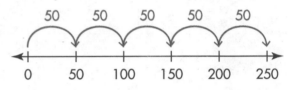

50    50    50    50    50

0    50    100    150    200    250

1 jump of 50 is 50.          1 × 50 =   50
2 jumps of 50 are 100.     2 × 50 = 100
3 jumps of 50 are 150.     3 × 50 = 150
4 jumps of 50 are 200.     4 × 50 = 200
5 jumps of 50 are 250.     5 × 50 = 250

There are place-value patterns when multiplying by multiples of 10.

There are 250 years in 5 half-centuries.

**Convince Me!** **Use Structure** Suppose the multiple of 10 in the table above was 40 years instead of 50. Explain how you can use place-value patterns to find each product.

Name _____

# ☆Guided Practice

## Do You Understand?

1. Explain how to use place-value patterns to multiply $9 \times 50$.

2. How are the products in Box B on the previous page like skip counting by 5?

## Do You Know How?

3. Draw or use place-value blocks to show $3 \times 60$. Then find the product.

4. Use the open number line to multiply $4 \times 60$.

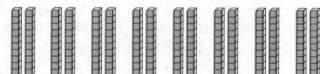

0

# Independent Practice ☆

**Leveled Practice** In **5–10**, use an open number line or draw place-value blocks to find each product.

5. $3 \times 70$

0

6. $8 \times 20$

7. $9 \times 30$

8. $5 \times 60$

9. $6 \times 60$

10. $2 \times 30$

# Problem Solving

**11.** The Aztecs had a solar calendar. How many days are in 7 of the longer months in all? Show how to use place value to solve.

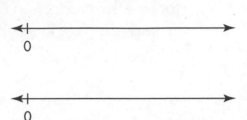

The longer months of the Aztec calendar are each 20 days long. After each of the longer months, there is a period of 5 days.

**12. Higher Order Thinking** On one open number line, show 4 × 30. On the other open number line, show 3 × 40. How are the problems alike? How are they different?

0

0

**13. Reasoning** Martina has $504. She spends $199 on new computer software. Use mental math to find how much money Martina has left.

**14.** Use place-value blocks to find 1 × 40, 2 × 40, 3 × 40, and 4 × 40. What is the same in each of the products you listed?

**15.** A package of crepe paper streamers has 2 rolls. Yen bought 3 packages. How many inches of crepe paper did Yen get?

70 inches long

## Assessment Practice

**16.** Select all the expressions that have a product of 300.

- ☐ 3 × 10
- ☐ 5 × 60
- ☐ 5 × 600
- ☐ 6 × 50
- ☐ 6 × 500

**17.** Select all the expressions that have a product of 240.

- ☐ 3 × 80
- ☐ 4 × 60
- ☐ 6 × 40
- ☐ 8 × 30
- ☐ 9 × 30

Name_____

## Solve & Share

Find the products of 4 × 50, 3 × 40, and 9 × 20. Describe the patterns you find.

**I can ...**
use different strategies to find products when one factor is a multiple of 10.

© **Content Standards** 3.NBT.A.3 Also 3.OA.A.3
**Mathematical Practices** MP.1, MP.4, MP.7

You can look for relationships. Think about how place-value patterns can help you solve the problems.

**Look Back!** How can you use place value to describe the patterns in the products?

**Essential Question** How Can Place Value Help You Use Mental Math to Multiply by a Multiple of 10?

**A**

*A regular box of crayons has 30 crayons. A jumbo box holds 60 crayons. There are 5 boxes of regular crayons on one shelf and 5 boxes of jumbo crayons on another shelf. How many crayons are on each shelf?*

? crayons

5 boxes →

You can use basic multiplication facts to multiply by multiples of 10.

**B** Find 5 × 30.

?

| 30 | 30 | 30 | 30 | 30 |

Think about tens.
Multiply 5 by the number of tens.

5 × 30 = 5 × 3 tens

5 × 30 = 15 tens

5 × 30 = 150

There are 150 crayons on one shelf.

**C** Find 5 × 60.

?

| 60 | 60 | 60 | 60 | 60 |

Sometimes the basic multiplication fact makes the product look different.

5 × 60 = 5 × 6 tens

5 × 60 = 30 tens

5 × 60 = 300

There are 300 crayons on the other shelf.

**Convince Me!** **Make Sense and Persevere** Suppose there are 50 crayons in each of the 5 boxes. Use mental math to find 5 × 50. How many crayons are in 5 boxes?

Name_____

# ☆ Guided Practice

## Do You Understand?

**1.** How can you find the product of 9 × 80? Explain.

**2.** Jon says, "4 × 6 is 4 groups of 6 ones. 4 times 6 equals 24."

Complete the sentences to describe 4 × 60 in a similar way.

4 × 60 is 4 groups of 6 _____.
4 times 60 equals _____.

## Do You Know How?

In **3–8**, complete each equation.

**3.** 6 × 6 = _____
   6 × 60 = _____

**4.** 3 × 2 = _____
   3 × 20 = _____

**5.** 5 × 4 = _____
   5 × 40 = _____

**6.** 8 × 2 = _____
   80 × 2 = _____

**7.** 4 × 9 = _____
   40 × 9 = _____

**8.** 7 × 8 = _____
   70 × 8 = _____

# Independent Practice ☆

**Leveled Practice** In **9–19**, complete each equation.

**9.** 6 × 70 = (6 × _____) tens
   6 × 70 = _____ tens
   6 × 70 = _____

**10.** 9 × 50 = (9 × _____) tens
   9 × 50 = _____ tens
   9 × 50 = _____

**11.** 2 × 6 = _____
   2 × 60 = _____

**12.** 5 × 8 = _____
   5 × 80 = _____

**13.** 9 × 4 = _____
   9 × 40 = _____

**14.** 2 × 30 = _____

**15.** 60 × 9 = _____

**16.** _____ = 8 × 20

**17.** 80 × 5 = _____

**18.** _____ = 90 × 2

**19.** 30 × 4 = _____

# Problem Solving

**20.** The horse conch can reach a length of 24 inches. Use multiplication to write 2 different equations that represent the conch's length.

**24 inches in length**

**21. Model with Math** Juanita buys 7 sheets of postage stamps at the post office. Each sheet has 20 stamps. How many stamps does she buy in all? Explain how you solved the problem. Tell why you chose that method.

**22. Algebra** What value makes the equation below true?

$9 \times ? = 630$

**23.** Janet bought 137 green beads. Now she has 349 beads. How many beads did Janet have before?

**24. Higher Order Thinking** Ali and his family are going to the amusement park. If there are 2 adults and 5 children, how much will the tickets cost?

AMUSEMENT PARK CHILD $20

AMUSEMENT PARK ADULT $30

---

### ☑ Assessment Practice

**25.** Mr. Ridley owns a clothing store. The table at the right shows the number of racks and the number of pieces of clothing on each rack. Match each equation with its product to find the number of pieces of each type of clothing that are on the racks.

|  | 80 | 120 |
|---|---|---|
| $2 \times 60 = ?$ | ☐ | ☐ |
| $3 \times 40 = ?$ | ☐ | ☐ |
| $4 \times 20 = ?$ | ☐ | ☐ |
| $2 \times 40 = ?$ | ☐ | ☐ |

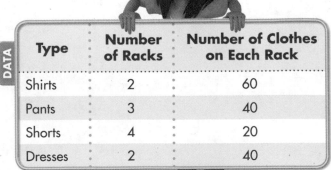

| DATA | Type | Number of Racks | Number of Clothes on Each Rack |
|---|---|---|---|
| | Shirts | 2 | 60 |
| | Pants | 3 | 40 |
| | Shorts | 4 | 20 |
| | Dresses | 2 | 40 |

Name_____

## Solve & Share

Three students found 5 × 30 in different ways. Which student is correct? Explain.

# Lesson 10-3
## Use Properties to Multiply

**I can ...**
use properties of multiplication to find a product when one factor is a multiple of 10.

© **Content Standards** 3.NBT.A.3 Also 3.OA.B.5
**Mathematical Practices** MP.3, MP.6, MP.8

**Janice**

I imagined 5 jumps of 30 on a number line and counted by 30s just like counting by 3s.
30, 60, 90, 120, 150

**Earl**

30 = 3 × 10. So, 5 × 30 = 5 × 3 × 10.
I multiplied 5 × 3 first to get 15.
Then, I multiplied 15 × 10 to get 150.

Properties can help you critique reasoning.

**Clara**

It is easier to count by 5 than 3.
I multiplied the 5 ×10 first to get 50, and then found 3 ×50 by counting 50, 100, 150.

**Look Back!** What property of multiplication did Earl use in his reasoning?

**Essential Question** How Can You Use Properties to Multiply by Multiples of 10?

**A**

How can you find the product of 4 × 20?

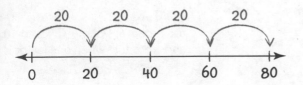

You know how to use an open number line to model multiplication.

You can use properties to explain a rule for finding a product when one factor is a multiple of 10.

Remember the 10s facts pattern. Think about the product of a number and 10. The product has a zero in the ones place. The other factor is written to the left of the zero.

**B** One Way

You can use the Associative Property of Multiplication to group the factors.

4 × 20 = 4 × (2 × 10)

4 × 20 = (4 × 2) × 10

4 × 20 = 8 × 10

4 × 20 = 80

Think of 20 as 2 × 10.

**C** Another Way

You can use the Distributive Property to decompose a factor.

4 × 20 = (2 + 2) × 20

4 × 20 = (2 × 20) + (2 × 20)

4 × 20 = 40 + 40

4 × 20 = 80

**Convince Me!** **Be Precise** Use properties of multiplication to explain why
3 × 60 = 18 × 10.

# ☆Guided Practice

## Do You Understand?

**1.** Why can you say that
$3 \times 20 = (2 \times 20) + 20$?

**2.** Why can you say that
$3 \times 20 = (3 \times 2) \times 10$?

## Do You Know How?

In **3** and **4**, find each product using properties of multiplication.

**3.** $9 \times 60 = 9 \times (\underline{\quad} \times 10)$

$9 \times 60 = (9 \times \underline{\quad}) \times 10$

$9 \times 60 = \underline{\quad} \times 10 = \underline{\quad}$

**4.** $4 \times 90 = (\underline{\quad} + 2) \times 90$

$4 \times 90 = (\underline{\quad} \times 90) + (\underline{\quad} \times 90)$

$4 \times 90 = \underline{\quad} + \underline{\quad} = \underline{\quad}$

# Independent Practice ☆

**Leveled Practice** In **5–12**, show how to find each product using properties of multiplication.

**5.** $7 \times 60 = 7 \times (\underline{\quad} \times 10)$

$7 \times 60 = (7 \times \underline{\quad}) \times 10$

$7 \times 60 = \underline{\quad} \times 10 = \underline{\quad}$

**6.** $5 \times 40 = \underline{\quad} \times (\underline{\quad} \times 10)$

$5 \times 40 = (\underline{\quad} \times \underline{\quad}) \times 10$

$5 \times 40 = \underline{\quad} \times \underline{\quad} = \underline{\quad}$

**7.** $8 \times 30$

**8.** $4 \times 70$

**9.** $5 \times 90$

**10.** $8 \times 80$

**11.** $6 \times 40$

**12.** $9 \times 80$

# Problem Solving

13. Look at the picture graph at the right. How many pounds of newspaper did Grade 3 collect?

**Newspaper Collected to Recycle**

Grade 2

Grade 3

Grade 4

Each ⬛ = 30 pounds.

14. How many pounds of newspaper did Grade 3 and Grade 4 collect together? Explain your plan for solving.

15. **Higher Order Thinking** Grade 5 collected 150 pounds of newspaper. How many more symbols would be in the row for Grade 5 than for Grade 2?

16. **Generalize** Without finding the products, how can you tell whether $4 \times 60$ or $7 \times 40$ is greater?

17. Explain how to use mental math to add $521 + 104$.

18. Tikie said that it is easy to count by 50s. Explain how she could use counting by 50s to find $5 \times 60$.

You can use properties and equations to help construct an argument!

✓ **Assessment Practice**

19. Which products are equal to 180? Select all that apply.

☐ $1 \times 80$     ☐ $6 \times (3 \times 10)$

☐ $6 \times 30$     ☐ $3 \times (6 \times 10)$

☐ $3 \times 60$

20. Which products are equal to 200? Select all that apply.

☐ $2 \times 10$     ☐ $5 \times (4 \times 10)$

☐ $5 \times 40$     ☐ $2 \times (1 \times 10)$

☐ $4 \times 50$

Name_____

### Solve & Share

Stefan says that he could use this multiplication table to help multiply 3 × 40 to get 120. Explain Stefan's strategy.

| ×  | 0 | 1 | 2  | 3  | 4  | 5  | 6  |
|----|---|---|----|----|----|----|----|
| 0  | 0 | 0 | 0  | 0  | 0  | 0  | 0  |
| 1  | 0 | 1 | 2  | 3  | 4  | 5  | 6  |
| 2  | 0 | 2 | 4  | 6  | 8  | 10 | 12 |
| 3  | 0 | 3 | 6  | 9  | 12 | 15 | 18 |
| 4  | 0 | 4 | 8  | 12 | 16 | 20 | 24 |
| 5  | 0 | 5 | 10 | 15 | 20 | 25 | 30 |
| 6  | 0 | 6 | 12 | 18 | 24 | 30 | 36 |

**I can ...**
use patterns to describe relationships between quantities.

© **Mathematical Practices** MP.7 Also MP.1, MP.3, MP.4
**Content Standards** 3.NBT.A.3 Also 3.OA.D.9

### Thinking Habits

*Be a good thinker!
These questions can help you.*

- What patterns can I see and describe?

- How can I use the patterns to solve the problem?

- Can I see expressions and objects in different ways?

**Look Back!** **Use Structure** Could Stefan also use the multiplication table to solve 4 × 40 in the same way? Explain how you decided.

**Essential Question**

# How Can I Use Structure to Multiply with Multiples of 10?

**A**

*Find the missing products in the multiplication table.*

| × | 10 | 20 | 30 | 40 | 50 | 60 | 70 | 80 | 90 |
|---|----|----|----|----|----|----|----|----|----|
| 4 | 40 | 80 |    |    |    | 240 |   | 320 |   |
| 5 | 50 |    | 150 |   |    |    | 350 |   |   |
| 6 | 60 |    | 180 |   |    |    | 420 |   |   |

You can look for relationships in the multiplication table.

**B**

**How can I make use of structure to solve this problem?**

**I can**

- look for patterns to help solve a problem.

- describe the patterns that I find.

- identify how numbers are organized.

**C**

Here's my thinking...

As I move down the columns, the numbers increase by the value of the column.

As I move across the rows, the numbers increase by the value in the column where 10 is a factor.

I used patterns I know for multiplying by multiples of 10.

| × | 10 | 20 | 30 | 40 | 50 | 60 | 70 | 80 | 90 |
|---|----|----|----|----|----|----|----|----|----|
| 4 | 40 | 80 | 120 | 160 | 200 | 240 | 280 | 320 | 360 |
| 5 | 50 | 100 | 150 | 200 | 250 | 300 | 350 | 400 | 450 |
| 6 | 60 | 120 | 180 | 240 | 300 | 360 | 420 | 480 | 540 |

**Convince Me!** **Use Structure** The ones digit never changes in the products in the multiplication table above. Explain why.

Practice  Tools  Assessment

# ☆Guided Practice

**Use Structure**

Sean is making muffins. He is choosing to make either 7 or 8 batches. He is also choosing whether to use 40, 50, 60, or 70 raisins for each batch. Sean starts this table to show the total number of raisins he will need for each choice.

You can use the structure of the products and factors to find a pattern.

1. Find the missing products in the table to show how many raisins Sean will use for each batch. Think about patterns or properties you know.

| × | 40 | 50 | 60 | 70 |
|---|----|----|----|----|
| 7 |    |    | 420 |    |
| 8 | 320 |   |    |    |

2. Sean uses 480 raisins in total. How many batches does he make? How many raisins does he use for each batch?

# Independent Practice ☆

**Use Structure**

Jolene is making a display with equal rows of stickers. She is choosing whether to use 20, 30, 40, or 50 stickers in each row. She is also choosing whether to have 2, 3, or 4 rows. Jolene starts this table to show the total number of stickers she will need for each choice.

3. Find the missing products in the table to show how many stickers Jolene will need for each choice. Think about patterns or properties you know.

| × | 20 | 30 | 40 | 50 |
|---|----|----|----|----|
| 2 | 40 | 60 |    |    |
| 3 | 60 |    |    |    |
| 4 |    |    |    | 200 |

4. Jolene uses 150 stickers in total. How many rows does she have in her display? How many stickers does she put in each row?

# Problem Solving

## ✓ Performance Task

**Music Lessons**

Four students each took music lessons for different instruments this month. They want to know who spent the most money on music lessons.

| Student | June | Li | Mick | Rita |
|---|---|---|---|---|
| Price Paid per Lesson (dollars) | 60 | 20 | 10 | 40 |
| Length of Lesson (minutes) | 60 | 60 | 50 | 90 |
| Number of Lessons | 4 | 8 | 9 | 7 |
| Total Cost (dollars) | ___ | ___ | ___ | ___ |

5. **Make Sense and Persevere** What do you need to do to solve the problem?

6. **Use Structure** How can you find the total amount for each student? Think about properties or patterns you know.

> Think about and look for relationships to help solve problems.

7. **Model with Math** Use math you know to complete the table. Circle the name of the student who spent the greatest amount.

8. **Construct Arguments** Did the student who spent the most per lesson also spend the greatest amount in total? Explain why or why not.

**Set A** pages 381–384

**Reteaching**

Find 5 × 70.

Show 5 jumps of 70 on the number line.

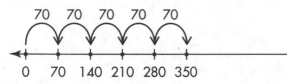

1 jump of 70 is 70.        1 × 70 = 70

2 jumps of 70 are 140.     2 × 70 = 140

3 jumps of 70 are 210.     3 × 70 = 210

4 jumps of 70 are 280.     4 × 70 = 280

5 jumps of 70 are 350.     5 × 70 = 350

There are place-value patterns when multiplying by 10.

**Remember** that you can skip count to show multiplication.

In **1–3**, use an open number line to solve.

**1.** 4 × 80

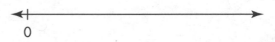

**2.** 7 × 20

**3.** 3 × 50

**Set B** pages 385–388

You can use basic multiplication facts to multiply by multiples of 10.

Find 6 × 30

Multiply the number of tens by 6.

6 × 30 = 6 × 3 tens
6 × 30 = 18 tens
6 × 30 = 180

Place-value patterns can help you learn a shortcut!

**Remember** to think about basic facts.

In **1–10**, find each product.

**1.** 3 × 30          **2.** 50 × 9

**3.** 6 × 60          **4.** 5 × 80

**5.** 8 × 40          **6.** 80 × 7

**7.** 70 × 4          **8.** 8 × 30

**9.** 7 × 70          **10.** 60 × 5

**Set C** pages 389–392

Find 7 × 80.

Think of 80 as 8 × 10. Then use the Associative Property of Multiplication.

$7 \times 80 = 7 \times (8 \times 10)$
$7 \times 80 = (7 \times 8) \times 10$
$7 \times 80 = 56 \times 10$
$7 \times 80 = 560$

You can use properties of operations, such as the Associative Property and the Distributive Property, to help multiply.

**Remember** that the Associative Property of Multiplication lets you regroup factors.

In **1** and **2**, find the product using properties.

**1.** $5 \times 80 = 5 \times (\underline{\phantom{xx}} \times 10)$

$5 \times 80 = (5 \times \underline{\phantom{xx}}) \times 10$

$5 \times 80 = \underline{\phantom{xx}} \times 10 = \underline{\phantom{xx}}$

**2.** $7 \times 40 = \underline{\phantom{xx}} \times (\underline{\phantom{xx}} \times 10)$

$7 \times 40 = (\underline{\phantom{xx}} \times \underline{\phantom{xx}}) \times 10$

$7 \times 40 = \underline{\phantom{xx}} \times 10 = \underline{\phantom{xx}}$

**Set D** pages 393–396

Think about these questions to help you **make use of structure**.

### Thinking Habits

- What patterns can I see and describe?

- How can I use the patterns to solve the problem?

- Can I see expressions and objects in different ways?

**Remember** to use patterns or properties to multiply by multiples of 10.

Christy is making a savings plan. She wants to know how much she will save if she saves $40 for 6, 7, 8, or 9 weeks.

**1.** How can you use patterns to help solve this problem?

**2.** Find the total amount Christy would save after 6, 7, 8, or 9 weeks. Think about patterns or properties you know.

**1.** Julia gives each of her 4 friends a sheet of stickers. Each sheet has 20 stickers. How many stickers do her friends have in all?

**2.** Select all of the expressions equal to 8 × 60.

- ☐ 48 × 10
- ☐ 6 × 80
- ☐ (8 × 6) × 10
- ☐ 8 × (8 × 10)
- ☐ 60 × 80

**3.** Mrs. Rode bought 80 packs of juice boxes for her school's party. The juice boxes came in packs of 8. How many juice boxes did Mrs. Rode buy? Explain how to solve.

**4.** The third-grade teachers at Jenny's school need 5 boxes of yellow folders and 4 boxes of red folders. Each box has 40 folders. How many folders do the teachers need?

- Ⓐ 160
- Ⓒ 320
- Ⓑ 200
- Ⓓ 360

**5.** Write each expression in the correct answer space to show expressions equal to 6 × 30 and 3 × 80.

| 6 × 30 | 3 × 80 |
| --- | --- |
|  |  |

(3 × 8) × 10            6 × (3 × 10)
3 × (6 × 10)            18 × 10
24 × 10                3 × (8 × 10)
8 × (3 × 10)           (6 × 3) × 10

**6.** Match each expression on the left to an equal expression.

|  | 42 × 10 | 24 × 10 | 36 × 10 | 28 × 10 |
| --- | --- | --- | --- | --- |
| 6 × 60 | ☐ | ☐ | ☐ | ☐ |
| 6 × 70 | ☐ | ☐ | ☐ | ☐ |
| 7 × 40 | ☐ | ☐ | ☐ | ☐ |
| 6 × 40 | ☐ | ☐ | ☐ | ☐ |

**7.** What is $4 \times 30$?

Ⓐ 22

Ⓑ 34

Ⓒ 120

Ⓓ 160

**8.** Tyler does 40 pushups each day. How many pushups does he do in 5 days?

**9.** The family membership to a children's museum is $90 for a year. On Friday 5 families bought memberships. How much did the museum receive for the new memberships?

**10.** Select all of the expressions that are equal to $7 \times 50$.

☐ $7 \times (5 \times 10)$

☐ $35 \times 10$

☐ $7 \times 5$

☐ $75 \times 10$

☐ $(7 \times 5) \times 10$

**11.** Tyrone drives 30 miles every day. How many miles does Tyrone drive in 7 days?

**A.** Use a number line to solve the problem.

**B.** Describe another way to solve the problem.

Name_____

**Pet Adoption**
Carson and Adriana volunteer at a local animal rescue center. The adoption fee is different based on the animal and its age.

Carson made an **Adoption Fee** graph to show the fees for adult dogs, puppies, adult cats, and kittens. Adriana recorded the number of each animal adopted during the summer in the **Animals Adopted** table.

Use the **Adoption Fee** graph and the **Animals Adopted** table to answer Questions **1–3**.

1. Carson wants to find the total adoption fees the rescue center received for adopted adult dogs. Show how Carson can use a number line to do this.

Adoption Fee

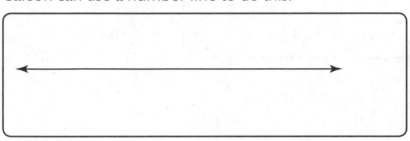

2. Adriana says that she can use (4 × 8) × 10 to find the total adoption fees for adopted puppies. Is she correct? Explain why or why not. Then find the total.

| Animals Adopted | |
|---|---|
| Adult Dog | 8 |
| Puppy | 4 |
| Adult Cat | 5 |
| Kitten | 3 |

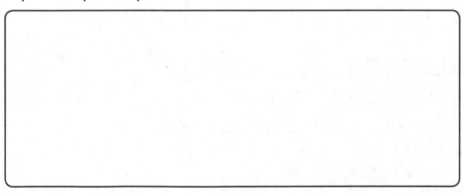

3. Find the adoption fees the rescue center received for kittens. Think about patterns or properties you know. Show your work.

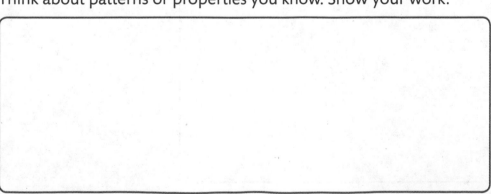

The animal rescue center sells toy packages for pets.

The **Toy Packages** graph shows the amount earned for different types of packages. The **Toy Packages Sold** table shows how many packages were sold in the summer.

Use the **Toy Packages** graph and the **Toy Packages Sold** table to answer Questions **4** and **5**.

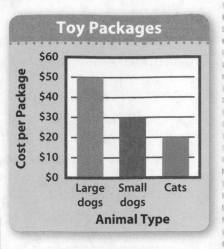

**Toy Packages**

4. How much money did the animal rescue center earn from toys for large dogs? Show your work.

| Toy Packages Sold | |
|---|---|
| Large Dog | 5 |
| Small Dog | 7 |

5. Carson says that the center earned more money selling toys for small dogs than from selling toys for large dogs. Is he correct? Explain why or why not.

Use the **Toy Packages** graph to answer Question **6**.

6. Adriana forgot to record the number of packages of cat toys that were sold. She knows that the center earned a total of $140 from the toys for cats. How many packages of cat toys did they sell?

# Use Operations with Whole Numbers to Solve Problems

**Essential Question:** What are ways to solve 2-step problems?

It is fun to build something that you designed! Here is a project on engineering.

Kites come in many shapes and sizes.

Engineers think about how much material, time, and money they need for a successful design.

## enVision STEM Project: Engineering Design

**Do Research** Use the Internet or other sources to find information about kites. Find two designs for building a kite. What materials do you need for each design? How much do those materials cost?

**Journal: Write a Report** Include what you found. Also in your report:

- Find the total cost for each design.

- Decide which design is less expensive.

- Write an equation to show how much less expensive that design is.

Name _____

# Review What You Know

## A-Z Vocabulary

Choose the best term from the box.
Write it on the blank.

| • equation | • quotient |
|---|---|
| • product | • unknown |

1. The equal sign shows that the left side of a(n) _____ has the same value as the right side.

2. A question mark can be a symbol for a(n) _____ value.

3. The answer to a division problem is the _____ .

## Addition and Subtraction

4. 739 − 104

5. 512 + 216

6. 710 − 569

7. 104 + 67

8. 664 + 78

9. 825 − 477

## Multiplication and Division

10. 60 ÷ 6

11. 40 × 4

12. 7 × 3

13. $(3 \times 10) \times 6 =$
    Ⓐ $(3 \times 10) + (6 \times 10)$
    Ⓑ $(3 \times 6) + (10 \times 6)$
    Ⓒ $3 \times (10 \times 6)$
    Ⓓ $(10 + 10 + 10) + 6$

14. $4 \times (20 \times 2) =$
    Ⓐ $(4 \times 20) \times 2$
    Ⓑ $(4 \times 20) + (4 \times 2)$
    Ⓒ $4 + (20 + 20)$
    Ⓓ $(4 + 20) + (4 + 2)$

## Model with Math

15. Caleb has 8 toy cars. Each car has 4 wheels. He wants to know how many wheels are on all of his cars. Represent this problem using a bar diagram and an equation. Then solve.

Name_____

**PROJECT 11A**

**Why do stores have sales and other promotions?**

**Project:** Write a Skit About a Sale

**PROJECT 11B**

**How did grapefruit first come to Florida?**

**Project:** Create a Poster About Citrus Groves

**PROJECT 11C**

**How would you make a budget for selling lemonade in a lemonade stand?**

**Project:** Perform a Song About Lemonade

Math Modeling

## Cash Bucket

Video

Before watching the video, think:

Selling tickets to the play helps pay for the costumes the actors wear.

**I can ...**
model with math to solve a problem that involves computing with whole numbers.

© **Mathematical Practices** MP.4 Also MP.1, MP.7
**Content Standards** 3.OA.D.8 Also 3.OA.A.3, 3.NBT.A.2

Name_____

Activity

☆ ☆
**Solve & Share**

Jen buys a backpack and a sleeping bag. She gets $10 off if the total is more than $200. What is the final cost of Jen's order? Complete the bar diagram below. Then draw another diagram to solve the problem.

**I can ...**
draw diagrams and write equations to show how the quantities in a problem are related.

© **Content Standards** 3.OA.D.8 Also 3.NBT.A.2
**Mathematical Practices** MP.2, MP.3, MP.4

| Item | Price |
|------|-------|
| Grill | $138 |
| Backpack | $89 |
| Lantern | $78 |
| Sleeping Bag | $128 |

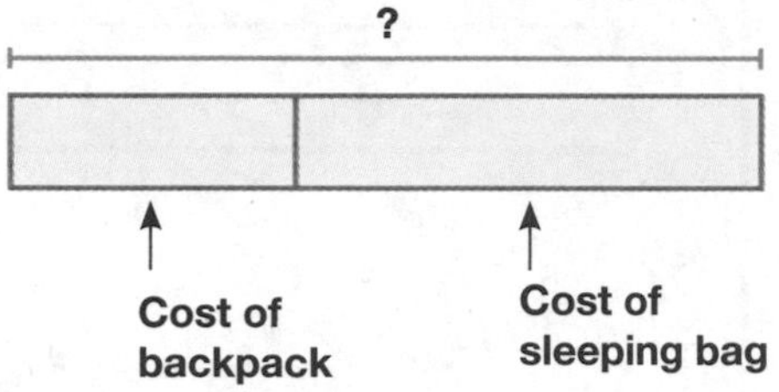

DATA

?
⎡_____⎤
| | |

↑ Cost of backpack    ↑ Cost of sleeping bag

Use reasoning. You can draw more than one diagram and write more than one equation to solve 2-step problems.

**Look Back!** How can you use an estimate to show that the final cost of the backpack and sleeping bag you found makes sense?

**Essential Question** **How Can You Use Diagrams to Solve 2-Step Problems?**

**A**

The results of a car survey are shown in the table. How many fewer cars in the survey have poor fuel efficiency than have either good or average fuel efficiency? Use estimation to check the answer.

You can draw bar diagrams to help. You can use a letter to stand for the unknown quantity.

| DATA | Survey of Fuel-Efficient Cars | |
|---|---|---|
| | Fuel Efficiency | Number of Cars |
| | Good | 98 |
| | Average | 165 |
| | Poor | 224 |

**B** Find and answer the hidden question.

How many total cars in the survey have either good or average fuel efficiency?

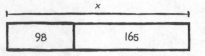
x

$x$ is the unknown total.

$x = 98 + 165$

$\begin{array}{cc} +2 & -2 \end{array}$

$= 100 + 163$

$= 263$

You can round 98 to 100 to estimate: $100 + 165 = 265$. 265 is close to 263. The answer is reasonable.

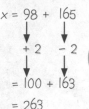

263 cars have good or average fuel efficiency.

**C** Answer the original question.

How many fewer cars in the survey have poor fuel efficiency?

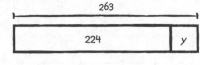
263

224   $y$

$y$ is the unknown difference.

$y = 263 - 224$

$\begin{array}{r} 263 \\ -200 \\ \hline 63 \\ -20 \\ \hline 43 \\ -3 \\ \hline 40 \\ -1 \\ \hline 39 \end{array}$

You can round $263 - 234$ to $260 - 230$ to estimate. 30 is close to 39. The answer is reasonable.

39 fewer cars have poor fuel efficiency.

**Convince Me!** **Critique Reasoning** Jane used estimation to check the reasonableness of the work above. Explain whether Jane's work makes sense.

165 and 98 is about 200.
224 minus 200 equals 24, which is close to 39.

Name _____

# ☆ Guided Practice

## Do You Understand?

**1.** How do the bar diagrams help you write equations for the problem on the previous page?

## Do You Know How?

**2.** Josie has $145. She buys a bike for $127. The next week she saves $15. How much money does Josie have now? Complete the bar diagrams and write equations to solve.

_____

| _____ | $a$ | ← Money left after buying a bike |

$s$ ← Money now

| _____ . | _____ |

# Independent Practice ☆

In **3**, use the map. Draw diagrams and write equations to solve. Use letters to represent unknown quantities.

**3.** Manuel's family drove from Louisville to Indianapolis to Detroit and then directly back to Louisville. How much farther did they drive going to Detroit than returning from Detroit?

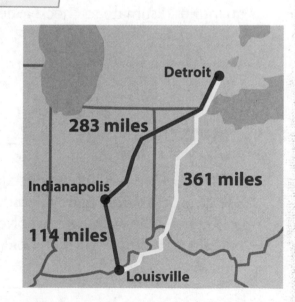

Detroit

283 miles

Indianapolis

361 miles

114 miles

Louisville

**4.** How can you estimate to check if your answer above is reasonable? Explain.

# Problem Solving

5. Write equations to find how many more tickets were sold for the roller coaster on Saturday than for the swings on both days combined. Use letters to represent the unknown quantities. You can draw diagrams to help.

| DATA | Number of Tickets Sold | | |
|---|---|---|---|
| | Ride | Saturday | Sunday |
| | Ferris Wheel | 368 | 302 |
| | Roller Coaster | 486 | 456 |
| | Swings | 138 | 154 |

6. **Higher Order Thinking** Write a two-step problem about buying or selling books that can be solved using addition or subtraction. Solve your problem.

7. **enVision®** STEM Lindsay has 6 boxes of toothpicks. There are 80 toothpicks in each box. Lindsay uses all of the toothpicks to build a model bridge. How many toothpicks does Lindsay use in all?

8. **Model with Math** Matt had 327 plastic bottles for recycling. He recycled 118 bottles on Monday. He recycled 123 bottles on Tuesday. How many bottles does Matt have left to recycle? Use representations such as bar diagrams or equations to model with math. Use letters to represent the unknown quantities. Estimate to check your work.

When checking, remember to estimate for each step.

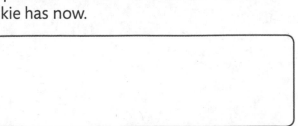
## Assessment Practice

9. Ukie has 142 leaves in her collection. She gives 25 to her brother and then collects 19 more. Create and solve equations to find the number of leaves Ukie has now.

10. Richard had $236 in his savings account. He got $45 for his birthday and saved all but $16 of it. Create and solve equations to find the amount in Richard's savings account now.

Name_____

Activity

**Lesson 11-2**
Solve 2-Step
Word Problems:
Multiplication
and Division

**Solve & Share**

Two friends decide to share equally all of the apples they picked. They filled the bags shown with 4 apples in each bag. How many apples will each friend get?

**I can ...**
draw diagrams and write equations to show how the quantities in a problem are related.

Use reasoning. You can use diagrams and equations to show how the numbers in 2-step problems are related.

© **Content Standards** 3.OA.D.8 Also 3.OA.C.7
**Mathematical Practices** MP.1, MP.2, MP.6

*t*

6

**Look Back!** Tell why multiplication can be used to find the total number of apples.

**A**

The teams for the City Baseball Tournament are divided equally into 3 leagues. Each league is divided into 2 regions with the same number of teams in each region. How many teams are in each region?

**City Baseball Tournament**

• 24 teams

• 3 leagues

You can represent this problem with bar diagrams. You can use a letter to stand for the unknown quantity.

**B Step 1**

**Find and answer the hidden question.**

How many teams are in each league?

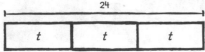

*t* is the unknown number of teams in each league.

$t = 24 \div 3$

$t = 8$

There are 8 teams in each league.

**C Step 2**

**Use the answer to the hidden question to answer the original question.**

How many teams are in each region?

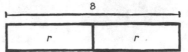

*r* is the unknown number of teams in each region.

$r = 8 \div 2$

$r = 4$

There are 4 teams in each region.

**Convince Me!** **Make Sense and Persevere** Another tournament has 2 leagues with 9 teams in each league. An equal number of teams will play on each of the 3 days of the tournament. Each team will play once. How many teams will play on each day?

**Practice  Tools  Assessment**

# ☆ Guided Practice

## Do You Understand?

**1.** Why do you need to solve the hidden question first for the problem in Box A on the previous page?

**2.** What multiplication equation could be written for the bar diagram in Box C on the previous page?

Remember that multiplication can help you solve division problems.

## Do You Know How?

In **3**, complete the bar diagrams and write equations to solve.

**3.** There are 8 students in 2 school vans with the same number of students in each van. The admission fee for each student is $5. What is the total admission fee for all of the students in one van?

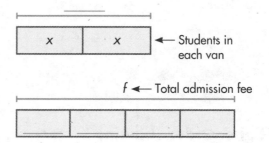

## ☆ Independent Practice ☆

In **4**, draw diagrams and write equations to solve. Use letters to represent the unknown quantities.

**4.** Arif saves $4 each week. After 6 weeks, he spends all the money he saved on 3 items. Each item costs the same amount. How much does each item cost?

**5.** Georgia says that because she knows 5 × 4 = 20, she knows Arif will have saved more than $20. Is Georgia correct? Explain.

# Problem Solving

6. **Be Precise** One Grade 3 class collected 86 pounds of newspaper. The other Grade 3 class collected 65 pounds of newspaper. Which grade collected the greatest number of pounds of newspaper?

**DATA**

| Pounds of Newspaper Collected | |
| --- | --- |
| Grade | Pounds of Newspaper |
| 3 | ? |
| 4 | 75 |
| 5 | 125 |

7. Six pounds of pecans are shared equally between 2 friends. Each pound has 60 pecans. How many pecans does each friend get? Write equations to solve. Use letters to represent the unknown quantities.

8. **Higher Order Thinking** A store can buy boxes of 8 calculators each for $32 or boxes of 5 calculators each for $30. How much less is each calculator if the store buys boxes of 8 calculators each instead of boxes of 5 calculators each? Complete the bar diagrams and solve.

| c | c | c | c | c | c | c | c |
| --- | --- | --- | --- | --- | --- | --- | --- |

| p | p | p | p | p |
| --- | --- | --- | --- | --- |

Think about what you know and what you need to find.

9. In a basketball game, Morgan made 9 shots, each worth 2 points. Jim scored the same number of points in the game. Jim's shots were worth 3 points each. How many shots did Jim make?

   Ⓐ 4 shots     Ⓒ 8 shots

   Ⓑ 6 shots     Ⓓ 9 shots

10. Mia saved an equal amount of money each week for 6 weeks. Heather saved $3 a week for 8 weeks. Mia and Heather saved the same total amount. Which equation could you use to help find how much Mia saved each week?

   Ⓐ $s = 8 \times 6$     Ⓒ $s = 6 \div 3$

   Ⓑ $s = 6 \times 3$     Ⓓ $s = 24 \div 6$

Name_____

## Solve & Share

An aquarium had 75 clownfish in a large water tank. The clownfish represented in the graph were added to this tank. How many clownfish are in the tank now? Write and explain how you found the answer.

**I can ...**
solve two-step word problems involving different operations.

Ⓒ **Content Standards** 3.OA.D.8 Also 3.OA.C.7, 3.NBT.A.2, 3.MD.B.3
**Mathematical Practices** MP.1, MP.7, MP.8

Make Sense and Persevere. Think about the information you need to solve the problem.

**Recent Arrivals at the Aquarium**

Clownfish △ △ △ △ △ △ △ △ △

Sea Stars △ △ △ △ △

Crabs △ △ △ △ △ △

Each △ = 5 animals.

**Look Back!** What operations did you use to solve this problem? Tell why you needed those operations.

**Essential Question**

# How Can You Solve 2-Step Problems?

**A**

*Jill can rent a car and GPS device for $325 for 7 days. What is the cost to rent the car for a week without the GPS device? Use estimation to check the answer.*

| Car Rental Extras | |
|---|---|
| DVD player | $6 a day |
| GPS | $9 a day |
| Child seat | $10 a day |

DATA

$a$ = cost to rent the GPS for 7 days

$b$ = cost to rent the car without the GPS for 7 days

There are two operations needed to solve this problem.

**B**

To solve a two-step problem, you first have to find and answer the hidden question.

The hidden question is:

How much does it cost to rent the GPS for 7 days?

Write and solve an equation for the hidden question. Use a letter for the unknown quantity.

$7 \times \$9 = a$

$\$63 = a$

It costs $63 to rent the GPS for 7 days.

**C**

Write and solve an equation for the problem. Use a letter for the unknown quantity.

$\$325 - \$63 = b$

$\$262 = b$

It costs $262 to rent the car without the GPS for 7 days.

You can use compatible numbers and mental math to estimate. $7 \times 9 = 63$. 63 is close to 75 and $325 - 75$ is 250. 250 is close to 262, so the answer is reasonable.

**Convince Me!** **Use Structure** Jill can rent a different car and a DVD player for $384 for 7 days. She wants to know the cost to rent the car for a week without the DVD player. Explain how this problem is different from the problem above. Then solve.

# ☆ Guided Practice

## Do You Understand?

**1.** Dotty says you also can use $63 + b = $325 instead of $325 − $63 = b for the problem on the previous page. Can this equation be used to get the correct answer? Explain.

*no*

**2.** When solving a two-step problem, why should you answer the hidden question first?

*it will help you*

## Do You Know How?

In **3**, write equations to solve. Use letters to represent unknown quantities.

**3.** Look at Box A on the previous page. How much would it cost Jill to rent the car for a week with the GPS and DVD player?

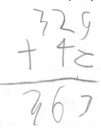
```
  329
+  4
─────
  967
```
*967*

# ☆ Independent Practice ☆

In **4** and **5**, write equations to solve. Use letters to represent the unknown quantities.

**4.** Trish bought 4 yards of rope to make a swing. Judy spent $18 on rope. How much did the two girls spend in all?

*$40*

$3 PER YARD

**5.** Martha has 12 stamps. Toni has 21 stamps. Toni divides her stamps into 3 equal groups. She gives one group to Martha. How many stamps does Martha have now?

```
19  + 7
    12
    19
```

Check that your equation represents the problem before you solve.

# Problem Solving

In **6** and **7**, use the fruit shown at the right.

**6.** Maurice needs 36 apples for his party. How much will the apples cost?

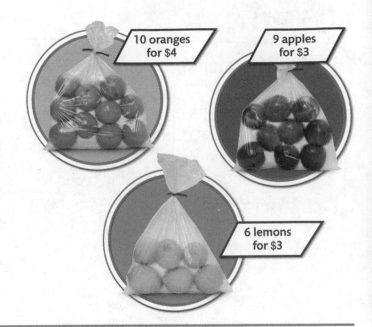

10 oranges for $4

9 apples for $3

6 lemons for $3

**7. Higher Order Thinking** Delia bought 24 lemons and 63 apples. How much did she spend on fruit?

**8.** **A-Z** **Vocabulary** Fill in the blank.

When you _____ 72 to the nearest ten, you get 70.

**9. Generalize** Carla collected 328 shells. Dan collected 176 shells. How can you use compatible numbers to estimate how many shells they collected?

**10. enVision® STEM** Sasha is using the engineering design process to plan a scratching post for her cat. There will be 3 levels. Sasha will spend $10 on the pole. She will spend $7 on each level. Sasha's plan to find the total cost is shown at the right. Is she correct? Explain.

$3 \times \$10 = \$30$
$\$30 + \$7 = \$37$

## ✓ Assessment Practice

**11.** Use the fruit from Exercises **6** and **7**. Kaylie bought 4 bags of oranges and 1 bag of apples. How many pieces of fruit did she buy? Write equations to solve. Use letters to represent any unknown quantities.

Name_____

### Solve & Share

Concert tickets for adults cost $12. Concert tickets for students cost $9. Marie has $190. She wants to buy 1 adult and 20 student tickets.

Skip says, "$190 is enough for all the tickets because $9 \times 20 = $180 and $180 is less than $190."

Does Skip's reasoning make sense? Explain.

**I can ...**
critique the reasoning of others using what I know about estimating.

**©** **Mathematical Practices** MP.3 Also MP.1, MP.5, MP.6
**Content Standards** 3.OA.D.8 Also 3.OA.C.7, 3.NBT.A.2

### Thinking Habits

*Be a good thinker!*
*These questions can help you.*

- What questions can I ask to understand other people's thinking?

- Are there mistakes in other people's thinking?

- Can I improve other people's thinking?

**Look Back!** **Critique Reasoning** What did Skip get correct in his reasoning and what did he get wrong?

Essential Question

# How Can You Critique the Reasoning of Others?

**A**

Gina has $68. She earns $9 an hour babysitting. She wants to buy a computer program for $130.

Will Gina have enough money to buy the program if she babysits for 6 hours?

Danielle solved this problem.

Her work is shown at the right.

6 × $9 = $54, which is about $60.
Gina has $68, which is about $70.
$60 + $70 = $130
Gina can buy the program.

## What is Danielle's reasoning to support her conclusion?

Danielle used an estimate to add the amount Gina made babysitting to the amount she already had.

**B**

## How can I critique the reasoning of others?

**I can**

- ask questions for clarification.

- decide if the strategy used makes sense.

- look for flaws in estimates or calculations.

**C**

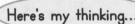 Here's my thinking...

Danielle's reasoning has flaws. Because Danielle rounded up each time, her total estimate adds up to more than the actual amount Gina will have.

6 × 9 = $54

$54 + $68 = $122

Danielle's conclusion is not correct because the actual amount Gina will have is less than $130.

**Convince Me!** **Critique Reasoning** Tony says that if Gina babysits for 8 hours, she will have enough money. He reasons that 8 × $9 = $72, which rounds to $70, and $70 + $60 = $130. Does his reasoning make sense? Explain.

# ☆ Guided Practice

### Critique Reasoning

Miguel's and Nita's goal is to collect 600 box tops. Miguel collects 253 box tops in January and 158 box tops in February. Nita collects 209 box tops in all.

Teri estimates they have already collected more than their goal. She estimates that $250 + 150 = 400$ and $400 + 200 = 600$.

> When you critique reasoning, you can look for good strategies and mistakes. You can see whether you can clarify or improve the reasoning.

**1.** What is Teri's argument? How does she support it?

**2.** Does Teri's conclusion make sense? Explain.

# ☆ Independent Practice ☆

### Critique Reasoning

Gill gets 24 stickers on Monday. She gets the same number of stickers on Tuesday. Gill then shares all of her stickers equally among 8 friends.

Liam concluded that each friend gets fewer than 5 stickers. His work is shown at the right.

> **Liam's work**
>
> $8 \times 3 = 24$
> So, $24 \div 8 = 3$.
>
> Each friend gets 3 stickers.
> 3 is less than 5.

**3.** What is Liam's argument? How does he support it?

**4.** Does Liam's reasoning make sense? Explain.

**5.** Explain the strategy you would use to improve Liam's work.

# Problem Solving

### Selling Buttons

A Grade 3 class is going to buy buttons like the ones shown. Each package costs $8. Each package is 40 cm long. They need to know if $50 is enough money to buy 200 buttons.

**30 buttons**

Jim's work

6 × 30 = 180 buttons, which is not enough.
7 × 30 = 210 buttons, so the class needs to buy 7 packages.
7 × $8 = $48
48 < 50
$50 is enough.

**6. Make Sense and Persevere** Which given information do you **NOT** need to solve this problem?

**7. Critique Reasoning** Jim solved the problem as shown above. Does Jim's strategy make sense? Explain.

When you critique reasoning, you need to carefully consider all parts of an argument.

**8. Be Precise** Are Jim's calculations correct? Explain how you decided.

**9. Use Appropriate Tools** Can place-value blocks be used to check whether Jim's math is correct? Explain.

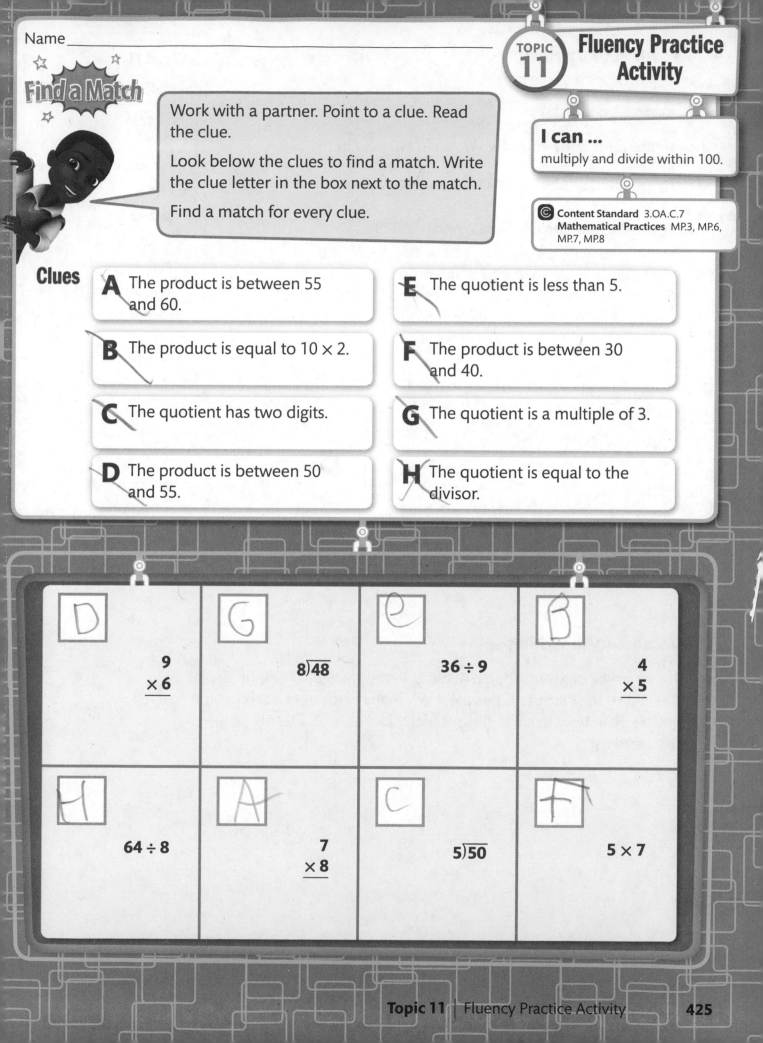

**Find a Match**

Work with a partner. Point to a clue. Read the clue.

Look below the clues to find a match. Write the clue letter in the box next to the match.

Find a match for every clue.

**I can ...**
multiply and divide within 100.

© **Content Standard** 3.OA.C.7
**Mathematical Practices** MP.3, MP.6, MP.7, MP.8

**Clues**

**A** The product is between 55 and 60.

**E** The quotient is less than 5.

**B** The product is equal to $10 \times 2$.

**F** The product is between 30 and 40.

**C** The quotient has two digits.

**G** The quotient is a multiple of 3.

**D** The product is between 50 and 55.

**H** The quotient is equal to the divisor.

| | | | |
|---|---|---|---|
| D $\begin{array}{r} 9 \\ \times 6 \\ \hline \end{array}$ | G $8\overline{)48}$ | E $36 \div 9$ | B $\begin{array}{r} 4 \\ \times 5 \\ \hline \end{array}$ |
| H $64 \div 8$ | A $\begin{array}{r} 7 \\ \times 8 \\ \hline \end{array}$ | C $5\overline{)50}$ | F $5 \times 7$ |

A-Z
Glossary

**Word List**

- difference
- dividend
- divisor
- equation
- factor
- product
- quotient
- sum
- unknown

## Understand Vocabulary

Choose the right term from the Word List. Write it in the blank.

**1.** The missing number in an equation is a(n) _____.

**2.** A multiplication problem has more than one _____.

**3.** A bar diagram can help you write a(n) _____.

**4.** In a division problem, you divide the _____ by the _____.

Draw a line to match the term to the result of a relationship between the numbers 80 and 4.

**5.** difference                          20

**6.** product                             76

**7.** quotient                            84

**8.** sum                                320

## Use Vocabulary in Writing

**9.** There are 52 cards in a deck. Al turns 4 cards face up. Then he deals the rest of the cards to 6 people. How many cards does each person get? Explain how to solve this problem. Use at least 2 terms from the word list.

**Set A** pages 409–412

You can use more than one step to solve problems.

Use bar diagrams to help write equations.

A ship has 439 passengers. One hundred seventy-nine new passengers get on at a port. Then 250 passengers get off. How many passengers are on the ship now?

Total passengers ⟶ *p*

| 439 | 179 |
|-----|-----|

$p = 439 + 179; p = 618$

There are 618 passengers in all.

618

| 250 | *l* | ⟵ Passengers left |
|-----|-----|

$l = 618 - 250; l = 368$

There are 368 passengers left on the ship.

**Remember** to check for reasonableness after each step.

In **1**, draw bar diagrams and write equations to solve the problem.

1. Mr. Sato has $800. He spends $600 on rent. Then he spends $85 on groceries. How much money does he have left?

**Set B** pages 413–416

You can use bar diagrams and equations to show how numbers are related.

Roger reads a poem with 16 lines. Each line has 7 words. The poem is on 2 pages with the same number of lines on each page. How many words are on each page?

16

| *a* | *a* |
|-----|-----|

$16 \div 2 = a$ lines on each page

$a = 8$ lines

*w*

$8 \times 7 = w$ words on each page

$w = 56$ words

**Remember** to use unknowns to stand for the numbers you need to find.

In **1**, draw bar diagrams and write equations to solve the problem.

1. A rancher has 24 cows. He puts an equal number of cows in 4 fields. Each cow produces 5 gallons of milk. How much milk do the cows in one field produce?

Ryan reads a book with 420 pages. He also reads 7 magazine articles. Each article has 6 pages. How many pages does Ryan read?

First, write and solve an equation for the hidden question. Use a letter for the unknown quantity.

$n$ = number of article pages

$7 \times 6 = n$

$42 = n$

Then, write and solve an equation for the problem. Use a letter for the unknown quantity.

$t$ = total pages read

$420 + 42 = t$

$462 = t$

Ryan reads 462 pages.

**Remember** to perform the operations in the correct order for the problem.

In **1** and **2**, write equations to solve. Use letters to stand for unknown quantities.

1. Destiny gets $168 for selling mint cookies and chocolate cookies. She sells 8 boxes of chocolate cookies at $9 per box. How much does Destiny get for selling mint cookies?

2. Mary buys three books that cost $7 and one book that costs $12. How much did Mary spend on books?

Think about these questions to help you **critique the reasoning of others**.

**Thinking Habits**

- What questions can I ask to understand other people's thinking?

- Are there mistakes in other people's thinking?

- Can I improve other people's thinking?

**Remember** to consider all parts of an explanation.

Pat needs to practice guitar for at least 40 hours this month. He has practiced 9 hours a week for the last 3 weeks. He practiced for 15 hours this week. Pat says, "3 × 9 is less than 40. So I have not practiced enough."

1. Does Pat's reasoning make sense? Explain.

2. How can you clarify or improve Pat's reasoning?

Name_____

1. Emma works at a diner. On Monday, she served 7 tables with 6 people at each table. On Tuesday, she served 72 people. She wants to know how many more people she served on Tuesday than on Monday.

Choose the correct operations to represent this problem using equations. Write each operation on the blanks.

7 _____ 6 = m

72 _____ 42 = d

+    −    ×    ÷

2. Madison has a jar of 160 jelly beans. She saves 88 for herself. She divides the rest equally among 8 friends. She wants to find how many jelly beans each friend gets.

Which equations should she use? Select all that apply.

☐ $80 \div 8 = a$

☐ $88 - 8 = b$

☐ $160 - 88 = c$

☐ $160 \div 80 = d$

☐ $72 \div 8 = e$

3. Alberto sells magazine subscriptions to his neighbors. Three neighbors each buy 3 subscriptions. There are 8 issues in each subscription. Write and solve equations to find the total number of magazine issues all of his neighbors get.

4. Ro's diner has a jar of 585 toothpicks. At lunch, 315 toothpicks are used. At dinner, 107 toothpicks are used. Ro says that $315 - 107 = t$ toothpicks are used in all, and that $585 - 208 = r$ toothpicks are left. Is her answer reasonable? Explain why or why not.

5. Tyler has 127 trading cards in his collection. Chloe has 63 cards in her collection. Then Chloe gives her collection away. She divides it equally among Tyler and 8 other friends. How many cards does Tyler have now?

**6.** Ten people each bring 4 platters of food to a family reunion. The 120 guests all share the platters equally.

**A.** How many guests share 1 platter?

**B.** Landon thinks that the answer is 12 guests. He says, "10 + 4 = 14, and 14 rounds to 10. Then 10 × 12 = 120." Do you agree with his reasoning? Explain.

**7.** Jeri collects flags of the United Nations. She wants to know how many cases she needs to display her collection. She can fit 9 flags in one case. There are 193 countries in the United Nations. Jeri does not have flags for 130 countries. Which equation could she use first to solve this problem?

Ⓐ $c = 193 + 130$  Ⓒ $f = 72 \div 9$

Ⓑ $c = 193 - 130$  Ⓓ $f = 9 \times 7$

**8.** Mrs. Lazio lives 8 miles from her office. She drives to her office and back 5 days each week. On Saturday she also drives 173 miles to visit her sister. How many miles does Mrs. Lazio drive each week?

**9.** José counted beetles for a project. He saw 5 beetles at the park each month and 3 beetles in his backyard each month. How many beetles did he count in 4 months?

Ⓐ 7

Ⓑ 32

Ⓒ 30

Ⓓ 8

**10.** Gail wants to save $68 for a jacket. She saves money for 3 weeks. Each week she saves $5. What is a good estimate for how much more money Gail needs to save? Select all that apply.

☐ $55

☐ $50

☐ $60

☐ $40

☐ $35

Name_____

## Filmmaking Camp

Mrs. Radner and Mr. Yu teach filmmaking at a summer camp. The students work in crews to make movies. The summer ends with the crew and actors watching all the movies.

### Class Details

- Mrs. Radner helps the students who make the action and drama films.
- Mr. Yu helps the students who make the comedy films.
- There are 246 actors in all.

| Film Types | | |
| --- | --- | --- |
| **Type** | **Number of Films** | **Pages of Script per Film** |
| Action | 2 | 126 |
| Comedy | 3 | 178 |
| Drama | 4 | 157 |

Use the **Class Details** list and **Film Types** table to answer Questions **1–3**.

1. There are 20 actors working on each drama film. How many actors are not working on drama films?

2. Mrs. Radner has read 139 pages of the action-film scripts. How many more pages does she need to read to finish reading all of the action-script pages?

3. Mr. Yu says, "I have read 169 pages of the scripts for each comedy film. I need to read 27 more pages to finish reading all of the pages." Do you agree with his reasoning? Explain why or why not.

**4.** Mrs. Radner wants to find $t$, the total time to watch all the student films. Use the **Film Lengths** table to answer the following questions.

**Film Lengths**

| Length (min) | Number of Films | Crew per Film |
|---|---|---|
| 30 | 1 | 12 |
| 60 | 3 | 10 |
| 90 | 5 | 20 |

**Part A**

Mrs. Radner estimates $t = 810$ minutes. She reasons, "There are 9 films. Most of the films are 90 minutes long. Nine times 90 equals 810." Do you agree with her reasoning? Explain why or why not.

**Part B**

Use bar diagrams or equations to represent $t$. Then find $t$.

**5.** Mrs. Radner sets up chairs for the crew and actors to watch the films. Use the **Film Lengths** table and **Class Details** list to answer the following questions.

**Part A**

How many students are in the crew in all?

**Part B**

Find the number of chairs Mrs. Radner needs if 147 students cannot watch the films. Use estimation to check your work.

# Understand Fractions as Numbers

**Essential Question:** What are different interpretations of a fraction?

Most fossils form when living things die and get buried in sediment.

Scientists dig up and study fossils. They help to show a picture of Earth's past environments.

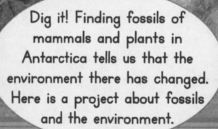

Dig it! Finding fossils of mammals and plants in Antarctica tells us that the environment there has changed. Here is a project about fossils and the environment.

## enVision STEM Project: Fossils and Environment

**Do Research** Use the Internet or other sources to find out more about what fossils tell us about past environments. Research and make a booklet of fossils found in your state. Find at least 5 fossils and use one page for each fossil. Include where each fossil was found and what type of environment each location is now.

**Write a Report: Journal** Include what you found. Also in your report:

- List the types of food each of the 5 creatures ate when they were alive.

- Explain whether each of the 5 creatures on your list could live in today's environment.

- Find the lengths of different fossils to the nearest half inch. Record the lengths in a line plot.

Name _____

# Review What You Know

**A-Z Vocabulary**

Choose the best term from the box.
Write it on the blank.

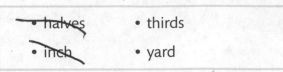
- ~~halves~~    • thirds
- ~~inch~~    • yard

1. If a shape is divided into 2 equal parts, the parts can be called ___halves___.

2. The width of an adult's thumb is about 1 ___inch___.

3. If a shape is divided into 3 equal parts, the parts can be called ___thirds___.

## Skip Counting on the Number Line

Skip count on the number line. Write the missing numbers.

4.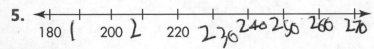
110   115   120   125   130   135   140   145   150   155

5.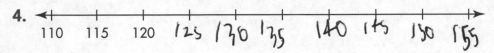
180   |   200   |   220   230   240   250   260   270

## Equal Parts

6. Circle the shapes that show halves.

7. Circle the shapes that show fourths.

## Measurement

8. How long is the nail to the nearest inch?
   Explain how you know.

   2 inches

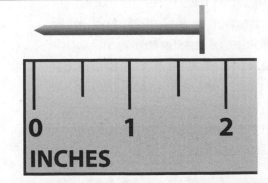

Name _____

**PROJECT 12A**

How long would it take to drive across the Florida Keys?

**Project:** Make a Map

**PROJECT 12B**

Why are there so many different types of floors in every building?

**Project:** Create a Flooring Design

## PROJECT 12C

### What is the most common hat size?

**Project:** Collect Hat Size Data and Create a Line Plot

## PROJECT 12D

### What are the most popular fruits and vegetables?

**Project:** Draw a Garden Plot

Name_____

★ ☆ ★
**Solve & Share**

Show two different ways to divide a 2 × 6 region into 6 equal parts. How do you know the parts are equal?

**I can ...**
read and write a unit fraction.

© **Content Standards** 3.G.A.2 Also 3.NF.A.1
**Mathematical Practices** MP.1, MP.3, MP.6

Be precise. Think about the area of each part as you divide the regions.

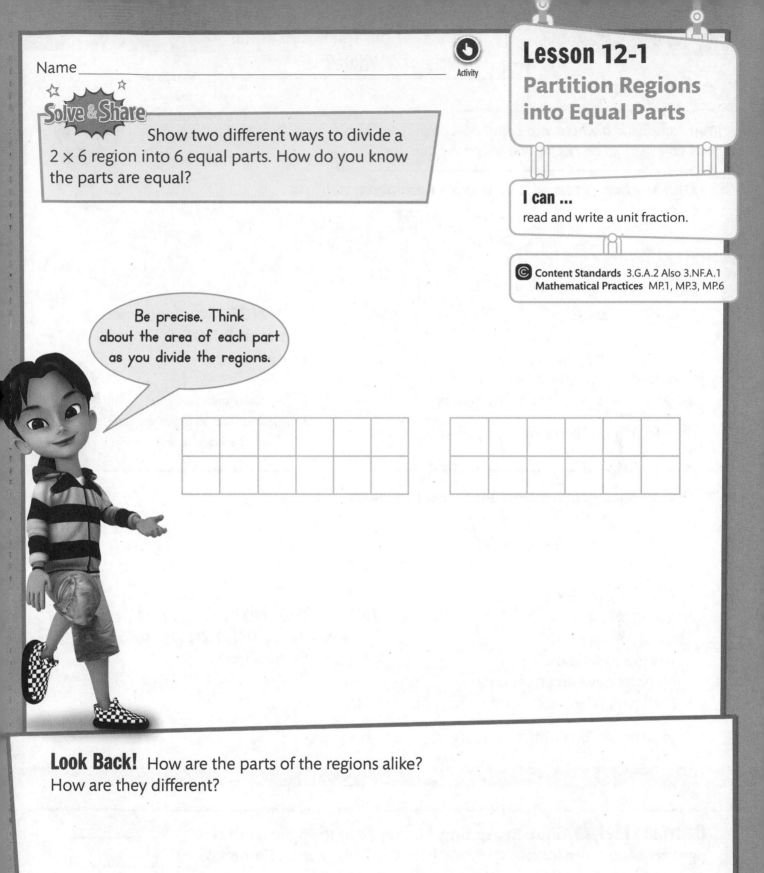

**Look Back!** How are the parts of the regions alike? How are they different?

**Essential Question**

# How Can You Name the Equal Parts of a Whole?

**A**

You can divide a whole into equal parts. What fraction can you write to represent one of these equal parts?

 A fraction is a part of a whole.

### Divide each green whole into four equal parts.

Has 4 equal parts

Has 4 equal parts

Does **NOT** have 4 equal parts
Each part is **NOT** one fourth of the whole.

In the green wholes:
- All parts have an equal area.
- Each part is one fourth of the area of the whole.

One fourth can be written as the fraction $\frac{1}{4}$.

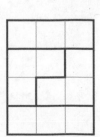 $\frac{1}{4}$ is a unit fraction. A unit fraction represents one of the equal parts.

**B**

### Divide each green whole into six equal parts.

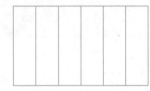
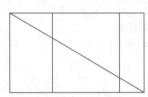

Has 6 equal parts

Has 6 equal parts

Does **NOT** have 6 equal parts
Each part is **NOT** one sixth of the whole.

In the green wholes:
- All parts have an equal area.
- Each part is one sixth of the area of the whole.

One sixth can be written as the fraction $\frac{1}{6}$.

**Convince Me!** **Critique Reasoning** Kim says that the figure at the right is divided into fourths because there are 4 equal parts. Carrie says it is not divided into fourths because the parts are not the same shape. Who is correct? Explain.

# Guided Practice

## Do You Understand?

**1.** In the examples in Box A on the previous page, explain how you know the 4 parts are equal.

Samesize

In **2** and **3**, tell if each shape shows equal or unequal parts. If the parts are equal, label 1 of the parts using a unit fraction.

**2.**

**3.**

## Do You Know How?

**4.** Draw lines to divide the shape into 8 equal parts. Then write the fraction that represents 1 part.

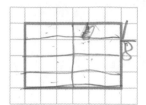

# Independent Practice

In **5–7**, tell if each shape shows equal or unequal parts. If the parts are equal, label 1 of the parts using a unit fraction.

**5.**

no

**6.**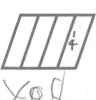

Yes

**7.**

Yes

In **8–10**, draw lines to divide the shape into the given number of equal parts. Then write the fraction that represents one part.

**8.** 6 equal parts

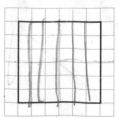

**9.** 3 equal parts

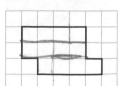

**10.** 4 equal parts

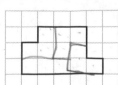

# Problem Solving

In **11–14**, use the table of flags to answer the questions.

**11.** What fraction represents the white part of Nigeria's flag?

$\frac{1}{3}$

**12.** Which nation's flag is $\frac{1}{2}$ red?

Poland

**13.** **Higher Order Thinking** The flag of this nation has more than 3 equal parts. Which nation is it, and what fraction represents 1 part of its flag?

Mauritius

$\frac{1}{4}$

| Flags of Different Nations | |
|---|---|
| **Nation** | **Flag** |
| Mauritius | |
| Nigeria | |
| Poland | |
| Seychelles | |

**14.** Which nation's flag is **NOT** divided into equal parts?

Seychelles

**15.** Maryann buys 24 cans of soda. The soda comes in packs of 6 cans. How many packs does she purchase? Write a multiplication equation and a division equation to show your answer.

4

**16.** **Make Sense and Persevere** Jim has stickers in an array of 8 rows and 4 columns. He also has a packet of 14 stickers. How many stickers does Jim have in all?

46

**17.** Draw lines to show how to divide this square into 8 equal pieces. Then select the fraction that represents 1 of the pieces.

Ⓐ $\frac{1}{2}$

Ⓑ $\frac{1}{3}$

Ⓒ $\frac{1}{4}$

Ⓓ $\frac{1}{8}$

Name _____

## Solve & Share

Pat made a garden in the shape of a rectangle and divided it into 4 equal parts. She planted flowers in 3 of the parts. Draw a picture of what Pat's garden might look like.

Activity

**I can ...**
use a fraction to represent multiple copies of a unit fraction.

© **Content Standards** 3.NF.A.1 Also 3.G.A.2
**Mathematical Practices** MP.4, MP.6, MP.8

Model with math. You can use what you know to draw a picture to represent Pat's garden.

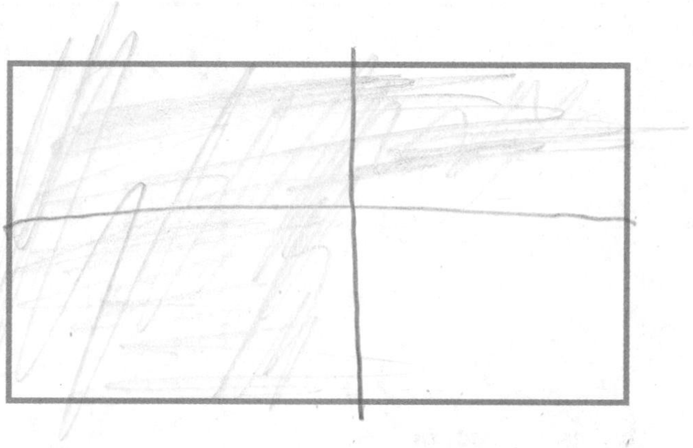

**Look Back!** How many parts of Pat's garden do **NOT** have flowers? Explain.

$$\frac{1}{4}$$

**Essential Question** **How Can You Show and Name Parts of a Region?**

**A**

*Mr. Peters served part of a pan of enchiladas to a friend. What does each part of the whole pan represent? What part was served? What part is left?*

You can use fractions to represent more than one of the equal parts.

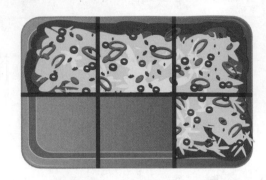

**B** The whole pan is divided into 6 equal parts. Each part is $\frac{1}{6}$ of the whole.

6 copies of $\frac{1}{6}$ is $\frac{6}{6}$. So, the whole is $\frac{6}{6}$. The unit fraction is $\frac{1}{6}$.

The number below the bar in a fraction shows the number of equal parts in the whole. It is called the denominator.

**C** 2 copies of $\frac{1}{6}$ is $\frac{2}{6}$.

$\frac{2}{6}$ of the pan was served.

4 copies of $\frac{1}{6}$ is $\frac{4}{6}$.

$\frac{4}{6}$ of the pan is left.

The number above the bar in a fraction shows the number of copies of the unit fraction. It is called the numerator.

**Convince Me!** **Be Precise** Below is a picture of a pie pan. Draw lines and use shading to show that five $\frac{1}{8}$-pieces are still in the pan, and that three $\frac{1}{8}$-pieces were eaten. Use a fraction to label the part of the pie that is in the pan.

Name_____

 **Guided Practice**

Practice  Tools  Assessment

## Do You Understand?

1. In the problem in Box A on the previous page, what fraction names all of the pieces in the pan?

$\frac{1}{6}$

2. Mrs. Patel made a cake. What fraction of the whole cake does each piece represent?

3. In the picture in Exercise **2**, how many $\frac{1}{8}$-pieces were eaten? What fraction of the whole cake was eaten?

## Do You Know How?

 In **4–6**, use the figure below.

4. How many $\frac{1}{3}$-parts are blue?

2

5. What fraction of the whole is blue?

$\frac{2}{3}$

6. What fraction names *all* of the parts in the whole?

$\frac{3}{3} = 1$

## Independent Practice

In **7–10**, write the unit fraction that represents each part of the whole.
Then write the number of blue parts and the fraction of the whole that is blue.

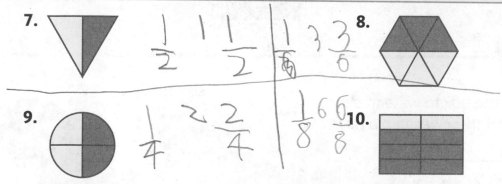

7.  $\frac{1}{2}$   1   $\frac{1}{2}$   |   $\frac{1}{6}$   3   $\frac{3}{6}$   **8.**

9.   $\frac{1}{4}$   2   $\frac{2}{4}$   |   $\frac{1}{8}$   6   $\frac{6}{8}$  **10.**

11. Draw a rectangle that shows 6 equal parts. Write the unit fraction that represents each part. Then shade $\frac{2}{6}$ of the rectangle. Explain how you know you shaded $\frac{2}{6}$ of the rectangle.

**Topic 12** | Lesson 12-2    **443**

# Problem Solving

**12.** **Vocabulary** Fill in the blanks. In the fraction $\frac{4}{7}$, 4 is the _numerator_ and 7 is the _denominator_.

**13.** **Generalize** Divide the grid below into fourths. Shade 3 of the parts. Write a fraction that represents the shaded area. Write a fraction that represents the unshaded area. What can you generalize about your fractions?

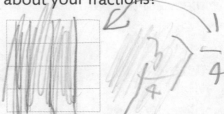

$\frac{3}{4}$   $\frac{1}{4}$

**14.** Christine has 6 red scarves and 3 blue scarves. Each scarf has 2 stripes. How many stripes does Christine have on her scarves? Write equations to represent and solve the problem.

18 stripes

**15.** **Higher Order Thinking** Draw a circle that shows 6 equal parts. Shade more than $\frac{3}{6}$ of the circle, but less than $\frac{5}{6}$ of the circle. What fraction have you shaded?

$\frac{4}{6}$

**16.** **Number Sense** What is the area of the baseball card? Show your work.

140

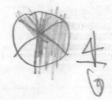

10 cm

7 cm

**17.** Select numbers from the box to write fractions to show 3 parts of each of these vegetable trays.

1   2   3   4   5   6   7   8

$\frac{3}{4}$ , $\frac{3}{6}$ , $\frac{3}{8}$

**Size of Tray**

Small

Medium

Large

Name _____

☆ Solve & Share ☆

Mrs. Garcia's third-grade class is planting a flower garden and a vegetable garden.

Draw a picture of the whole flower garden and the whole vegetable garden based on the parts shown. How did you decide what the whole of each garden looked like?

**I can ...**
identify the whole by seeing a part.

© **Content Standards** 3.NF.A.3c Also 3.NF.A.1
**Mathematical Practices** MP.2, MP.3

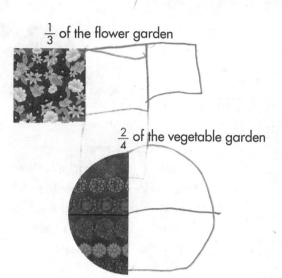

$\frac{1}{3}$ of the flower garden

$\frac{2}{4}$ of the vegetable garden

You can use reasoning. Think about the parts you know and how many parts you need to make the whole.

**Look Back!** What do the fractions $\frac{1}{3}$ and $\frac{2}{4}$ tell you about the number of equal parts in the whole?

**Essential Question** **How Can You Use a Fractional Part to Find the Whole?**

**A**

Anya and Novi are running in different races. The diagrams below show how much of their races each runner has completed. Draw a picture of the whole of each track. Write a fraction to represent the whole.

You can look at the fraction to find how many parts will make up the whole.

Anya $\frac{1}{6}$ ├────────┤

Novi $\frac{1}{6}$ ├───────┤

**B**

You know Anya and Novi have each completed $\frac{1}{6}$ of their races.

Six lengths of $\frac{1}{6}$ make $\frac{6}{6}$, or 1 whole.

These diagrams show the whole of Anya's and Novi's races. The sixths are different sizes because the tracks for the races (the wholes) are different sizes.

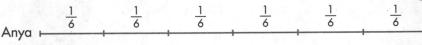

Anya $\frac{1}{6}$ $\frac{1}{6}$ $\frac{1}{6}$ $\frac{1}{6}$ $\frac{1}{6}$ $\frac{1}{6}$

Novi $\frac{1}{6}$ $\frac{1}{6}$ $\frac{1}{6}$ $\frac{1}{6}$ $\frac{1}{6}$ $\frac{1}{6}$

$1 = \frac{6}{6}$

**Convince Me!** **Reasoning** Why is Novi's track longer than Anya's track?

## Another Example!

The part of a race Rob completed is shown at the right. You can use fractional parts like this to identify the whole.

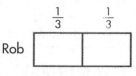

Rob

$\frac{2}{3}$

$\frac{2}{3}$ is 2 copies of $\frac{1}{3}$. Divide Rob's track into 2 equal parts.

$\frac{1}{3}$ $\frac{1}{3}$

Rob

Three copies of $\frac{1}{3}$ make $\frac{3}{3}$, or 1 whole. Draw one more third.

$\frac{1}{3}$ $\frac{1}{3}$ $\frac{1}{3}$

$1 = \frac{3}{3}$

Rob

## Guided Practice

### Do You Understand?

1. If the distance Anya ran was $\frac{1}{5}$ of the length of the track, what fraction would you use to represent the whole track?

2. What is true about the numerator and denominator of each fraction that represents one whole?

### Do You Know How?

3. Draw a picture of the whole and write a fraction to represent the whole.

$\frac{2}{8}$

$1 = \frac{\square}{\square}$

## Independent Practice

In **4–7**, draw a picture of the whole and write a fraction to represent the whole.

4. $\frac{2}{3}$

$1 = \frac{\square}{\square}$

5. $\frac{1}{2}$

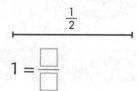

$1 = \frac{\square}{\square}$

6. $\frac{3}{4}$

$1 = \frac{\square}{\square}$

7. $\frac{2}{6}$

$1 = \frac{\square}{\square}$

**Topic 12** | Lesson 12-3    **447**

# Problem Solving

**8.** Ronnie and Gina were shown $\frac{1}{2}$ of a table. They each drew a picture of the whole table. Whose drawing could be correct? Explain.

 $\frac{1}{2}$ of table    Ronnie's drawing of the whole table   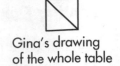 Gina's drawing of the whole table

*Gina*

---

**9.** **Higher Order Thinking** If the part shown in Exercise **8** is $\frac{1}{4}$ of a table, what could the whole table look like? Draw a picture and write a fraction to represent the whole.

**10.** The Florida panther is endangered. In 1970, the population was estimated at 20 panthers. In 2017, the population was estimated at 230 panthers. About how many more panthers were there in 2017 than in 1970?

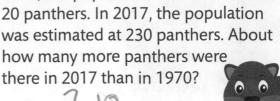

*210*

---

**11.** **Construct Arguments** Jenna and Jamal are making rugs. They have finished the parts shown. Draw pictures to show each whole rug. Whose rug will be longer when it is finished? Explain.

*Jamal*

$\frac{1}{3}$ of Jenna's rug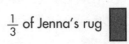

$\frac{1}{3}$ of Jamal's rug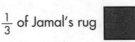

---

 **Assessment Practice**

**12.** The picture shows $\frac{2}{3}$ of a granola bar. Which shows the whole granola bar?

Ⓐ

Ⓑ

Ⓒ

Ⓓ

**13.** Each part below is $\frac{1}{2}$ of a different whole. Which is part of the largest whole?

Ⓐ ├────────────┤

Ⓑ ├──────┤

Ⓒ ├────┤

Ⓓ ├──┤

Name_____

**Solve & Share**

At a state park, there is a 1-mile hiking path between the park entrance and the beach. Scenic lookouts are located at points $\frac{1}{3}$ and $\frac{2}{3}$ of the distance from the park entrance to the beach. Show about where the lookout points are located on the line below.

**I can ...**
represent fractions on a number line.

**Content Standards** 3.NF.A.2a Also 3.NF.A.2b
**Mathematical Practices** MP.3, MP.4

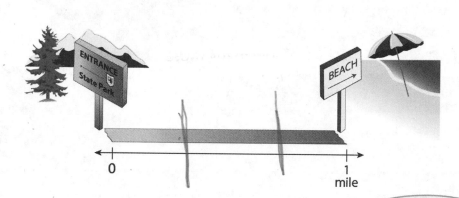

Model with math. You can represent this problem on a number line.

**Look Back!** If you know about where the point for $\frac{1}{3}$ is located, how can you find about where the point for $\frac{2}{3}$ is located?

**Essential Question** **How Can You Record Fractions on a Number Line?**

**A**

Mr. Singer is picking up his daughter, Greta, from school to go to soccer practice. Greta's school is located at $\frac{3}{4}$ of the distance from the Singers' house to the soccer field. How can you represent $\frac{3}{4}$ on a number line?

Every number on a number line represents a distance from 0.

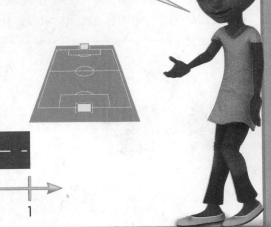

0          1

**B** **Step 1**

Draw a number line from 0 to 1.

0 represents the Singers' house.

1 represents the distance from the Singers' house to the soccer field.

0          1

**C** **Step 2**

Divide the distance from 0 to 1 into 4 equal parts.

Each length is $\frac{1}{4}$ of the whole distance between 0 and 1.

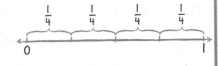

**D** **Step 3**

Start at 0. Draw a point at the end of the **third fourth** on the line. Write $\frac{3}{4}$. This represents the distance from the Singers' house to Greta's school.

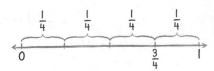

$\frac{3}{4}$ is the same as 3 lengths of $\frac{1}{4}$.

**Convince Me!** **Critique Reasoning**

Jenna and Benito each marked $\frac{1}{4}$ on a number line. The length of the part from 0 to $\frac{1}{4}$ on Jenna's number line is shorter than on Benito's. Did someone make a mistake? Explain your thinking.

Jenna
0   $\frac{1}{4}$         1

Benito
0      $\frac{1}{4}$            1

**450** **Topic 12** | Lesson 12-4

Practice   Tools   Assessment

# ☆ Guided Practice

## Do You Understand?

**1.** Maliya divides a number line from 0 to 1 into 6 equal lengths. What unit fraction represents each equal length? What should Maliya label the tick mark just to the left of 1? Explain.

$\frac{1}{6}$          $\frac{5}{6}$

**2.** Josh divides a number line from 0 to 1 into 8 equal lengths. What should he label the first tick mark just to the right of 0? Explain.

$\frac{1}{8}$

## Do You Know How?

In **3** and **4**, divide the number line into the given number of equal lengths. Then mark and label the given fraction on the number line.

**3.** 2 equal lengths; $\frac{1}{2}$

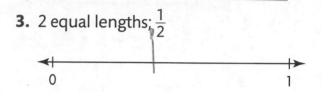

**4.** 4 equal lengths; $\frac{2}{4}$

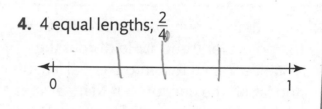

# ☆ Independent Practice ☆

**Leveled Practice** In **5** and **6**, divide the number line into the given number of equal lengths. Then mark and label the given fraction on the number line.

**5.** 3 equal lengths; $\frac{2}{3}$

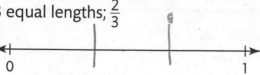

**6.** 6 equal lengths; $\frac{2}{6}$

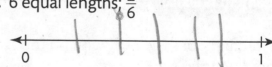

In **7** and **8**, draw a number line from 0 to 1. Divide the number line into equal lengths for the given fraction. Then mark and label the given fraction on the number line.

**7.** $\frac{4}{6}$

**8.** $\frac{5}{8}$

# Problem Solving

**9.** **Construct Arguments** Terrance and Dana each drew a number line and marked $\frac{3}{4}$. Did each person represent $\frac{3}{4}$ in the correct place on his or her line? Explain.

Terrance ⟵|—|—|—●—|—⟶
$\quad$ 0 $\qquad\quad$ $\frac{3}{4}$ $\quad$ 1

Dana ⟵|—|—|—●—|—⟶
$\quad$ 0 $\qquad\qquad$ $\frac{3}{4}$ $\quad$ 1

yes

**10.** A gymnast starts at the left end of the balance beam and does some handsprings. When she is finished, she is at the point shown on the diagram. What fraction represents how far she went on the balance beam?

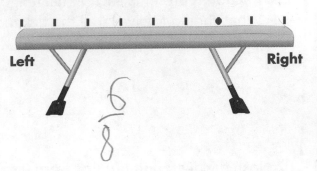

**Left** $\qquad\qquad\qquad\qquad\qquad$ **Right**

$\frac{6}{8}$

**11.** Mark draws a number line and labels the points for 0 and 1. He divides the distance from 0 to 1 into 2 equal lengths and labels the fraction $\frac{1}{2}$. If Mark divides each half into 2 equal lengths, what fractions can Mark label on his number line?

$\frac{2}{4}$

**12.** **Higher Order Thinking** Show 3 ways you can represent three eighths.

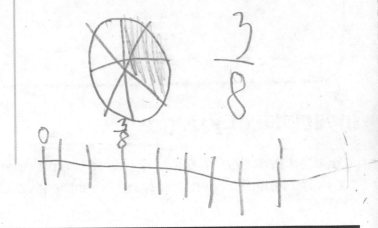

$\frac{3}{8}$

**13.** What fraction does the red point on this number line represent?

$\quad$ 0 $\qquad\qquad\qquad\qquad$ 1

Ⓐ $\frac{1}{6}$

Ⓑ $\frac{2}{6}$

Ⓒ $\frac{3}{6}$

Ⓓ $\frac{4}{6}$

**14.** Which number line has a red point at $\frac{1}{3}$?

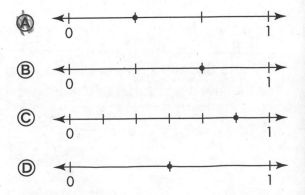

Ⓐ ⟵|—●—|—|—⟶
$\quad$ 0 $\qquad\qquad\qquad$ 1

Ⓑ ⟵|—|—●—|—⟶
$\quad$ 0 $\qquad\qquad\qquad$ 1

Ⓒ ⟵|—|—|—|—|—●—|—⟶
$\quad$ 0 $\qquad\qquad\qquad$ 1

Ⓓ ⟵|—●—|—⟶
$\quad$ 0 $\qquad\qquad\qquad$ 1

Activity

**Solve & Share**

The length of one strip of paper is 1 whole unit. Fold two strips of paper in half. Open the two strips and place them end to end.

How many halves do you have? Use fractions to name each fold line. Tell how you decided. Draw a picture to show your work.

**I can ...**
represent fractions equal to or greater than 1 on a number line.

© **Content Standards** 3.NF.A.2b Also 3.NF.A.2a
**Mathematical Practices** MP.3, MP.5, MP.6

Use appropriate tools. Think about how your paper strips show copies of unit fractions.

**Look Back!** If you added a third strip of paper folded in half, how could you use halves to name the fold lines? Explain.

**Essential Question** **How Can You Use a Number Line to Represent Fractions Greater Than 1?**

**A**

A marsh rabbit hopped $\frac{7}{4}$ the length of a rabbit trail. How can you show this on a number line?

Number lines can represent fractions that are greater than 1 whole. $\frac{7}{4}$ is greater than 1 whole, but less than 2 wholes. The whole is the distance between 0 and 1.

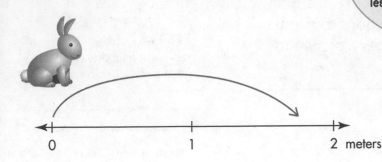

**B** Divide each whole into 4 equal lengths.

Each length is $\frac{1}{4}$ of the whole.

$\frac{4}{4}$ is the same as 1 whole.

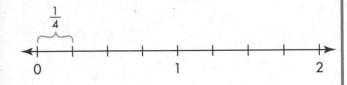

**C** The marsh rabbit hopped 7 lengths of the unit fraction $\frac{1}{4}$.

The point showing 7 lengths of $\frac{1}{4}$ can be labeled as $\frac{7}{4}$.

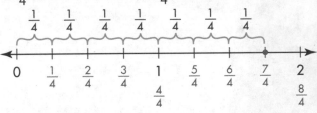

Each additional length is one more copy of the unit fraction. So, the numerator increases by 1 for each additional length.

**Convince Me! Be Precise** One tick mark on the number line below has been named with the fraction $\frac{2}{3}$. On the number line the lengths marked are equal. Write fractions for the other tick marks shown.

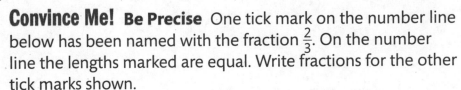

Name_____

## Do You Understand?

1. Name a fraction that is to the right of the tick mark for 2 on a number line.

2. Quinn says that $\frac{10}{8}$ comes to the right of $\frac{9}{8}$ on a number line. Do you agree? Why or why not?

## Do You Know How?

In **3** and **4**, each number line has equal lengths marked. Write the missing fractions.

3.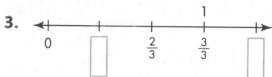

4.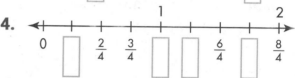

# Independent Practice

**Leveled Practice** In **5–7**, each number line has equal lengths marked. Write the missing fractions.

5.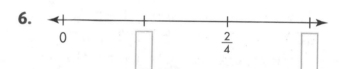

6.

7.

The length of each unit depends on the size of the whole.

In **8** and **9**, divide the number lines into equal lengths. Write the missing fractions.

8.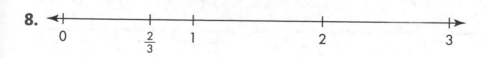

9.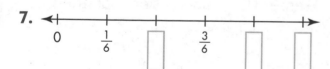

# Problem Solving

In **10** and **11**, use the number line below.

The distance from 0 to 1 is 1 mile.

School         Grocery Store      Post Office      Swimming Pool

0              $\frac{3}{6}$             1

**10.** What fraction tells how far the swimming pool is from the school? Explain how you know.

**11. Higher Order Thinking** The hospital is halfway between the grocery store and the post office. What fraction tells how far the hospital is from the school? Explain.

**12.** Tim has 78 board games. He has 10 boxes. Each box holds 9 games. If Tim puts all the games he has into the boxes, how many more games can he fit? Complete the bar diagram and solve the problem.

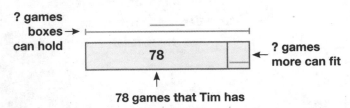

? games
boxes → can hold

78

? games more can fit

↑ 78 games that Tim has

**13. Critique Reasoning** Rachel says that she can find $(7 \times 5) \times 2$ by calculating $(7 \times 2) + (5 \times 2) = 14 + 10$. Then add to get 24. Does Rachel's reasoning make sense? Use properties of operations to explain.

## Assessment Practice

**14.** What fraction is represented by the total length marked on the number line? Select the correct fraction from the box.

$\frac{1}{2}$    $\frac{2}{3}$    $\frac{3}{4}$    $\frac{4}{2}$    $\frac{4}{3}$

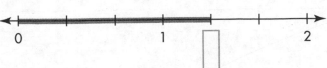

0               1               2

    

Name_____

☆ **Solve & Share** ☆

Jamie measured the lengths of 6 beetles. She measured each beetle's length to the nearest inch and to the nearest half inch. She recorded the lengths in the two line plots below. Measure the length of each beetle below to the nearest inch and to the nearest half inch. Record your measurements in Jamie's line plots.

**I can ...**
measure to the nearest half inch and show the data on a line plot.

© **Content Standards** 3.MD.B.4 Also 3.NF.A.2a, 3.NF.A.2b
**Mathematical Practices** MP.1, MP.2, MP.6

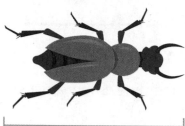

Be precise. First measure each beetle to the nearest inch. Then measure each beetle to the nearest half inch.

**Lengths of Beetles to Nearest Inch**

```
        •       •
        •       •
        •       •
  •——————•——————•——————•——————•——→
  0      1            2
```
**Length (Inches)**

**Lengths of Beetles to Nearest Half Inch**

```
         •      •
         •      •     •
  •——————•——————•——————•——————•——→
  0     1/2     1    1 1/2    2
```
**Length (Inches)**

**Look Back!** What tool did you use to measure the length of each beetle? How did you use this tool?

**How Can You Measure Lengths and Use Line Plots to Show the Data?**

**A**

*Julio is measuring some lengths of yarn in inches. How can he use a ruler to measure to the nearest half inch?*

The distance between each whole number on this ruler is 1 inch. Each tick mark shows $\frac{1}{2}$ inch. So, you can think of each whole inch as two $\frac{1}{2}$ inches.

Line up one end of the object with 0.

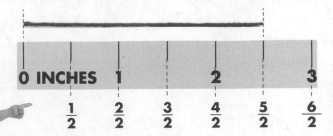

The fifth $\frac{1}{2}$-inch tick mark is closest to the end of the length of yarn.

So, to the nearest half inch, the yarn measures $\frac{5}{2}$ inches.

This length is two whole inches and one $\frac{1}{2}$ inch. You can write this length as $2\frac{1}{2}$ inches.

**B** Julio measured 9 other lengths of yarn in inches:

$2\frac{1}{2}$  $3\frac{1}{2}$  3  $3\frac{1}{2}$  4  3  3  $3\frac{1}{2}$  4  $3\frac{1}{2}$

Then he recorded the data in a line plot.

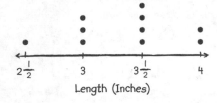

**C Steps to Make a Line Plot**

- Draw a number line. Show a scale based on the data.
- Write a title for the line plot.
- Mark a dot for each data value.

You have used number lines to show fractions. A line plot is a way to organize data on a number line.

**Convince Me! Reasoning** Suppose you measured a length of yarn that was about $4\frac{1}{2}$ inches. How would you need to change the line plot above to record this length?

Name _____

# ☆ Guided Practice

## Do You Understand?

1. Draw a line that is $1\frac{1}{2}$ inches long.

_____

2. If a line measures halfway between 3 and $3\frac{1}{2}$ inches and you need to measure to the nearest $\frac{1}{2}$ inch, what length will you record? Why?

## Do You Know How?

3. Measure the length of each of your fingers. List the measurements to the nearest half inch.

4. Make a line plot to show the measurements of your fingers.

# ☆ Independent Practice ☆

5. Measure the lengths of the pieces of yarn at the right to the nearest half inch. Write the length for each piece.

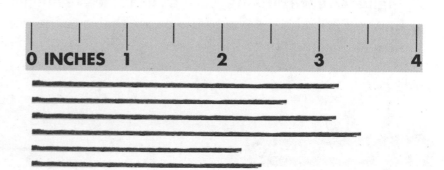

6. Draw a line to represent another length of yarn. Measure your line to the nearest half inch.

7. Make a line plot to show the measurements of the yarn.

You can use dots or Xs to record data in a line plot.

# Problem Solving

8. Measure the lengths of 10 classroom objects to the nearest half inch. Choose objects that are between 1 and 6 inches long. Record your measurements.

9. On grid paper, draw a line plot to show your data from Exercise 8.

10. **Make Sense and Persevere** Raymond weighed his three dogs. The oldest dog weighs 74 pounds. The other two dogs each weigh 34 pounds. How many more pounds does the oldest dog weigh than the other two dogs combined?

11. Draw a number line from 0 to 2. Label the wholes. Divide each whole into thirds. Label each fraction.

In **12** and **13**, use the table at the right.

12. How many more of the shortest paper chains does Rico have than the longest paper chains? Explain.

| DATA | Rico's Paper Chains | |
| --- | --- | --- |
| | Number of Paper Chains | Length |
| | 3 | $6\frac{1}{2}$ in. |
| | 2 | $7\frac{1}{2}$ in. |
| | 4 | 8 in. |
| | 1 | $8\frac{1}{2}$ in. |

13. **Higher Order Thinking** Look at Rico's measurements. Can you tell if he measured the paper chains to the nearest half inch or to the nearest inch? Explain.

## Assessment Practice

14. Jessica used 4 of Nail A, 2 of Nail B, and 3 of Nail C to build a birdhouse. Measure each nail to the nearest half inch. Then complete the line plot.

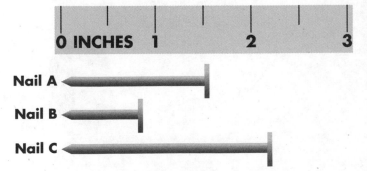

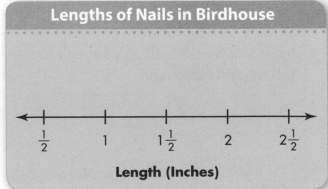

**Lengths of Nails in Birdhouse**

$\frac{1}{2}$　1　$1\frac{1}{2}$　2　$2\frac{1}{2}$

Length (Inches)

Name_____

☆ ★ ☆
**Solve & Share**

Monica and her friends measured the lengths of their shoes. Show this data by marking a dot for each length on the line plot below.

Measure the length of three classmates' shoes. Add a dot to represent each length on the line plot. What length was the most common?

**I can ...**
measure to the nearest fourth inch and show the data on a line plot.

© **Content Standards** 3.MD.B.4 Also 3.NF.A.2a, 3.NF.A.2b
**Mathematical Practices** MP.1, MP.7

DATA

| Lengths of Shoes | |
|---|---|
| **Friend** | **Length (Inches)** |
| A | 8 |
| B | $8\frac{2}{4}$ |
| C | $9\frac{1}{4}$ |
| D | $8\frac{2}{4}$ |
| E | $9\frac{1}{4}$ |
| F | $9\frac{1}{4}$ |
| G | 9 |
| H | $9\frac{1}{4}$ |
| I | 9 |
| J | $8\frac{1}{4}$ |

**Lengths of Shoes**

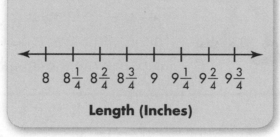

Length (Inches)

Make sense and persevere. How will marking the data on the line plot help you solve the problem?

**Look Back!** Are there different ways to record the results of a data collection? Explain.

Essential Question

# How Can You Make and Use Line Plots?

**A**

*Anna is measuring the length of her crayons. How can she use a ruler to measure to the nearest fourth inch?*

The distance between each whole number on this ruler is 1 inch. Each tick mark shows $\frac{1}{4}$ inch. So, each whole inch is divided into four $\frac{1}{4}$ inches.

Line up one end of the object with 0.

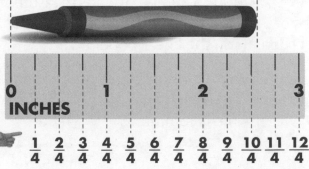

$$\frac{1}{4} \quad \frac{2}{4} \quad \frac{3}{4} \quad \frac{4}{4} \quad \frac{5}{4} \quad \frac{6}{4} \quad \frac{7}{4} \quad \frac{8}{4} \quad \frac{9}{4} \quad \frac{10}{4} \quad \frac{11}{4} \quad \frac{12}{4}$$

The tenth $\frac{1}{4}$-inch tick mark is closest to the end of the length of the crayon.

So, to the nearest fourth inch, the crayon measures $\frac{10}{4}$ inches.

This length is two whole inches and two $\frac{1}{4}$ inches. You can write this length as $2\frac{2}{4}$ inches.

**B**

Anna measured her other crayons.

She then recorded the data in a line plot.

Lengths of Crayons

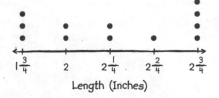

Length (Inches)

You can use this line plot to see that the crayon length that occurred most often was $2\frac{3}{4}$ inches. The crayon length that occurred least often was $2\frac{2}{4}$ inches.

---

## Convince Me! Make Sense and Persevere

Nathan also made a line plot to show the lengths of his crayons. Tell three things you know about the lengths of Nathan's crayons.

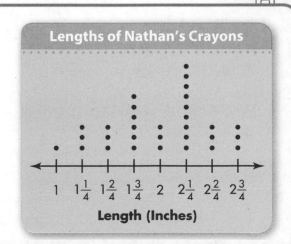

Lengths of Nathan's Crayons

Length (Inches)

Name _____

# Guided Practice

## Do You Understand?

**1.** Measure the length of this line to the nearest fourth inch.

_____

**2.** Describe how you would show this measurement on a line plot.

## Do You Know How?

**3.** Draw a line plot to show the data.

| Lengths of Sandy's Pencils in Inches | | | | |
| --- | --- | --- | --- | --- |
| $5\frac{1}{4}$ | $5\frac{3}{4}$ | $5\frac{1}{4}$ | 6 | $5\frac{2}{4}$ |

**4.** Measure your pencil to the nearest fourth inch. Show the length on your line plot.

# Independent Practice

**5.** Daisy measured the lengths of her toy dinosaurs to the nearest fourth inch. She listed the lengths. Make a line plot to show the data.

$1\frac{2}{4}$ in., $2\frac{1}{4}$ in., 1 in., $1\frac{2}{4}$ in., $1\frac{3}{4}$ in.

**6.** Measure the lengths of the toy dinosaurs at the right to the nearest fourth inch. Write the length for each toy. Show the lengths on your line plot.

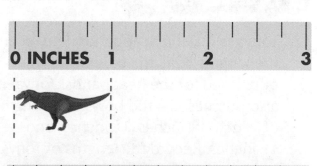

# Problem Solving

In **7** and **8**, use the line plot at the right.

Arty used Xs to record the data in a line plot.

**7.** Arty made a line plot to show the number of inches that different snails crawled in a 5-minute race. What was the most common distance that the snails crawled?

**8. Higher Order Thinking** How many more snails crawled a length more than $8\frac{3}{4}$ inches than a length less than $8\frac{3}{4}$ inches?

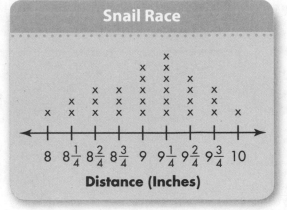

**Snail Race**

Distance (Inches)

---

**9.** Measure the lengths of 10 classroom objects to the nearest fourth inch. Choose objects that are between 1 and 5 inches long. Record your measurements.

**10.** On grid paper, draw a line plot to show your data from Exercise **9**.

---

**11.** Jackson bought 5 books that cost $7 each. How much change did he get from $40?

**12. Use Structure** Use the digits 2, 6, and 8 to make as many 3-digit numbers as you can. Use place value to arrange the numbers in order from least to greatest.

---

### ☑ Assessment Practice

**13.** Tonya is making headbands. She recorded the lengths of all the blue bows she purchased for the headbands. Tonya also purchased 4 red bows with lengths of 1 inch, $1\frac{1}{4}$ inches, $1\frac{2}{4}$ inches, and $1\frac{2}{4}$ inches. Record the lengths of Tonya's red bows in the line plot.

Each dot on the line plot represents a different bow Tonya bought.

**Lengths of Different Bows**

Length (Inches)

Name _____

Activity

## Solve & Share

Marcus, Mariah, and Tony painted a mural. They divided it into equal parts. Marcus painted 2 parts, Mariah painted 3 parts, and Tony painted the rest. What fraction of the mural did each student paint?

This problem may have missing or extra information. If information you need is missing, make up some reasonable information and then solve the problem.

**I can ...**
make sense of problems and keep working if I get stuck.

Ⓒ **Mathematical Practices** MP.1 Also MP.2, MP.3
**Content Standard** 3.NF.A.1

### Thinking Habits

*Be a good thinker! These questions can help you.*

• What do I need to find?

• What do I know?

• What's my plan for solving the problem?

• What else can I try if I get stuck?

• How can I check that my solution makes sense?

**Look Back!** **Make Sense and Persevere** What information was not given in the problem? How did you still solve the problem?

## Essential Question: How Can You Make Sense of a Problem and Persevere in Solving It?

**A**

Suki divides her garden into 6 equal parts. She plants daisies, roses, and violets. It takes Suki 1 hour to plant the flowers. She plants daisies in 1 part, roses in 2 parts, and violets in the rest of the garden.

*In what fraction of the garden does Suki plant violets?*

### What is a good plan for solving the problem?

I need to make sense of the given information. I need to think about what I can use to help me solve the problem.

*To make sense and persevere, you can use a picture to help develop a strategy.*

**B**

### How can I make sense of and solve this problem?

**I can**

- identify the quantities given.

- understand which quantities are needed to solve the problem.

- choose and implement an appropriate strategy.

- check to be sure my work and answer make sense.

**C**

The information about *1 hour to plant the flowers* is not needed to solve the problem.

I can use a picture to help make sense.

1 equal part for daisies is $\frac{1}{6}$ of the whole.

2 equal parts for roses is $\frac{2}{6}$ of the whole.

There are 3 equal parts left for violets.

3 copies of $\frac{1}{6}$ is $\frac{3}{6}$. So, Suki plants violets in $\frac{3}{6}$ of the garden.

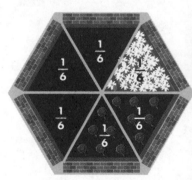

**Convince Me!** **Make Sense and Persevere** How can you check to make sure the work and answer given above make sense?

Name _____

# Guided Practice

**Make Sense and Persevere**

Keira and Matt cut a sandwich into 4 equal parts. They each ate 1 part. Keira is 9 years old. Matt is the same age as Keira. What fraction of the sandwich is not eaten?

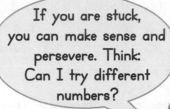

*If you are stuck, you can make sense and persevere. Think: Can I try different numbers?*

1. Is there any missing or extra information? Explain.

2. What do you need to find before you can determine how much of the sandwich is left?

3. Solve the problem. If information you need is missing, make up some reasonable information for the problem.

# Independent Practice

**Make Sense and Persevere**

Marni planted a vegetable garden. She put lettuce in 1 part, carrots in 4 parts, and broccoli in the rest of her garden. In what fraction of the garden did Marni plant broccoli?

4. Is there any missing or extra information?

5. Solve the problem. If information you need is missing, make up some reasonable information for the problem.

6. Can you use a different number of parts and still solve the problem? Explain.

# Problem Solving

**Sports Day**

Green School divides its school gym into 8 equal parts for a sports day. Basketball is in 2 parts, soccer is in 1 part, and volleyball and tennis are in the rest.

| Green School Sports Day | | |
| --- | --- | --- |
| **Sport** | **Parts of the Gym Needed** | **Number of Coaches Needed** |
| Basketball | 2 | 2 |
| Soccer | 1 | 1 |
| Tennis | ? | 3 |
| Volleyball | ? | 2 |

7. **Make Sense and Persevere** The gym teacher wants to know what fraction of the gym is used for tennis. What missing information do you need to solve the problem?

In **8** and **9**, draw a picture to represent the number of parts in each plan.

8. **Reasoning** What fraction of the gym would be used for tennis if 2 parts were for volleyball?

You can look for extra or missing information to help make sense and persevere in solving a problem.

9. **Reasoning** What fraction of the gym would be used for tennis if 3 parts were used for volleyball?

10. **Construct Arguments** To have the same fraction for tennis as for basketball, which plan, Exercise **8** or **9**, should be used? Justify your answer.

Name_____

**Follow the Path**

Shade a path from **START** to **FINISH**.
Follow the sums and differences where the
digit in the hundreds place is greater than
the digit in the tens place. You can only
move up, down, right, or left.

**I can ...**
add and subtract within 1,000.

 **Content Standard** 3.NBT.A.2
**Mathematical Practices** MP.2, MP.6,
MP.7

| Start | | | | |
|---|---|---|---|---|
| 822 − 514 | 814 − 128 | 499 + 182 | 210 + 484 | 580 − 434 |
| 753 − 536 | 768 + 29 | 723 − 461 | 555 − 320 | 253 + 234 |
| 951 − 96 | 195 + 474 | 964 − 532 | 672 − 127 | 725 − 314 |
| 125 + 424 | 244 − 147 | 279 + 531 | 365 − 97 | 230 + 757 |
| 921 − 614 | 989 − 239 | 572 + 346 | 992 − 539 | 495 + 485 |

Finish

**A-Z**
Glossary

**Word List**

- denominator
- fraction
- line plot
- nearest fourth inch
- nearest half inch
- numerator
- unit fraction

## Understand Vocabulary

**1.** Circle each *unit fraction.*

$\frac{1}{4}$ (circled)    $\frac{3}{8}$    $\frac{1}{6}$ (circled)    $\frac{1}{8}$ (circled)    $\frac{2}{3}$

**2.** Circle each fraction where 6 is the *denominator.*

$\frac{3}{6}$ (circled)    $\frac{6}{8}$    $\frac{1}{6}$ (circled)    $\frac{5}{6}$ (circled)    $\frac{4}{8}$

**3.** Circle each fraction where 4 is the *numerator.*

$\frac{2}{4}$    $\frac{4}{8}$ (circled)    $\frac{1}{4}$    $\frac{3}{4}$    $\frac{4}{6}$ (circled)

**4.** Circle the lengths that could be measurements to the *nearest half inch.*

$2\frac{1}{2}$ in.    4 in.    $3\frac{3}{4}$ in. (circled)    $7\frac{1}{4}$ in. (circled)    6 in.

**5.** Circle the lengths that could be measurements to the *nearest fourth inch.*

$8\frac{3}{4}$ in.    $1\frac{1}{4}$ in.    11 in.    $7\frac{1}{4}$ in.    6 in.

Write *always, sometimes,* or *never.*

**6.** The numerator in a fraction is ____?____ greater than the denominator.    _Never_

**7.** A fraction ____?____ has a numerator and denominator.    _always_

**8.** A line plot ____?____ shows measurements of lengths.    _sometimes_

## Use Vocabulary in Writing

**9.** Use at least 2 terms from the Word List to explain how to find the unit fraction of the shape shown below.

## Set A | pages 437–440

This is one way to divide a whole into fourths.

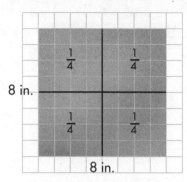

8 in.

8 in.

Because each of the 4 parts has the same area, each part is one fourth of the whole.

You can write this fraction as $\frac{1}{4}$.

A unit fraction represents one of the equal parts. $\frac{1}{4}$ is a unit fraction.

**Remember** that fractions can name equal parts of a whole.

In **1** and **2**, draw lines to divide the shape into the given number of equal parts. Then write the fraction that represents 1 part.

**1.** 6 equal parts    **2.** 2 equal parts

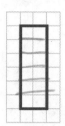   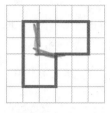

**3.** Martin divides a shape into 3 equal parts. What unit fraction can he write to represent 1 part?

## Set B | pages 441–444

What fraction of this rectangle is shaded?

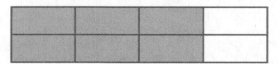

The rectangle is divided into 8 equal parts. So, the unit fraction of the rectangle is $\frac{1}{8}$.

In the whole rectangle, there are 8 parts of $\frac{1}{8}$.

8 copies of $\frac{1}{8}$ is $\frac{8}{8}$.

For the shaded part there are 6 parts of $\frac{1}{8}$.

$$\frac{\text{numerator}}{\text{denominator}} = \frac{\text{the number of repetitions of the unit fraction}}{\text{what fractional part is being counted}} = \frac{6}{8}$$

6 copies of $\frac{1}{8}$ is $\frac{6}{8}$.

So, $\frac{6}{8}$ of the rectangle is shaded.

**Remember** that you need to think about how many parts there are in all and how many parts are shaded.

In **1–4**, write the unit fraction that represents each part of the whole. Next, write the number of shaded parts. Last, write the fraction of the whole that is shaded.

**1.**    **2.**

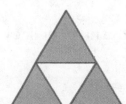   

**3.**    **4.**

## Set C | pages 445–448

This shape is $\frac{2}{4}$ of a piece of fabric Tina used in a quilt. You can draw a picture and write a fraction to represent the whole piece of fabric.

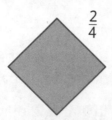
$\frac{2}{4}$

$\frac{2}{4}$ is 2 copies of $\frac{1}{4}$.

Divide the piece of fabric into 2 equal parts.

4 copies of $\frac{1}{4}$ makes $\frac{4}{4}$, or 1 whole.

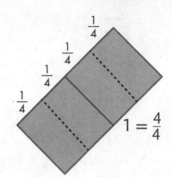
$1 = \frac{4}{4}$

**Remember** that the denominator shows the total number of equal parts in a whole.

In **1** and **2**, draw a picture and write a fraction to represent the whole.

1. $\frac{1}{4}$

$1 = \dfrac{\square}{\square}$

2. $\frac{3}{8}$

$1 = \dfrac{\square}{\square}$

## Set D | pages 449–452

You can show fractions on a number line.

The fraction $\frac{5}{6}$ is labeled. What are the missing fractions?

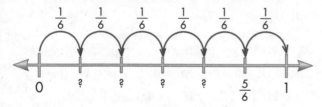

First, find the unit fraction. The line is divided into six equal lengths. So, the number line shows sixths.

Each jump represents $\frac{1}{6}$. So, the first tick mark is labeled $\frac{1}{6}$. The second tick mark is labeled $\frac{2}{6}$, and so on.

The missing fractions on the number line are $\frac{1}{6}, \frac{2}{6}, \frac{3}{6},$ and $\frac{4}{6}$.

**Remember** to first decide what unit fraction is shown on each number line.

In **1** and **2**, write the missing fractions on each number line.

1.

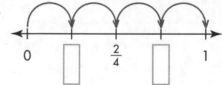

2.

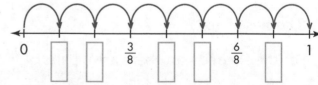

3. Divide the number line below into 3 equal parts and mark $\frac{2}{3}$ on the line.

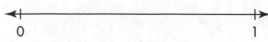

Name_____

Reteaching
Continued

**Set E** pages 453–456

Number lines can have fractions greater than 1.

The number line below is divided into thirds.

The denominator is 3 because the unit fraction is $\frac{1}{3}$. The numerator shows how many copies of the unit fraction each point represents.

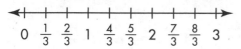

$0 \quad \frac{1}{3} \quad \frac{2}{3} \quad 1 \quad \frac{4}{3} \quad \frac{5}{3} \quad 2 \quad \frac{7}{3} \quad \frac{8}{3} \quad 3$

**Remember** that the numerator increases by 1 because each part of the number line is 1 more copy of the unit fraction.

1. The number line has equal lengths marked. Write the missing fractions.

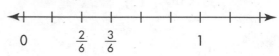

$0 \qquad \frac{2}{6} \quad \frac{3}{6} \qquad 1$

2. Divide the number line into fourths. Label each point.

$0 \qquad 1 \qquad 2 \qquad 3$

**Set F** pages 457–460

You can use a line plot to show data, such as lengths measured to the nearest half inch.

Steps to make a line plot:

- Draw a number line and choose a scale.

- The scale should show data values from the least to the greatest.

- Write a title for the line plot.

- Mark a dot for each value.

**DATA**

| **Lengths of Lilly's Ribbons** | | | | |
|---|---|---|---|---|
| $5\frac{1}{2}$ in. | 4 in. | $5\frac{1}{2}$ in. | $4\frac{1}{2}$ in. | $4\frac{1}{2}$ in. |

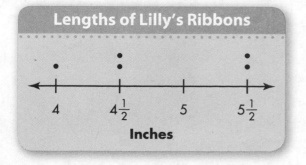

**Remember** to mark a dot for each length. Check your completed line plot against the data in the chart.

**DATA**

| **Lengths of Carl's Strings** | | | | |
|---|---|---|---|---|
| 3 in. | $2\frac{1}{2}$ in. | $2\frac{1}{2}$ in. | $2\frac{1}{2}$ in. | 4 in. |
| $2\frac{1}{2}$ in. | $3\frac{1}{2}$ in. | $3\frac{1}{2}$ in. | 3 in. | 3 in. |

1. Draw a line plot to show the data.

2. How many strings does Carl have in all?

3. Draw a line that is the same length as the most common string length.

**Topic 12** | Reteaching   **473**

**Set G** pages 461–464

You can measure to different lengths, such as to the nearest fourth inch.

The closest fourth-inch mark to the end of the length of the rectangle is the $2\frac{1}{4}$-inch mark.

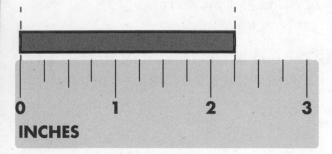

The lengths can be shown on a line plot.

**Remember** to think about the scale of the line plot. It needs to include the least and greatest values.

1. Measure and record the lengths of 5 classroom objects to the nearest fourth inch. Use objects that are between 1 and 3 inches long.

2. Draw a line plot to show your data.

**Set H** pages 465–468

Think about these questions to help you **make sense and persevere** in solving problems.

### Thinking Habits

- What do I need to find?
- What do I know?
- What's my plan for solving the problem?
- What else can I try if I get stuck?
- How can I check that my solution makes sense?

**Remember** to make sense of the problem by identifying the quantities. Then use what you know to solve.

Gavin divided his notebook into 8 equal parts. He plans to use 3 parts to take notes for math and 2 parts for reading. He has school from 8:30 A.M. to 3:30 P.M. What fraction of his notebook does he have left?

1. Is there any missing or extra information? Explain.

2. Solve the problem. If information you need is missing, make up some reasonable information for the problem. You can draw a picture to help.

Name _____

1. What fraction of the whole is colored green? What fraction of the whole is colored yellow?

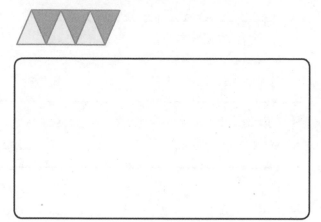

3. This line segment represents $\frac{1}{3}$ of the distance from Mal's house to the library. Which represents the whole distance and has an accurate explanation?

Ⓐ ⊢————————⊣ The line segment represents $\frac{1}{3}$ the distance from Mal's house to the library. So, the whole distance is 3 times as long.

Ⓑ ⊢———————⊣ The line segment represents $\frac{1}{3}$ the distance from Mal's house to the library. So, the whole distance is 2 times as long.

Ⓒ ⊢——————————————⊣ The line segment represents $\frac{1}{3}$ the distance from Mal's house to the library. So, the whole distance is 4 times as long.

Ⓓ ⊢———⊣ The line segment represents the distance from Mal's house to the library. So, the whole distance is the identical line segment.

2. Write a fraction to name the equal parts of the whole pizza. How many parts would you need to make two whole pizzas? Explain.

4. Which point is at $\frac{3}{6}$ on the number line?

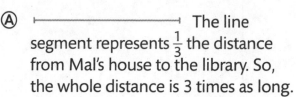

Ⓐ Point A          Ⓒ Point C

Ⓑ Point B          Ⓓ Point D

5. Which of the fractions would be to the right of 1 on a number line? Select all that apply.

☐ $\frac{3}{4}$          ☐ $\frac{1}{3}$

☐ $\frac{5}{4}$          ☐ $\frac{2}{5}$

☐ $\frac{4}{2}$

**6. A.** Draw a picture to show $\frac{2}{4}$.

**B.** Explain how you knew you had shaded the correct amount of your picture.

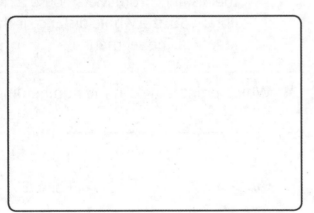

**7.** Jeremy put pepperoni on $\frac{1}{2}$ of a pizza. He put olives on $\frac{1}{3}$ of the pizza. What fraction of the pizza did **NOT** have pepperoni? What fraction of the pizza did **NOT** have olives?

**8.** One point on the number line below has been named with the fraction $\frac{2}{4}$. Write a fraction for each of the other points shown.

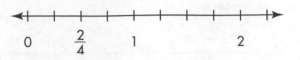

**9.** Explain how you know $\frac{3}{3}$ represents a whole.

**10.** Jared folded a piece of paper 9 inches by 12 inches into sections as shown below. What fraction of the total area is in each section? Explain.

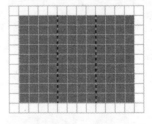

**11.** How many $\frac{2}{8}$s do you need to get $\frac{8}{8}$?

**14.** Which point represents 6 lengths of $\frac{1}{8}$ on the number line? Explain.

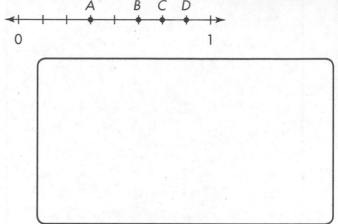

**12.** Lane's class is painting a mural with 6 equal parts. They spent 45 minutes painting on each of 2 days. On the first day, the class painted $\frac{1}{6}$ of the mural. The next day, the class painted another $\frac{1}{6}$ of the mural. How many $\frac{1}{6}$-parts did the class paint in the two days?

Ⓐ 1

Ⓑ 2

Ⓒ 3

Ⓓ 4

**15.** Divide the circle into 8 equal parts. What fraction does each part represent?

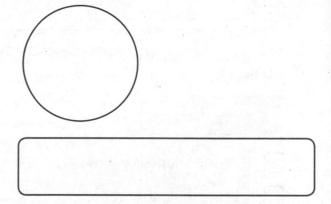

**13.** How many $\frac{1}{8}$s do you need to get $\frac{5}{8}$? Use the number line below for help.

Ⓐ 1

Ⓑ 3

Ⓒ 5

Ⓓ 8

**16.** Seth drew $\frac{2}{4}$ of a shape below. Draw a picture to show the whole shape and write a fraction to represent the whole.

$\frac{2}{4}$

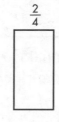

**17.** Mara believes the point marked on the number line is $\frac{2}{3}$. Is she correct? Explain.

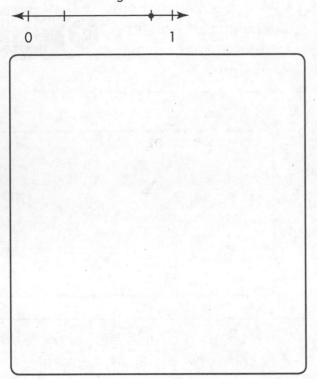

0                  1

**18.** Select all the sentences that describe this shape.

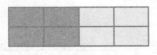

- ☐ $\frac{8}{8}$ of the shape is yellow.
- ☐ $\frac{8}{8}$ represents the whole.
- ☐ $\frac{5}{8}$ of the shape is green.
- ☐ $\frac{4}{8}$ of the shape is green.
- ☐ $\frac{4}{8}$ of the shape is yellow.

**19.** Divide the number line into equal lengths. Then mark and label the given fraction.

6 equal lengths; $\frac{5}{6}$

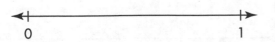

0                  1

**20.** Tony collects colored strings. The table shows the lengths of some of his strings.

DATA

| Lengths of Tony's Strings | |
| --- | --- |
| String Colors | Length (nearest fourth inch) |
| Black String | $3\frac{2}{4}$ in. |
| Blue String | 3 in. |
| White String | $3\frac{2}{4}$ in. |
| Yellow String | $2\frac{1}{4}$ in. |
| Green String | $2\frac{3}{4}$ in. |

**A.** Measure the lengths of Tony's red and brown strings shown below to the nearest fourth inch.

_____

_____

_____

_____

**B.** Draw a line plot to show the lengths of Tony's 7 strings to the nearest fourth inch.

**478**    **Topic 12** | Assessment Practice

Name _____

**Art Display**

Three students, Zach, Allie, and Paige, are making an art display.

Use the **Paint Colors** list and the design at the right to answer
Questions **1–4**.

1. The display will be divided into 8 equal parts.
   Draw lines to show one way to do this. Then
   write the fraction that describes the area of
   the total shape that is represented by
   1 equal part.

**Paint Colors**
- Allie is painting the blue parts.
- Paige is painting the red parts.
- Zach is painting the yellow parts.
- Each student will paint at least 2 parts.

2. Shade the parts blue, yellow, or red to show how many parts
   each student could paint. Write fractions to show how much
   of the total display Allie and Paige painted.

3. Divide the number line into the number of equal parts of the
   display. Then mark a dot to show the fraction of the display
   that Zach painted on the number line.

   0                                               1

4. Which fraction represents the whole display? Explain.
   Then mark a dot to show where this fraction is located
   on the number line above.

Use the **Ribbon Lengths** diagram on the right and the **Number of Ribbons** table below to answer Question **5**.

5. The students will use the ribbon lengths at the right in their display.

**Part A**

Measure and record the lengths of each of these ribbons to the nearest fourth inch.

**Part B**

The **Number of Ribbons** table shows how many of each color ribbon will be used. Draw a line plot to show this data.

| Number of Ribbons | |
|---|---|
| **Color** | **Number Used** |
| Blue | 4 |
| Green | 4 |
| Red | 2 |

6. In order to complete the display, the students recorded the number of half-hour sessions they spent working together.

The number line below is divided into equal parts. Each part represents half an hour. Write the missing fractions on the number line.

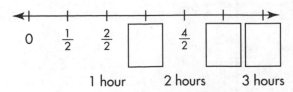

480     **Topic 12** | Performance Task

# Fraction Equivalence and Comparison

**Essential Question:** What are different ways to compare fractions?

**Digital Resources**

Interactive Student Edition · Activity · Visual Learning · Video · Practice

Assessment · Games · Tools · Glossary

Animals and plants change and grow during their life cycles.

Some animals and plants even change their forms.

A caterpillar changes into a butterfly! Here is a project on life cycles and fractions.

## enVision STEM Project: Life Cycles

**Do Research** A frog egg hatches into a tadpole that lives in water. The tadpole will change and eventually become an adult frog. Use the Internet or another source to gather information about the life cycle of a frog and other animals.

**Journal: Write a Report** Include what you found. Also in your report:

- Tell about what is in a frog's habitat to support changes the frog goes through in its life cycle.

- Compare the life cycles of the different animals you studied.

- For the animals you studied, make up and solve problems using fractions. Draw fraction strips to represent the fractions.

Name _____

# Review What You Know

**(A-Z) Vocabulary**

Choose the best term from the box. Write it on the blank.

> • <          • numerator
>
> • >          • unit fraction

1. The symbol ___>___ means *is greater than*.

2. The symbol ___<___ means *is less than*.

3. A _____ represents one equal part of a whole.

## Comparing Whole Numbers

Compare. Write <, >, or =.

4. 48 (>) 30

5. 6 (=) 6

6. 723 (<) 732

7. 152 (<) 183

8. 100 (>) 10

9. 189 (>) 99

10. 456 (=) 456

11. 123 (<) 223

12. 421 (>) 399

13. 158 (<) 185

14. 117 (=) 117

15. 900 (>) 893

## Identifying Fractions

For each shape, write the fraction that is shaded.

16.  $\frac{4}{8}$

17. $\frac{1}{5}$

18. $\frac{2}{4}$

## Division

Divide.

19. 30 ÷ 5

20. 72 ÷ 8

21. 28 ÷ 4

22. 48 ÷ 6

23. 81 ÷ 9

24. 45 ÷ 5

25. 32 ÷ 8

26. 42 ÷ 6

27. 49 ÷ 7

28. How can you check if the answer to 40 ÷ 5 is 8?

Name _____

**PROJECT 13A**

**Do you want to ride a horse?**

**Project:** Design a Racetrack for Horses

**PROJECT 13B**

**How deep do you have to dig before you reach water?**

**Project:** Create a Picture of a Well

**PROJECT 13C**

**How many coffee beans does it take to fill up a container?**

**Project:** Plot Fractions on a Number Line

Video

## Math Modeling

## What's the Beef?

Before watching the video, think:

Cooking is even more fun when you do it with a friend. Today I'm going to be a handy helper.

**I can ...**

model with math to solve a weight comparison problem that involves adding unit fractions and comparing.

 **Mathematical Practices**  MP.4 Also MP.3, MP.6
**Content Standards**  3.NF.A.3a Also 3.NF.A.1, 3.NF.A.3c

Name_____

☆ ☆
**Solve & Share**

Gregor threw a softball $\frac{3}{4}$ of the length of the yard in front of his house. Find as many fractions as you can that name the same part of the length of the yard that Gregor threw the ball. Explain how you decided.

**I can ...**
find equivalent fractions that name the same part of a whole.

© **Content Standards** 3.NF.A.3b Also 3.NF.A.3a
**Mathematical Practices** MP.2, MP.5, MP.7

You can use appropriate tools. Think about what you need to find. Think about the tools or models you can use to help solve the problem.

**Gregor's yard**

---

**Look Back!** How can fraction strips help you tell if a fraction with a denominator of 2, 3, or 6 would name the same part of a whole as $\frac{3}{4}$?

**Essential Question**

# How Can Different Fractions Name the Same Part of a Whole?

**A**

*The Chisholm Trail was used to drive cattle to market. Ross's herd has walked $\frac{1}{2}$ the distance to market. What is another way to name $\frac{1}{2}$?*

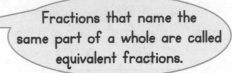

Different fractions can name the same part of a whole.

Fractions that name the same part of a whole are called equivalent fractions.

**B**

$\frac{1}{2} = \dfrac{\square}{\square}$  You can use fraction strips.

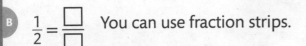

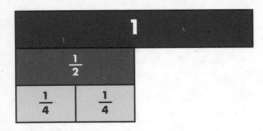

The fractions $\frac{1}{2}$ and $\frac{2}{4}$ represent the same part of the whole.

Two $\frac{1}{4}$ strips are equal to $\frac{1}{2}$, so $\frac{1}{2} = \frac{2}{4}$.

Another name for $\frac{1}{2}$ is $\frac{2}{4}$.

**C**

You can find other equivalent fractions. Think about fractions that name the same part of the whole.

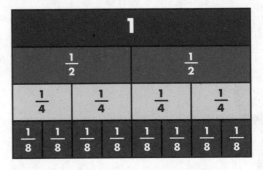

Four $\frac{1}{8}$ strips are equal to $\frac{1}{2}$, so $\frac{1}{2} = \frac{4}{8}$.

Another name for $\frac{1}{2}$ is $\frac{4}{8}$.

**Convince Me!** **Look for Relationships** In the examples above, what pattern do you see in the fractions that are equivalent to $\frac{1}{2}$? What is another name for $\frac{1}{2}$ that is not shown above?

Practice   Tools   Assessment

## Another Example!

You can find an equivalent fraction for $\frac{4}{6}$ using an area model.

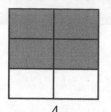 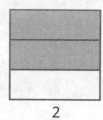

$\frac{4}{6}$          $\frac{2}{3}$

Both area models have the same-sized whole.
One is divided into sixths. The other shows thirds.
The shaded parts show the same part of a whole.

Because $\frac{4}{6} = \frac{2}{3}$, another name for $\frac{4}{6}$ is $\frac{2}{3}$.

## ☆ Guided Practice

### Do You Understand?

1. Divide the second area model into sixths. Shade it to show a fraction equivalent to $\frac{1}{3}$.

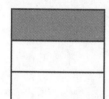 

$\frac{1}{3} = \boxed{\phantom{0}}$

### Do You Know How?

2. Use the fraction strips to help find an equivalent fraction.

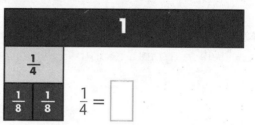

$\frac{1}{4} = \boxed{\phantom{0}}$

## ☆ Independent Practice ☆

3. Use the fraction strips to help find an equivalent fraction.

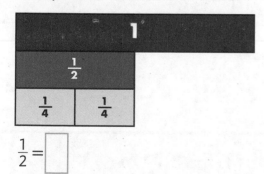

$\frac{1}{2} = \boxed{\phantom{0}}$

4. Divide the second area model into eighths. Shade it to show a fraction equivalent to $\frac{1}{2}$.

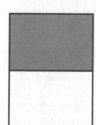

$\frac{1}{2} = \boxed{\phantom{0}}$

In **5–8**, find each equivalent fraction. Use fraction strips or draw area models to help.

5. $\frac{3}{4} = \frac{\boxed{\phantom{0}}}{8}$

6. $\frac{6}{6} = \frac{\boxed{\phantom{0}}}{8}$

7. $\frac{2}{6} = \frac{\boxed{\phantom{0}}}{3}$

8. $\frac{4}{8} = \frac{\boxed{\phantom{0}}}{2}$

# Problem Solving

In **9** and **10**, use the fraction strips at the right.

9. Marcy used fraction strips to show equivalent fractions. Complete the equation.

$$\frac{\square}{4} = \boxed{\phantom{x}}$$

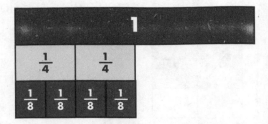

10. Rita says the fraction strips show fractions that are equivalent to $\frac{1}{2}$. Explain what you could do to the diagram to see if she is correct.

Both fractions represent the same part of the whole.

---

11. **Reasoning** A band learns 4 to 6 new songs every month. What is a good estimate for the number of songs the band will learn in 8 months? Explain.

12. Three eighths of a playground is covered by grass. What fraction of the playground is **NOT** covered by grass?

---

13. **Higher Order Thinking** Aiden folded 2 strips of paper into eighths. He shaded a fraction equal to $\frac{1}{4}$ on the first strip and a fraction equal to $\frac{3}{4}$ on the second strip. Use eighths to show the fractions Aiden shaded on the pictures to the right. Which fraction of each strip did he shade?

---

## Assessment Practice

14. Which fractions are equivalent? Select all that apply.

☐ $\frac{1}{4}$ and $\frac{1}{8}$     ☐ $\frac{3}{4}$ and $\frac{3}{8}$

☐ $\frac{1}{4}$ and $\frac{2}{8}$     ☐ $\frac{3}{4}$ and $\frac{6}{8}$

☐ $\frac{2}{4}$ and $\frac{4}{8}$

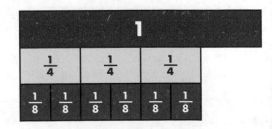

Name_____

## Lesson 13-2
### Equivalent Fractions: Use the Number Line

☆ ☆
**Solve & Share**

The top number line shows a point at $\frac{1}{4}$. Write the fraction for each of the points labeled A, B, C, D, E, and F. Which of these fractions show the same distance from 0 as $\frac{1}{4}$?

**I can ...**
use number lines to represent equivalent fractions.

© **Content Standards** 3.NF.A.3a Also 3.NF.A.3b
**Mathematical Practices** MP.3, MP.4

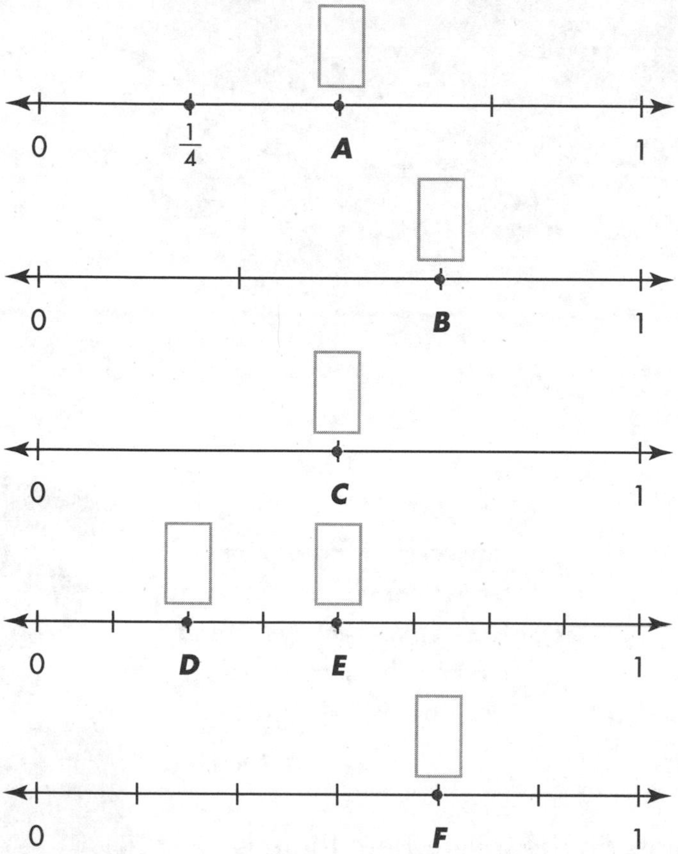

0     $\frac{1}{4}$     **A**                  1

0                       **B**                  1

0              **C**                           1

0        **D**        **E**                    1

0                 **F**                        1

Model with math. You can represent equivalent fractions on a number line.

**Look Back!** How can number lines show that two fractions are equivalent?

**A**

The Circle W Ranch 1-mile trail has water for cattle at each $\frac{1}{4}$-mile mark. The Big T Ranch 1-mile trail has water for cattle at the $\frac{1}{2}$-mile mark. What fractions name the points on the trails where there is water for cattle at the same distance from the start of each trail?

Circle W Ranch Trail

Big T Ranch Trail

**B** You can use number lines to find the fractions.

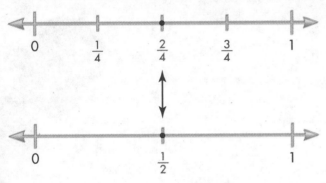

$$\frac{2}{4} = \frac{1}{2}$$

Equivalent fractions are different names for the same point on a number line. $\frac{2}{4}$ and $\frac{1}{2}$ name the same part of the whole.

The fractions $\frac{2}{4}$ and $\frac{1}{2}$ name the same points on the trails where there is water for cattle. They are at the same distance from the start of the trails.

**Convince Me!** **Model with Math** Ian paints $\frac{6}{8}$ of a fence. Anna paints $\frac{3}{4}$ of another fence of equal size and length. How can you show that Ian and Anna have painted the same amount of each fence?

Name_____

Practice  Tools  Assessment

# ☆Guided Practice

## Do You Understand?

**1.** Complete the number line to show that $\frac{2}{6}$ and $\frac{1}{3}$ are equivalent fractions.

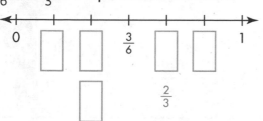

**2.** Sheila compares $\frac{4}{6}$ and $\frac{4}{8}$. She discovers that the fractions are **NOT** equivalent. How does Sheila know?

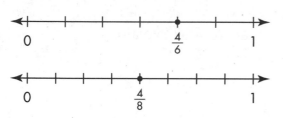

## Do You Know How?

In **3** and **4**, find the missing equivalent fractions on the number line. Then write the equivalent fractions below.

**3.**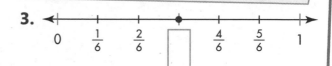

**4.**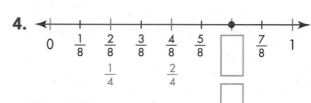

# Independent Practice

In **5–8**, find the missing equivalent fractions on the number line. Then write the equivalent fractions below.

**5.**

**6.**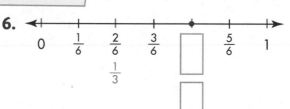

**7.**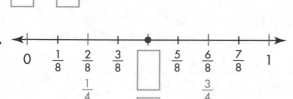

**8.**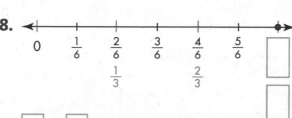

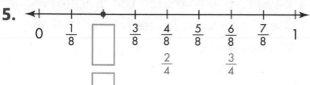 

# Problem Solving

**9. Number Sense** Bradley had 40 slices of pizza to share. How many pizzas did he have? Explain how you solved the problem.

Each of Bradley's pizzas was cut into 8 slices.

**10.** Ms. Owen has 15 magazines to share among 5 students for an art project. How many magazines will each student get? Use the bar diagram to write an equation that helps solve the problem.

15 magazines

| ? | ? | ? | ? | ? | ← 5 students

**11.** Yonita has 28 different apps on her computer. Casey has 14 music apps and 20 game apps on his computer. How many more apps does Casey have than Yonita? Explain.

**12. Construct Arguments** How can you tell, just by looking at the fractions, that $\frac{2}{4}$ and $\frac{3}{4}$ are **NOT** equivalent? Construct an argument to explain.

**13. Higher Order Thinking** Fiona and Gabe each had the same length of rope. Fiona used $\frac{2}{3}$ of her rope. Using sixths, what fraction of the length of rope will Gabe need to use to match the amount Fiona used? Draw a number line as part of your answer.

## ☑ Assessment Practice

**14.** Use the number line to find which fraction is equivalent to $\frac{3}{6}$.

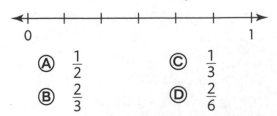

Ⓐ $\frac{1}{2}$   Ⓒ $\frac{1}{3}$

Ⓑ $\frac{2}{3}$   Ⓓ $\frac{2}{6}$

**15.** Use the number line to find which fraction is equivalent to $\frac{4}{8}$.

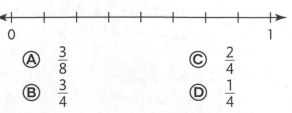

Ⓐ $\frac{3}{8}$   Ⓒ $\frac{2}{4}$

Ⓑ $\frac{3}{4}$   Ⓓ $\frac{1}{4}$

Name_____

## Solve & Share

Maria and Evan are both jogging a mile.
Maria has jogged $\frac{7}{8}$ mile, and Evan has jogged $\frac{3}{8}$ mile.
Show how far each has jogged. Use any model you
choose. Who jogged farther? How do you know?

**I can ...**
compare fractions that refer to the
same-sized whole and have the
same denominator by comparing
their numerators.

© **Content Standard** 3.NF.A.3d
**Mathematical Practices** MP.2, MP.5, MP.8

You can use appropriate
tools. Think about fraction strips
and why they can be good tools to
show fractions.

**Maria** [ ]

**Evan** [ ]

**Look Back!** Suppose Evan had jogged $\frac{5}{8}$ mile instead of $\frac{3}{8}$ mile.
Now, who has jogged farther? Explain.

**Essential Question** **How Can You Compare Fractions with the Same Denominator?**

**A**

Two banners with positive messages are the same size. One banner is $\frac{4}{6}$ yellow, and the other banner is $\frac{2}{6}$ yellow. Which is greater, $\frac{4}{6}$ or $\frac{2}{6}$?

Remember, comparisons are valid, or true, only if they refer to the same-sized whole.

Use fraction strips to reason about the sizes of these two fractions.

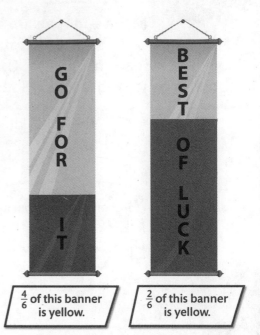

$\frac{4}{6}$ of this banner is yellow.

$\frac{2}{6}$ of this banner is yellow.

**B**

$\frac{4}{6}$ is 4 of the unit fraction $\frac{1}{6}$.

$\frac{2}{6}$ is 2 of the unit fraction $\frac{1}{6}$.

So, $\frac{4}{6}$ is greater than $\frac{2}{6}$.

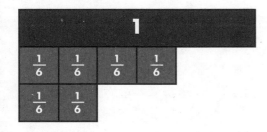

**C** Record the comparison using symbols or words.

$$\frac{4}{6} > \frac{2}{6}$$

*Four sixths* is greater than *two sixths*.

If two fractions have the same denominator, the fraction with the greater numerator is the greater fraction.

**Convince Me!** **Reasoning** Write a number for each numerator to make each comparison true. Use a picture and words to explain how you decided.

$$\frac{\square}{8} < \frac{\square}{8} \qquad \frac{\square}{3} > \frac{\square}{3}$$

Name_____

# ☆ Guided Practice

## Do You Understand?

**1.** Explain how you can use fraction strips to show whether $\frac{5}{6}$ or $\frac{3}{6}$ of the same whole is greater.

**2.** Which is greater, $\frac{3}{4}$ or $\frac{2}{4}$? Draw $\frac{1}{4}$-strips to complete the diagram and answer the question.

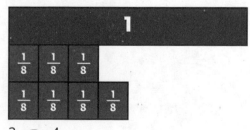

## Do You Know How?

In **3** and **4**, compare. Write <, >, or =. Use the fraction strips to help.

**3.**

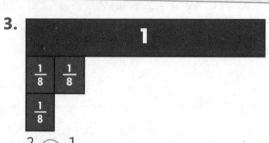

$\frac{2}{8}$ ◯ $\frac{1}{8}$

**4.**

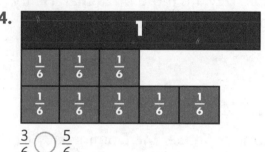

$\frac{3}{6}$ ◯ $\frac{5}{6}$

# ☆ Independent Practice ☆

**Leveled Practice** In **5–14**, compare. Write <, >, or =. Use or draw fraction strips to help. The fractions refer to the same whole.

**5.**

$\frac{3}{8}$ ◯ $\frac{4}{8}$

**6.**

$\frac{3}{4}$ ◯ $\frac{3}{4}$

**7.** $\frac{6}{8}$ ◯ $\frac{3}{8}$

**8.** $\frac{5}{8}$ ◯ $\frac{7}{8}$

**9.** $\frac{1}{2}$ ◯ $\frac{1}{2}$

**10.** $\frac{1}{3}$ ◯ $\frac{2}{3}$

**11.** $\frac{6}{6}$ ◯ $\frac{3}{6}$

**12.** $\frac{2}{8}$ ◯ $\frac{3}{8}$

**13.** $\frac{3}{3}$ ◯ $\frac{1}{3}$

**14.** $\frac{1}{4}$ ◯ $\frac{3}{4}$

# Problem Solving

In **15** and **16**, use the pictures of the strips that have been partly shaded.

**15.** Compare. Write <, >, or =.
The green strips show $\frac{1}{6}$ ◯ $\frac{2}{6}$.

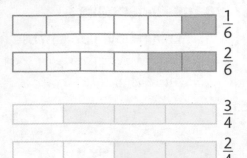

**16.** Do the yellow strips show $\frac{2}{4} > \frac{3}{4}$? Explain.

---

**17.** Izzy and Henry have two different pizzas. Izzy ate $\frac{3}{8}$ of her pizza. Henry ate $\frac{3}{8}$ of his pizza. Izzy ate more pizza than Henry. How is this possible? Explain.

**18.** **Generalize** Two fractions are equal. They also have the same denominator. What must be true of the numerators of the fractions? Explain.

---

**19.** **Number Sense** Mr. Domini had $814 in the bank on Wednesday. On Thursday, he withdrew $250, and on Friday, he withdrew $185. How much money did he have in the bank then?

**20.** **Higher Order Thinking** Tom's parents let him choose whether to play his favorite board game for $\frac{7}{8}$ hour or for $\frac{8}{8}$ hour. Explain which amount of time you think Tom should choose and why.

---

## ✓ Assessment Practice

**21.** Paul and Enrique each have equal-sized pizzas cut into 8 equal slices. Paul eats 3 slices. Enrique eats 2 slices. Select numbers and symbols from the box to write a comparison for the fraction of pizza Paul and Enrique have each eaten.

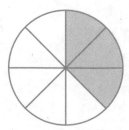

Paul's Pizza

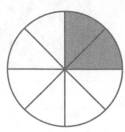

Enrique's Pizza

| 2  3  4  6  8  <  >  = |

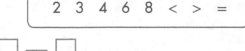

Name_____

### Solve & Share

Krista, Jamal, and Rafe each had 1 serving of vegetables. Krista ate $\frac{2}{6}$, Jamal ate $\frac{2}{3}$, and Rafe ate $\frac{2}{8}$ of his serving. Arrange the fractions in order from least to greatest to show who ate the least and who ate the greatest amount of vegetables.

**I can ...**
compare fractions that refer to the same whole and have the same numerator by comparing their denominators.

© **Content Standard** 3.NF.A.3d
**Mathematical Practices** MP.3, MP.6

Be precise.
Use pictures, words, and symbols to represent and compare fractions in different ways.

$\frac{2}{6}$     $\frac{2}{3}$     $\frac{2}{8}$

**Look Back!** Tamika ate $\frac{2}{2}$ of a serving of vegetables. In order from least to greatest, arrange the fractions of a serving Krista, Jamal, Rafe, and Tamika each ate. Explain your reasoning.

**Essential Question: How Can You Compare Fractions with the Same Numerator?**

**A**

$\frac{5}{6}$ of this scarf is orange.

Claire bought 2 scarves as souvenirs from her visit to a Florida university. The scarves are the same size. One scarf is $\frac{5}{6}$ orange, and the other scarf is $\frac{5}{8}$ orange. Which is greater, $\frac{5}{6}$ or $\frac{5}{8}$?

$\frac{5}{8}$ of this scarf is orange.

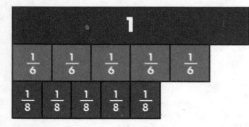

You can compare fractions that have the same numerator by reasoning about their size.

**B What You Show**

Use fraction strips to reason about the size of $\frac{5}{6}$ compared to the size of $\frac{5}{8}$.

| 1 |
| $\frac{1}{6}$ | $\frac{1}{6}$ | $\frac{1}{6}$ | $\frac{1}{6}$ | $\frac{1}{6}$ |
| $\frac{1}{8}$ | $\frac{1}{8}$ | $\frac{1}{8}$ | $\frac{1}{8}$ | $\frac{1}{8}$ |

There are 5 sixths. There are 5 eighths. The parts are different sizes.

The greater the denominator, the smaller each part will be.

**C What You Write**

Describe the comparison using symbols or words.

$\frac{5}{6} > \frac{5}{8}$

*Five sixths* is greater than *five eighths*.

If two fractions have the same numerator, the fraction with the lesser denominator is the greater fraction.

**Convince Me!** **Critique Reasoning** Julia says $\frac{1}{8}$ is greater than $\frac{1}{4}$ because 8 is greater than 4. Critique Julia's reasoning. Is she correct? Explain.

# ☆ Guided Practice

## Do You Understand?

**1.** How can fraction strips help you reason about whether $\frac{4}{6}$ or $\frac{4}{8}$ of the same whole is greater?

**2.** Which is greater, $\frac{1}{4}$ or $\frac{1}{6}$? Draw fraction strips to complete the diagram and answer the question.

| **1** |
|---|

## Do You Know How?

In **3** and **4**, compare. Write <, >, or =. Use fraction strips to help.

**3.**

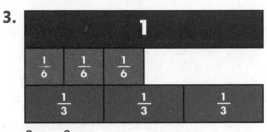

$\frac{3}{6} \bigcirc \frac{3}{3}$

**4.**

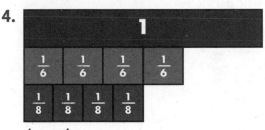

$\frac{4}{6} \bigcirc \frac{4}{8}$

# ☆ Independent Practice ☆

**Leveled Practice** In **5–14**, compare. Write <, >, or =. Use or draw fraction strips to help. The fractions refer to the same whole.

**5.**

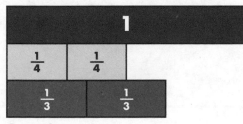

$\frac{2}{4} \bigcirc \frac{2}{3}$

**6.**

| **1** |
|---|

$\frac{4}{4} \bigcirc \frac{4}{6}$

**7.** $\frac{2}{3} \bigcirc \frac{2}{2}$     **8.** $\frac{4}{8} \bigcirc \frac{4}{8}$     **9.** $\frac{5}{6} \bigcirc \frac{5}{8}$     **10.** $\frac{1}{4} \bigcirc \frac{1}{3}$

**11.** $\frac{1}{3} \bigcirc \frac{1}{6}$     **12.** $\frac{4}{6} \bigcirc \frac{4}{6}$     **13.** $\frac{1}{8} \bigcirc \frac{1}{2}$     **14.** $\frac{2}{6} \bigcirc \frac{2}{3}$

# Problem Solving

**15.** James uses blue and white tiles to make the two designs shown here. James says that the total blue area in the top design is the same as the total blue area in the bottom design. Is he correct? Explain.

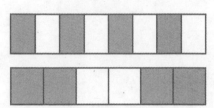

Each whole is the same size. So, you can compare the fractions the blue tiles represent in each whole.

**16.** Amy sold 8 large quilts and 1 baby quilt. How much money did she make from selling quilts?

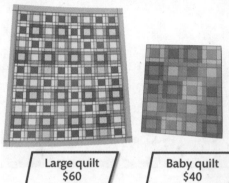

Large quilt $60

Baby quilt $40

**17. Be Precise** Write two comparison statements about the fractions shown below.

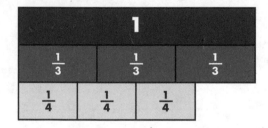

**18. Higher Order Thinking** John says that when you compare two fractions with the same numerator, you look at the denominators because the fraction with the greater denominator is greater. Is he correct? Explain, and give an example.

## Assessment Practice

**19.** These fractions refer to the same whole. Which of these comparisons are correct? Select all that apply.

☐ $\frac{5}{6} < \frac{5}{8}$   ☐ $\frac{2}{4} > \frac{2}{3}$

☐ $\frac{1}{2} > \frac{1}{4}$   ☐ $\frac{5}{6} = \frac{5}{6}$

☐ $\frac{3}{4} > \frac{3}{6}$

### Solve & Share

Mr. Evans wrote $\frac{2}{8}, \frac{4}{8}, \frac{6}{8}, \frac{1}{8}, \frac{3}{8}, \frac{5}{8}$ and $\frac{7}{8}$ on the board. Then he circled the fractions that are closer to 0 than to 1. Which fractions did he circle? Which fractions did he not circle? Explain how you decided.

**I can ...**
use what I know about the size of benchmark numbers to compare fractions.

| 0 | $\frac{1}{2}$ | 1 |
|---|---|---|
|   |   |   |

© **Content Standard** 3.NF.A.3d
**Mathematical Practices** MP.1, MP.2

You can use reasoning. Benchmarks like 0, $\frac{1}{2}$, and 1 are useful when comparing fractions of the same whole.

**Look Back!** Eric says that $\frac{3}{8}$ is closer to 1 than to 0 because $\frac{3}{8}$ is greater than $\frac{1}{8}$. Is he correct? Use benchmark numbers to evaluate Eric's reasoning and justify your answer.

**Essential Question** **How Can Benchmark Numbers Be Used to Compare Fractions?**

**A**

Keri wants to buy $\frac{2}{6}$ of a container of roasted peanuts. Alan wants to buy $\frac{2}{3}$ of a container of roasted peanuts. The containers are the same size. Who will buy more peanuts?

Another strategy to compare fractions is to use common benchmark numbers such as 0, $\frac{1}{2}$, and 1.

Roasted Peanuts

Full

**B** Compare each fraction to the benchmark number $\frac{1}{2}$. Then see how they relate to each other in size.

About $\frac{2}{6}$ full   About $\frac{1}{2}$ full   About $\frac{2}{3}$ full

$\frac{2}{6}$ is less than $\frac{1}{2}$.

$\frac{2}{3}$ is greater than $\frac{1}{2}$.

**C** So, $\frac{2}{6}$ is less than $\frac{2}{3}$.

$$\frac{2}{6} < \frac{2}{3}$$

Alan will buy more peanuts than Keri.

**Convince Me!** **Make Sense and Persevere** Candice buys $\frac{2}{8}$ of a container of roasted peanuts. The container is the same size as those used by Keri and Alan. She says $\frac{2}{8}$ is between $\frac{1}{2}$ and 1, so she buys more peanuts than Alan. Is Candice correct? Explain.

# Guided Practice

## Do You Understand?

**1.** Tina used benchmark numbers to decide that $\frac{3}{8}$ is less than $\frac{7}{8}$. Do you agree? Explain.

**2.** Write two fractions with a denominator of 6 that are closer to 0 than to 1.

**3.** Write two fractions with a denominator of 8 that are closer to 1 than to 0.

## Do You Know How?

In **4–6**, choose from the fractions $\frac{1}{8}$, $\frac{1}{4}$, $\frac{6}{8}$, and $\frac{3}{4}$. Use fraction strips to help.

**4.** Which fractions are closer to 0 than to 1?

**5.** Which fractions are closer to 1 than to 0?

**6.** Use the two fractions with a denominator of 8 to write a true statement: ▦ < ▦.

# Independent Practice

In **7** and **8**, choose from the fractions $\frac{2}{3}$, $\frac{7}{8}$, $\frac{1}{4}$, and $\frac{2}{6}$.

**7.** Which of the fractions are closer to 0 than to 1?

**8.** Which of the fractions are closer to 1 than to 0?

In **9–14**, use a strategy to compare. Write <, >, or =.

Remember that you can write equivalent fractions, use models, number sense, or benchmarks to help compare fractions.

**9.** $\frac{5}{8} \bigcirc \frac{7}{8}$

**10.** $\frac{5}{8} \bigcirc \frac{2}{8}$

**11.** $\frac{3}{4} \bigcirc \frac{3}{6}$

**12.** $\frac{4}{6} \bigcirc \frac{4}{8}$

**13.** $\frac{2}{6} \bigcirc \frac{2}{4}$

**14.** $\frac{2}{3} \bigcirc \frac{1}{3}$

# Problem Solving

In **15–17**, use the table at the right.

**15.** Which people have walked closer to 1 mile than to 0 miles?

**16.** Which people have walked closer to 0 miles than to 1 mile?

**17.** Who has walked a fraction of a mile that is closer to neither 0 nor 1? Explain.

| Name | Fraction of Mile Walked |
|------|------|
| Mrs. Avery | $\frac{1}{6}$ |
| Mr. Nunez | $\frac{5}{6}$ |
| Ms. Chang | $\frac{1}{3}$ |
| Mr. O'Leary | $\frac{4}{8}$ |
| Miss Lee | $\frac{4}{6}$ |

**18.** Rahul compares two wholes that are the same size. He says that $\frac{2}{6} < \frac{2}{3}$ because $\frac{2}{6}$ is less than $\frac{1}{2}$, and $\frac{2}{3}$ is greater than $\frac{1}{2}$. Is he correct? Explain.

Think about fractions that are equivalent to one half.

**19. Make Sense and Persevere**
Manish drives 265 more miles than Janice. Manish drives 642 miles. How many miles does Janice drive?

**20. Algebra** Nika has 90 pencils. Forty of them are yellow, 13 are green, 18 are red, and the rest are blue. How many blue pencils does Nika have?

**21. Higher Order Thinking** Omar says that $\frac{2}{6} < \frac{4}{6}$ because $\frac{2}{6}$ is between 0 and $\frac{1}{2}$, and $\frac{4}{6}$ is between $\frac{1}{2}$ and 1. Is he correct? Explain.

Think about benchmark fractions you know.

## Assessment Practice

**22.** Each of the fractions in the comparisons at the right refer to the same whole. Use benchmark fractions to reason about the size of each fraction. Select all the correct comparisons.

☐ $\frac{2}{3} < \frac{2}{4}$

☐ $\frac{2}{4} < \frac{2}{3}$

☐ $\frac{3}{8} > \frac{5}{8}$

☐ $\frac{1}{4} < \frac{2}{4}$

☐ $\frac{3}{6} > \frac{3}{8}$

Name _____

☆ Solve & Share ☆

Tanya, Riaz, and Ryan each used a bag of flour to make modeling clay. The bags were labeled $\frac{3}{4}$ lb, $\frac{1}{4}$ lb, and $\frac{2}{4}$ lb. Show these fractions on a number line. How can you use the number line to compare two of these fractions?

**I can ...**
compare two fractions by locating them on a number line.

© **Content Standard** 3.NF.A.3a
**Mathematical Practices** MP.2, MP.6, MP.7

You can use reasoning to compare fractions. Think about the size of the fractions. You can also use models such as a number line.

$\frac{1}{4}$          $\frac{3}{4}$

0                                    1

**Look Back!** If the bags were labeled $\frac{4}{8}$ lb, $\frac{3}{8}$ lb, and $\frac{6}{8}$ lb, how could a number line help you solve this problem?

Marking

**Essential Question**

# How Can You Compare Fractions Using the Number Line?

**A**

*Talia has two different lengths of blue and red ribbon. Does she have more blue ribbon or more red ribbon?*

Look at the numerators and the denominators of each fraction. You can compare the fractions by reasoning about their size, using benchmarks, or models such as number lines.

$\frac{2}{3}$ yard

$\frac{1}{3}$ yard

**B**

The fractions both refer to 1 yard of ribbon. This is the whole.

You can use a number line to compare $\frac{1}{3}$ and $\frac{2}{3}$.

The farther the distance of the fraction from zero on the number line, the greater the fraction.

| 0 | | $\frac{1}{3}$ | | $\frac{2}{3}$ | | 1 |

On the number line, $\frac{2}{3}$ is farther to the right than $\frac{1}{3}$.

So, $\frac{2}{3} > \frac{1}{3}$.

Talia has more blue ribbon than red ribbon.

**Convince Me!** **Use Structure** Talia has an additional length of green ribbon that measures $\frac{2}{4}$ yard. How can you compare the length of the green ribbon to the lengths of the blue and red ribbons?

Practice    Tools    Assessment

## ☆ Guided Practice

### Do You Understand?

**1.** When two fractions refer to the same whole, what do you notice when the denominators you are comparing are the same?

**2.** Write a problem that compares two fractions with different numerators.

### Do You Know How?

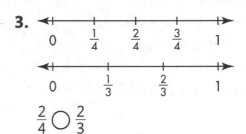

In **3–5**, compare fractions using <, >, or =. Use the number lines to help.

**3.**

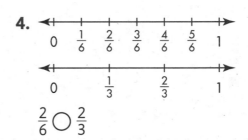

$\frac{2}{4} \bigcirc \frac{2}{3}$

**4.**

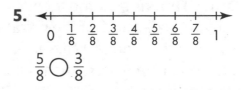

$\frac{2}{6} \bigcirc \frac{2}{3}$

**5.**

$\frac{5}{8} \bigcirc \frac{3}{8}$

## Independent Practice ☆

In **6–9**, use the number lines to compare the fractions. Write >, <, or =.

**6.**

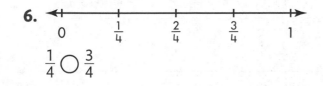

$\frac{1}{4} \bigcirc \frac{3}{4}$

**7.**

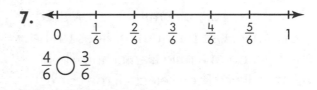

$\frac{4}{6} \bigcirc \frac{3}{6}$

**8.**

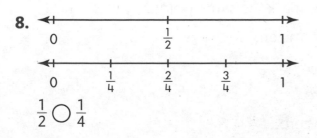

$\frac{1}{2} \bigcirc \frac{1}{4}$

**9.**

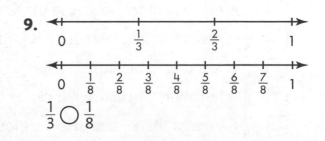

$\frac{1}{3} \bigcirc \frac{1}{8}$

# Problem Solving

10. **Number Sense** Randy wants to save $39. The table shows how much money he has saved. Explain how you can use estimation to decide if he has saved enough money.

| Money Saved | |
|---|---|
| **Month** | **Amount** |
| March | $14 |
| April | $11 |
| May | $22 |

DATA

---

11. Scott ate $\frac{2}{8}$ of a fruit bar. Anne ate $\frac{4}{8}$ of a same-sized fruit bar. Can you tell who ate more of a fruit bar, Scott or Anne? Explain.

12. **Be Precise** Matt and Adara have identical pieces of cardboard for an art project. Matt uses $\frac{2}{3}$ of his piece. Adara uses $\frac{2}{6}$ of her piece. Who uses more, Matt or Adara? Draw two number lines to help explain your answer.

---

13. **Higher Order Thinking** Some friends shared a pizza. Nicole ate $\frac{2}{8}$ of the pizza. Chris ate $\frac{1}{8}$ more than Johan. Mike ate $\frac{1}{8}$ of the pizza. Johan ate $\frac{1}{8}$ more than Mike. Who ate the most pizza?

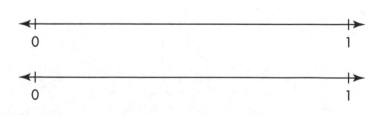

14. Inez has 2 rows of plants. There are 8 plants in each row. Each plant has 3 flowers. How many flowers are there in all?

---

## ✓ Assessment Practice

15. Daniel walked $\frac{3}{4}$ of a mile. Theo walked $\frac{3}{8}$ of a mile. Use the number lines to show the fraction of a mile Daniel and Theo each walked. Then select all the correct statements that describe the fractions.

```
←+——————————————+→
  0                1

←+——————————————+→
  0                1
```

- ☐ $\frac{3}{4}$ is equivalent to $\frac{3}{8}$ because the fractions mark the same point.
- ☐ $\frac{3}{4}$ is greater than $\frac{3}{8}$ because it is farther from zero.
- ☐ $\frac{3}{4}$ is less than $\frac{3}{8}$ because it is farther from zero.
- ☐ $\frac{3}{8}$ is less than $\frac{3}{4}$ because it is closer to zero.
- ☐ $\frac{3}{8}$ is greater than $\frac{3}{4}$ because it is closer to zero.

Name_____

**Solve & Share**

Jamie's family ate 12 pieces of apple pie during the week. Each piece was $\frac{1}{6}$ of a whole pie. How many whole pies did Jamie's family eat? What fraction of a pie was left over? Explain how you decided.

**I can ...**
use representations to find fraction names for whole numbers.

 **Content Standards** 3.NF.A.3c Also 3.NF.A.3a
**Mathematical Practices** MP.2, MP.7

Use reasoning. Think about the size of each piece and the size of the whole pie.

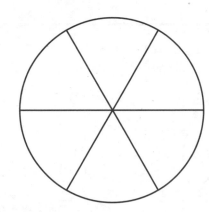

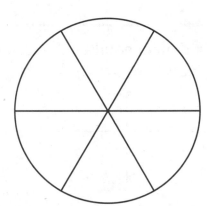

**Look Back!** Jamie cuts another pie into smaller pieces. Each piece of pie is $\frac{1}{8}$ of the whole. Jamie gives away 8 pieces. Does Jamie have any pie left over? Explain how you know.

Essential Question

# How Can You Use Fraction Names to Represent Whole Numbers?

**Visual Learning Bridge**

**A**

What are some equivalent fraction names for 1, 2, and 3?

You can write a whole number as a fraction by writing the whole number as the numerator and 1 as the denominator.

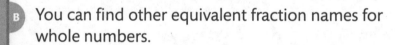

The number line shows 3 wholes. Each whole is divided into 1 equal part.

1 whole divided into 1 equal part can be written as $\frac{1}{1}$.

2 wholes each divided into 1 equal part can be written as $\frac{2}{1}$.

3 wholes each divided into 1 equal part can be written as $\frac{3}{1}$.

$1 = \frac{1}{1}$

$2 = \frac{2}{1}$

$3 = \frac{3}{1}$

**B** You can find other equivalent fraction names for whole numbers.

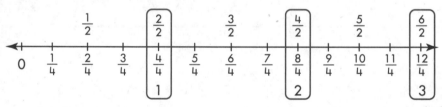

$1 = \frac{1}{1} = \frac{2}{2} = \frac{4}{4}$

$2 = \frac{2}{1} = \frac{4}{2} = \frac{8}{4}$

$3 = \frac{3}{1} = \frac{6}{2} = \frac{12}{4}$

There are many equivalent fraction names for whole numbers!

**Convince Me!** **Reasoning** What equivalent fraction names can you write for 4 using denominators of 1, 2, or 4?

## Another Example!

You can use fractions to name whole numbers.

| 1 | | | 1 | | | 1 | | | 1 | | |
|---|---|---|---|---|---|---|---|---|---|---|---|
| $\frac{1}{3}$ | $\frac{1}{3}$ | $\frac{1}{3}$ | $\frac{1}{3}$ | $\frac{1}{3}$ | $\frac{1}{3}$ | $\frac{1}{3}$ | $\frac{1}{3}$ | $\frac{1}{3}$ | $\frac{1}{3}$ | $\frac{1}{3}$ | $\frac{1}{3}$ |

Twelve $\frac{1}{3}$ fraction strips equal 4 whole fraction strips.

All whole numbers have fraction names. You can write $4 = \frac{12}{3}$.

You also know $4 = \frac{4}{1}$, so you can write $4 = \frac{4}{1} = \frac{12}{3}$.

## ☆Guided Practice

### Do You Understand?

1. Explain how you know that $\frac{4}{1} = 4$.

### Do You Know How?

2. Complete the number line.

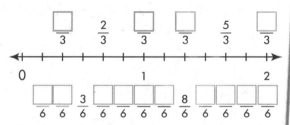

$\frac{\square}{3}$  $\frac{2}{3}$  $\frac{\square}{3}$  $\frac{\square}{3}$  $\frac{5}{3}$  $\frac{\square}{3}$

0           1           2

$\frac{\square}{6}$ $\frac{\square}{6}$ $\frac{3}{6}$ $\frac{\square}{6}$ $\frac{\square}{6}$ $\frac{\square}{6}$ $\frac{\square}{6}$ $\frac{8}{6}$ $\frac{\square}{6}$ $\frac{\square}{6}$ $\frac{\square}{6}$ $\frac{\square}{6}$

3. Look at the number line. Write two equivalent fractions for each whole number.

$1 = \dfrac{\square}{3} = \dfrac{\square}{6}$    $2 = \dfrac{\square}{3} = \dfrac{\square}{6}$

## ☆ Independent Practice ☆

In **4–7**, write two equivalent fractions for each whole number. You can draw number lines to help.

4. $4 = \dfrac{\square}{2} = \dfrac{\square}{1}$

5. $1 = \dfrac{\square}{4} = \dfrac{\square}{1}$

6. $2 = \dfrac{\square}{3} = \dfrac{\square}{1}$

7. $5 = \dfrac{\square}{2} = \dfrac{\square}{1}$

In **8–11**, for each pair of fractions, write the equivalent whole number.

8. $\frac{6}{2} = \frac{3}{1} =$

9. $\frac{3}{3} = \frac{6}{6} =$

10. $\frac{8}{4} = \frac{6}{3} =$

11. $\frac{9}{3} = \frac{12}{4} =$

# Problem Solving

12. Henry needs to fix or replace his refrigerator. It will cost $376 to fix it. How much more will it cost to buy a new refrigerator than to fix the current one?

New Refrigerator
$969

13. Declan says, "To write an equivalent fraction name for 5, I can write 5 as the denominator and 1 as the numerator." Do you agree with Declan? Explain.

14. **Look for Relationships** Describe a pattern in fractions equivalent to 1 whole.

15. **enVision® STEM** There are four stages in a butterfly's life cycle: egg, caterpillar, chrysalis, and butterfly. Dan makes one whole poster for each stage. Use a fraction to show the number of whole posters Dan makes.

16. Karen bought 4 movie tickets for $9 each. She has $12 left over. How much money did Karen have to start? Explain.

17. **Higher Order Thinking** Peggy has 4 whole sandwiches. She cuts each whole into halves. Then Peggy gives away 1 whole sandwich. Show the number of sandwiches Peggy has left as a fraction.

Each sandwich is cut into equal parts.

✅ **Assessment Practice**

18. Complete the equations. Match the fractions with their equivalent whole numbers.

| | 1 | 2 | 4 | 6 |
|---|---|---|---|---|
| $\frac{6}{1} = \frac{12}{2} = ?$ | ☐ | ☐ | ☐ | ☐ |
| $\frac{6}{3} = \frac{4}{2} = ?$ | ☐ | ☐ | ☐ | ☐ |
| $\frac{4}{4} = \frac{1}{1} = ?$ | ☐ | ☐ | ☐ | ☐ |
| $\frac{8}{2} = \frac{16}{4} = ?$ | ☐ | ☐ | ☐ | ☐ |

Name_____

**Solve & Share**

Lindsey and Matt are running in a 1-mile race. They have both run the same distance so far. Write a fraction that shows how far Lindsey could have run. Write a different fraction that shows how far Matt could have run. Construct a math argument to support your answer.

Running Track

**I can ...**
construct math arguments using what I know about fractions.

© **Mathematical Practices** MP.3 Also MP.1, MP.5, MP.6
**Content Standards** 3.NF.A.3d Also 3.NF.A.3b

**Thinking Habits**

*Be a good thinker! These questions can help you.*

• How can I use numbers, objects, drawings, or actions to justify my argument?

• Am I using numbers and symbols correctly?

• Is my explanation clear and complete?

**Look Back!** **Construct Arguments** Are the two fractions you wrote equivalent? Construct a math argument using pictures, words, and numbers to support your answer.

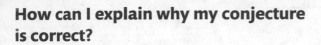 **Essential Question** **How Can You Construct Arguments?**

**A**

*Clara and Ana are making rugs. The rugs will be the same size. Clara has finished $\frac{3}{4}$ of her rug. Ana has finished $\frac{3}{8}$ of her rug. Who has finished more of her rug?*

Conjecture: Clara has finished a greater portion of her rug than Ana.

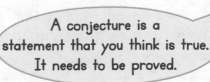

A conjecture is a statement that you think is true. It needs to be proved.

### How can I explain why my conjecture is correct?

I need to construct an argument to justify my conjecture.

Here's my thinking...

**B** **How can I construct an argument?**

**I can**

- use numbers, objects, drawings, or actions correctly to explain my thinking.

- make sure my explanation is simple, complete, and easy to understand.

**C** I will use drawings and numbers to explain my thinking.

The number lines represent the same whole. One is divided into fourths. One is divided into eighths.

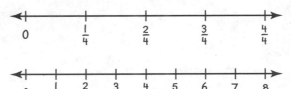

The number lines show that 3 of the fourths is greater than 3 of the eighths.

So, $\frac{3}{4} > \frac{3}{8}$. The conjecture is correct.

**Convince Me!** **Construct Arguments** Use numbers to construct another math argument to justify the conjecture above. Think about how you can look at the numerator and the denominator.

Name_____

# ☆ Guided Practice

**Construct Arguments**

Paul and Anna were eating burritos. The burritos were the same size. Paul ate $\frac{2}{6}$ of a burrito. Anna ate $\frac{2}{3}$ of a burrito. Conjecture: Paul and Anna ate the same amount.

1. Draw a diagram to help justify the conjecture.

An example can help you to construct an argument.

2. Is the conjecture correct? Construct an argument to justify your answer.

# Independent Practice ☆

**Construct Arguments**

Reyna has a blue ribbon that is 1 yard long and a red ribbon that is 2 yards long. She uses $\frac{2}{4}$ of the red ribbon and $\frac{2}{4}$ of the blue ribbon.

Conjecture: Reyna uses the same amount of red and blue ribbon.

3. Draw a diagram to help justify the conjecture.

4. Is the conjecture correct? Construct an argument to justify your answer.

5. Explain another way you could justify the conjecture.

# Problem Solving

## School Fair

Twenty-one students worked at the school fair. Mrs. Gold's students worked at a class booth. The table shows the fraction of 1 hour that her students worked. Mrs. Gold wants to know the order of the work times for the students from least to greatest.

| DATA | Student | Tim | Cathy | José | Pedro |
|------|---------|-----|-------|------|-------|
| | **Hours Worked** | $\frac{1}{4}$ | $\frac{2}{4}$ | $\frac{2}{6}$ | $\frac{3}{4}$ |

**6. Make Sense and Persevere** What comparisons do you need to make to find out who worked the least?

**7. Be Precise** What is the whole for each student's time? Do all the fractions refer to the same whole?

When you construct arguments, you explain why a conjecture is true.

**8. Use Appropriate Tools** What tool could you use to solve this problem? Explain how you would use this tool.

**9. Construct Arguments** What is the order of the work times from least to greatest? Construct a math argument to justify your answer.

☆ Find a Match ☆

Work with a partner. Point to a clue.

Read the clue.

Look below the clues to find a match. Write the clue letter in the box next to the match.

Find a match for every clue.

**I can ...**
multiply and divide within 100.

© **Content Standard** 3.OA.C.7
**Mathematical Practices** MP.3, MP.6, MP.7, MP.8

**Clues**

**A** Is equal to $3 \times 3$

**B** Is equal to $4 \times 4$

**C** Is equal to $9 \times 4$

**D** Is equal to $0 \div 10$

**E** Is equal to $35 \div 5$

**F** Is equal to $12 \div 4$

**G** Is equal to $5 \times 4$

**H** Is equal to $3 \times 8$

**I** Is equal to $2 \times 5$

**J** Is equal to $3 \times 10$

**K** Is equal to $9 \times 2$

**L** Is equal to $2 \times 4$

| C $6 \times 6$ | A $3\overline{)27}$ | H $6 \times 4$ |
| I $40 \div 4$ | D $0 \times 9$ | K $3 \times 6$ |
| L $32 \div 4$ | J $5 \times 6$ | E $4\overline{)28}$ |
| G $10 \times 2$ | F $7\overline{)21}$ | B $8 \times 2$ |

### Word List

- denominator
- equivalent fractions
- fraction
- number line
- numerator
- unit fraction

## Understand Vocabulary

Write T for *true* or F for *false*.

1. _____ $\frac{1}{6}$ and $\frac{2}{6}$ have the same numerator.

2. _____ $\frac{1}{2}$ and $\frac{4}{8}$ are equivalent fractions.

3. _____ $\frac{3}{8}$ is a unit fraction.

4. _____ A whole number can be written as a fraction.

5. _____ The denominators in $\frac{1}{3}$ and in $\frac{2}{3}$ are the same.

6. _____ A number line always shows fractions.

For each of these terms, give an example and a non-example.

| | Example | Non-example |
|---|---|---|
| 7. fraction | _____ | _____ |
| 8. unit fraction | _____ | _____ |
| 9. equivalent fractions | _____ | _____ |

## Use Vocabulary in Writing

10. Use at least 2 terms from the Word List to explain how to compare $\frac{1}{2}$ and $\frac{1}{3}$.

**Set A** pages 485–488

Two fractions are equivalent if they name the same part of a whole.

What is one fraction that is equivalent to $\frac{6}{8}$?

You can use fraction strips to find equivalent fractions.

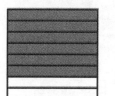

$\frac{6}{8} = \frac{3}{4}$

You also can use area models to see that $\frac{6}{8}$ and $\frac{3}{4}$ are equivalent fractions. The shaded fractions both show the same part of the whole.

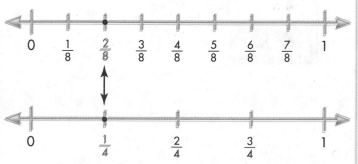

**Remember** to check that both sets of strips are the same length.

In **1** and **2**, find an equivalent fraction. Use fraction strips and models to help.

1.

$\frac{4}{6} = \boxed{\phantom{x}}$

2.

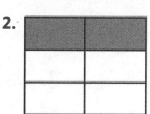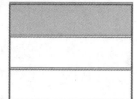

$\frac{2}{6} = \boxed{\phantom{x}}$

**Set B** pages 489–492

Riley says the library is $\frac{2}{8}$ of a mile from their house. Sydney says it is $\frac{1}{4}$ of a mile.

Use the number lines to find who is correct.

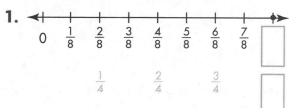

The fractions $\frac{2}{8}$ and $\frac{1}{4}$ are equivalent. They are the same distance from 0 on a number line. Riley and Sydney are both correct.

**Remember** that equivalent fractions have different names, but they represent the same point on a number line.

In **1** and **2**, write two fractions that name the same location on the number line.

1.

2.

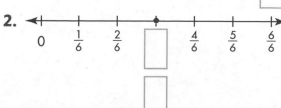

You can use fraction strips to compare fractions with the same denominator.

Compare $\frac{3}{4}$ to $\frac{2}{4}$.

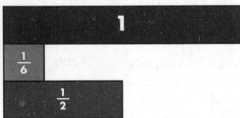

The denominator of each fraction is 4.

Three $\frac{1}{4}$ fraction strips show $\frac{3}{4}$.

Two $\frac{1}{4}$ fraction strips show $\frac{2}{4}$.

The fraction strips showing $\frac{3}{4}$ have 1 more unit fraction than the strips showing $\frac{2}{4}$.

So $\frac{3}{4} > \frac{2}{4}$.

**Remember** that if fractions have the same denominator, the greater fraction has a greater numerator.

In **1–3**, compare. Write <, >, or =. Use fraction strips to help.

1.
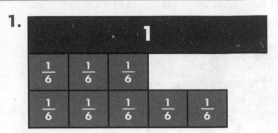

$\frac{3}{6} \bigcirc \frac{5}{6}$

2. $\frac{4}{6} \bigcirc \frac{5}{6}$    3. $\frac{5}{8} \bigcirc \frac{3}{8}$

You can use fraction strips to compare fractions with the same numerator.

Compare $\frac{1}{6}$ to $\frac{1}{2}$.

The numerator of each fraction is 1.

The $\frac{1}{6}$ fraction strip is less than the $\frac{1}{2}$ strip.

So $\frac{1}{6} < \frac{1}{2}$.

You can use reasoning to understand. Think about dividing a whole into 6 pieces and dividing it into 2 pieces. One of 6 pieces is less than 1 of 2 pieces.

**Remember** that if fractions have the same numerator, the greater fraction has a lesser denominator.

In **1–3**, compare. Write <, >, or =. Use fraction strips to help.

1.
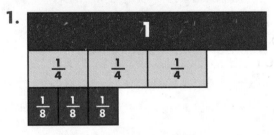

$\frac{3}{4} \bigcirc \frac{3}{8}$

2. $\frac{5}{6} \bigcirc \frac{5}{8}$    3. $\frac{1}{3} \bigcirc \frac{1}{2}$

Name _____

**Set E** pages 501–504

You can compare fractions using benchmark numbers such as 0, $\frac{1}{2}$, and 1.

Chris and Mary are painting pictures. The pictures are the same size. Chris painted $\frac{3}{4}$ of his picture. Mary painted $\frac{3}{8}$ of her picture. Who painted the greater amount?

$\frac{3}{4}$ is greater than $\frac{1}{2}$.

$\frac{3}{8}$ is less than $\frac{1}{2}$.

Chris painted the greater amount.

**Remember** that you can compare each fraction to a benchmark number to see how they relate to each other.

In **1** and **2**, use benchmark numbers to help solve.

1. Mike had $\frac{2}{6}$ of a candy bar. Sally had $\frac{4}{6}$ of a candy bar. Whose fraction of a candy bar was closer to 1? Closer to 0?

2. Paul compared two bags of rice. One weighs $\frac{4}{6}$ pound, and the other weighs $\frac{4}{8}$ pound. Which bag is heavier?

**Set F** pages 505–508

You can use a number line to compare fractions.

Which is greater, $\frac{3}{6}$ or $\frac{4}{6}$?

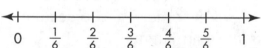

$\frac{4}{6}$ is farther from zero than $\frac{3}{6}$, so $\frac{4}{6}$ is greater.

You also can compare two fractions with the same numerator by drawing two number lines.

Which is greater, $\frac{2}{4}$ or $\frac{2}{3}$?

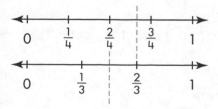

$\frac{2}{3}$ is farther from zero than $\frac{2}{4}$, so $\frac{2}{3}$ is greater.

**Remember** to draw two number lines that are equal in length when comparing fractions with different denominators.

In **1** and **2**, compare. Write <, >, or =. Use number lines to help.

1. $\frac{2}{6} \bigcirc \frac{3}{6}$

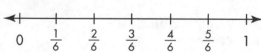

2. $\frac{3}{4} \bigcirc \frac{3}{6}$

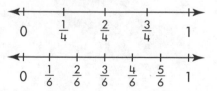

How many thirds are in 2 wholes?

You can use a number line or fraction strips to find a fraction name for 2 using thirds.

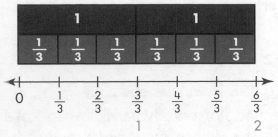

$2 = \frac{6}{3}$

The whole number 2 can also be written as the fraction $\frac{6}{3}$.

**Remember** that when you write whole numbers as fractions, the numerator can be greater than the denominator.

In **1–4**, write an equivalent fraction for each whole number.

**1.** 3          **2.** 2

**3.** 5          **4.** 1

In **5–8**, write the equivalent whole number for each fraction.

**5.** $\frac{6}{3}$          **6.** $\frac{10}{2}$

**7.** $\frac{14}{2}$          **8.** $\frac{8}{8}$

Think about these questions to help **construct arguments.**

**Thinking Habits**

• How can I use numbers, objects, drawings, or actions to justify my argument?

• Am I using numbers and symbols correctly?

• Is my explanation clear and complete?

**Remember** that when you construct an argument, you explain why your work is correct.

Odell and Tamra paint two walls with the same dimensions. Odell paints $\frac{1}{6}$ of a wall. Tamra paints $\frac{1}{3}$ of the other wall. Conjecture: Odell paints less than Tamra.

**1.** Draw a diagram to justify the conjecture.

**2.** Use the diagram to justify the conjecture.

Name _____

**1.** Two friends are working on a project. So far, Cindy has done $\frac{4}{8}$ of the project, and Kim has done $\frac{3}{8}$ of the project. Who has done more of the project? Explain.

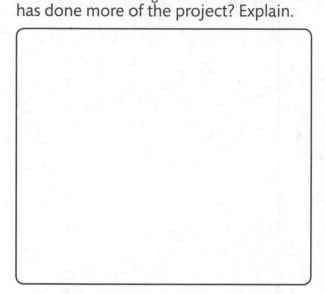

**2.** Serena can compare $\frac{3}{4}$ and $\frac{3}{6}$ without using fraction strips. She says that a whole divided into 4 equal parts will have larger parts than the same whole divided into 6 equal parts. Three larger parts must be more than three smaller parts, so $\frac{3}{4}$ is greater than $\frac{3}{6}$. Is Serena correct? If not, explain Serena's error. Then, write the correct comparison using symbols.

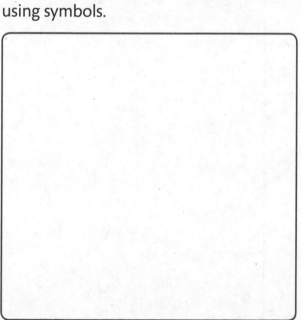

**3.** Jill finished reading $\frac{2}{3}$ of a book for a summer reading project. Owen read $\frac{2}{8}$ of the same book. Use the number lines to compare how much Jill and Owen each read. Who read more of the book?

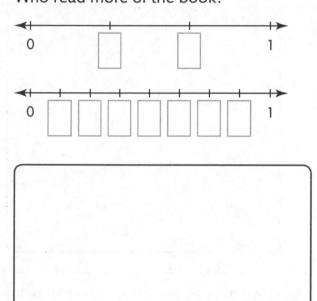

**4.** A small cake is cut into 4 equal pieces. What fraction represents the entire cake? Explain.

**5.** Mark and Sidney each have a piece of wood that is the same size. Mark paints $\frac{2}{8}$ of his piece of wood. Sidney paints $\frac{5}{8}$ of her piece of wood. Who painted a fraction that is closer to 1 than to 0? Explain how you found your answer. Then tell who painted less of his or her piece of wood.

**7.** Carl, Fiona, and Jen each had a sandwich. The sandwiches were the same size and cut into eighths. Carl ate $\frac{7}{8}$ of a sandwich, Fiona ate $\frac{3}{8}$ of a sandwich, and Jen ate $\frac{6}{8}$ of a sandwich. Who ate the most? Explain.

**6.** Greg colored the fraction model below.

**A.** Which fractions name the purple part of the model? Select all that apply.

☐ $\frac{1}{2}$   ☐ $\frac{3}{4}$

☐ $\frac{2}{3}$   ☐ $\frac{4}{6}$

☐ $\frac{6}{8}$

**B.** Does $\frac{1}{4}$ name the unshaded part of the model? Explain.

Name_____

**8.** George wants to know if two pieces of wire are the same length. One wire is $\frac{6}{8}$ foot. The other is $\frac{3}{4}$ foot. Are they the same length? Fill in the fractions on the number line to compare the lengths of the pieces of wire. Then explain your answer.

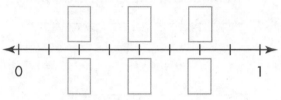

**9.** Lezlie hiked $\frac{3}{8}$ mile on Monday. On Wednesday she hiked $\frac{3}{6}$ mile. She hiked $\frac{3}{4}$ mile on Friday. Use benchmark fractions to arrange the lengths of the hikes in order from shortest to longest hike.

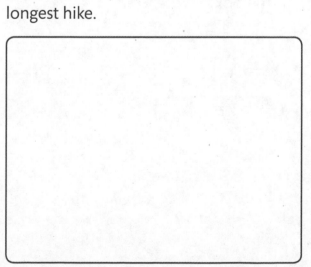

**10.** A mural is divided into 3 equal parts. What fraction represents the entire mural? Explain.

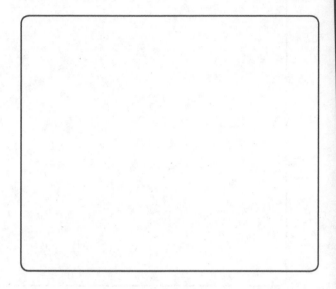

**11.** Meagan ate $\frac{3}{4}$ of a cookie. Write an equivalent fraction for the amount of cookie Meagan did **NOT** eat. Then write a fraction that is equivalent to the amount of the cookie that Meagan did eat, and explain why your answer is correct.

**12.** Circle each fraction that is equivalent to 1. Explain your reasoning. Then give another fraction that is equal to 1.

$$\frac{2}{4} \qquad \frac{3}{3} \qquad \frac{3}{6} \qquad \frac{4}{6} \qquad \frac{6}{6}$$

**13.** Use the number line to help order the fractions from least to greatest. Then explain how you found your answer.

$$\frac{6}{8} \qquad \frac{4}{4} \qquad \frac{1}{4} \qquad \frac{1}{2} \qquad \frac{0}{4}$$

**14.** Eva and Landon had the same math homework. Eva finished $\frac{2}{4}$ of the homework. Landon finished $\frac{2}{8}$ of the homework. Conjecture: Eva and Landon finished the same amount of their homework.

**A.** Complete the number lines to help think about the conjecture.

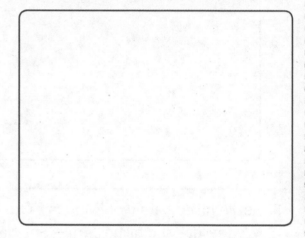

**B.** Use your diagram to decide if the conjecture is correct. Explain.

**15.** For each pair of fractions, write the equivalent whole number in the box.

$$\frac{16}{4} = \frac{8}{2} = \square$$

$$\frac{6}{3} = \frac{4}{2} = \square$$

$$\frac{8}{8} = \frac{6}{6} = \square$$

**Clothing Store**
Devin, Jenna, Eli, and Gabby work at a clothing store. On Saturday they each worked the same number of hours.

The **Time Spent at Cash Register** table shows the fraction of time each person spent checking out customers. The **Time Spent on Customer Calls** table shows the fraction of an hour Jenna spent answering phone calls for the store.

Use the **Time Spent at Cash Register** table to answer Questions **1–3**.

1. Draw fraction strips to show the fraction of time each person worked at the cash register.

| **1** |

| Time Spent at Cash Register | |
|---|---|
| **Name** | **Fraction of Work Day** |
| Devin | $\frac{3}{6}$ |
| Jenna | $\frac{2}{6}$ |
| Eli | $\frac{6}{6}$ |
| Gabby | $\frac{5}{6}$ |

2. Who spent the most time at the cash register?

3. Write a comparison to show the time Gabby spent at the cash register compared to the time Devin spent. Use >, <, or =.

4. Use the **Time Spent on Customer Calls** table to answer this question: On which day did Jenna spend closest to one hour on the phone? Explain how you know.

| Time Spent on Customer Calls | | | |
|---|---|---|---|
| **Day** | Saturday | Sunday | Monday |
| **Fraction of an Hour** | $\frac{3}{6}$ | $\frac{3}{5}$ | $\frac{3}{4}$ |

The store sells different colors of men's socks. The **Socks** table shows the fraction for each sock color in the store.

Use the **Socks** table to answer Questions **5** and **6**.

| Socks | |
|---|---|
| **Color** | **Fraction** |
| white | $\frac{1}{8}$ |
| black | $\frac{1}{4}$ |
| brown | $\frac{3}{8}$ |
| gray | $\frac{2}{8}$ |

5. **Part A**

Complete the fractions on the number line. Label the fraction that represents each sock color.

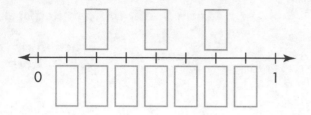

**Part B**

Does the store have more brown socks or more white socks?

6. Use the number line in Exercise **5** Part A to construct an argument to justify the following conjecture: The store has an equal number of gray socks and black socks.

7. Use the **Miguel's Socks** table to answer the question.

Miguel bought some socks at the clothing store. After he washed them, he counted the number of individual socks he has. Each sock is $\frac{1}{2}$ of a pair. How many pairs of black socks does he have? Write this number as a fraction.

| Miguel's Socks | |
|---|---|
| **Color** | **Number of Socks** |
| black | 6 |
| gray | 8 |

# Solve Time, Capacity, and Mass Problems

**Essential Question:** How can time, capacity, and mass be measured and found?

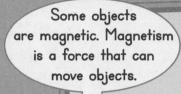

Some objects are magnetic. Magnetism is a force that can move objects.

A magnet interacts with certain metals, such as iron. But other materials do not interact with magnets, such as paper.

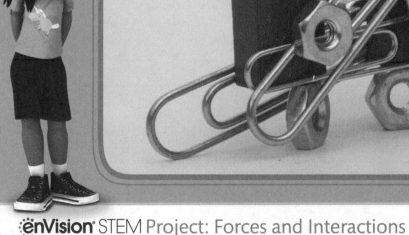

Here is a project on magnets.

## enVision STEM Project: Forces and Interactions

**Do Research** Use the Internet or other sources to find information about magnets. How are magnets used? What types of magnets are there? Attach different amounts of paper together using a metal paper clip. How can you lift the paper using the magnet? How much mass can the magnet lift?

**Journal: Write a Report** Include what you found. Also in your report:

- Give examples of magnetic and non-magnetic materials.

- Find the masses of the paper clip and of the paper.

- Write an equation to show how much mass you can lift using the magnet.

Name_____

# Review What You Know

## A-Z Vocabulary

Choose the best term from the box.
Write it on the blank.

| • denominator | • numerator |
| • number line | • unit fraction |

1. The _____ tells the number of repetitions of the unit fraction.

2. The _____ tells what fractional part is being counted.

3. One equal part of a whole can be represented using a _____.

## Solving 2-Step Problems

4. Mr. Vernon rides a train for 188 miles. Then he rides a subway for 9 stops. Each stop is 2 miles apart. How far does he travel?

5. Ms. Slate has a box of 320 new light bulbs. She replaces the light bulbs in 50 lamps. Each lamp has 5 sockets. How many new light bulbs does Ms. Slate have left?

## Number Lines

Label the missing numbers on the number lines.

6.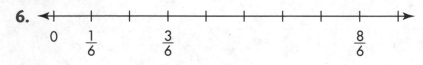

$0 \quad \frac{1}{6} \quad \frac{3}{6} \quad \frac{8}{6}$

7.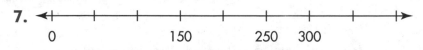

$0 \qquad 150 \qquad 250 \quad 300$

## Fractions

8. Rena divides a square into 8 equal parts. What unit fraction should she write as a label for each of the parts?

Ⓐ $\frac{0}{8}$　　　　Ⓑ $\frac{1}{8}$　　　　Ⓒ $\frac{8}{8}$　　　　Ⓓ $\frac{8}{1}$

9. Write two fractions that are equal to $\frac{1}{2}$.

Name_____

**PROJECT 14A**

### How do you show elapsed time on a clock?

**Project:** Write and Tell a Story About Time

**PROJECT 14B**

### What is the best way to plan for a full day?

**Project:** Create and Play a Matching Game

## PROJECT 14C

### How did people tell time before clocks?

**Project:** Design and Make a Sundial

---

## PROJECT 14D

### What is your favorite recipe?

**Project:** Perform a Song About the Masses of Objects

Activity

☆ Solve & Share ☆

Xander and his mother are visiting a store. In the store, there are many clocks on the shelves. The clocks show different times. Tell the times shown on each of the clocks below.

**I can ...**
show and tell time to the minute using clocks.

© Content Standard 3.MD.A.1
Mathematical Practices MP.4, MP.6, MP.7

Use structure. Recall that the space between each small tick mark on a clock represents a unit of 1 minute.

**Look Back!** Xander and his mother leave the store at 8:47. How can you use the clock to show this time?

# How Do You Tell Time to the Nearest Minute?

**A**

*The clock shows the time a train from Memphis is scheduled to arrive at Central Station. What time is the train scheduled to arrive? Write the time in digital form and in two other ways.*

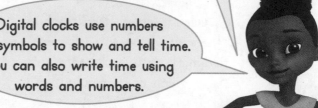

Analog clocks are tools that can help you show and tell time to the nearest minute using minute and hour hands.

Digital clocks use numbers and symbols to show and tell time. You can also write time using words and numbers.

---

**B** Step 1

The hour hand is between 12 and 1. The time is after 12:00 and before 1:00.

**C** Step 2

In 5 minutes, the minute hand moves from one number to the next.

Count by 5s from the 12 to the 8, which is 40 minutes.

**D** Step 3

In 1 minute, the minute hand moves from one mark to the next.

Count two more minutes. The digital time is 12:42. It is 42 minutes after 12:00 or 18 minutes before 1:00.

---

**Convince Me!** **Model with Math**  A train arrives from Atlanta one hour after the Memphis train. Write the arrival time of the Atlanta train in digital form and two other ways. Use a clock face to help.

☆ **Guided Practice**

## Do You Understand?

**1.** In the Memphis train example, why is 42 minutes after 12 o'clock the same as 18 minutes before 1 o'clock? Explain.

**2.** An airplane landed at 3:55. Does the clock show the time the airplane landed? Explain.

## Do You Know How?

In **3** and **4**, write the time shown on each clock in two ways.

**3.**

**4.**

---

☆ **Independent Practice** ☆

In **5–7**, write the time shown on each clock in two ways.

**5.**

**6.**

**7.**

# Problem Solving

In **8** and **9**, use the table.

**8.** Roy says that the scarf and the hat together cost about the same amount as a blanket and a hat. Is this a reasonable estimate? Explain.

**9.** What did Jorge buy at the sale if $19 + $19 + $19 + $18 stands for the total cost of his purchase?

| Winter Sale | | |
|---|---|---|
| Blanket |  | $19 |
| Hat | | $12 |
| Scarf | | $18 |

---

**10. Be Precise** Mia left her house at 25 minutes before 3 o'clock. Draw hands on the clock to show when she left.

**11. Higher Order Thinking** Sandra's party started at 7:00. Her friends Theo and Lily arrive at 10 minutes after 7 o'clock. Her friend Marcus arrives 35 minutes after Theo and Lily. What time did Marcus arrive? Write this time in two other ways.

---

### ✓ Assessment Practice

**12.** Clay and his family sit down to eat dinner at the time shown on the clock. Which of the following are other ways to write that time? Select all that apply.

☐ 3:25
☐ 5:16
☐ 16 minutes after 5 o'clock
☐ 44 minutes before 5 o'clock
☐ 16 minutes before 5 o'clock

**13.** Mary Ann called her grandmother. She ended the call at the time shown on the clock. Which of the following are **NOT** other ways to write this time? Select all that apply.

☐ 14 minutes before 9 o'clock
☐ 3:46
☐ 46 minutes after 3 o'clock
☐ 9:19
☐ 14 minutes before 4 o'clock

Name_____

## Solve & Share

Denise went to see a movie. The movie started at 1:05 P.M. It ended at 2:35 P.M. How long did the movie last? Explain your reasoning.

| Start | End |

Use reasoning. Use the clock faces to help determine the change in time.

**I can ...**
measure intervals of time in hours and minutes.

© Content Standard 3.MD.A.1
Mathematical Practices MP.1, MP.2

**Look Back!** Without counting hours and minutes, how do you know the movie Denise went to see was less than 2 hours long?

**Essential Question** How Can You Find Elapsed Time?

A

Start   End

*Janey took part in a charity walk. The walk started at 7:10 A.M. It ended at 11:20 A.M. How long did the walk last?*

Elapsed time is the total amount of time that passes from the starting time to the ending time.

The hours between midnight and noon are A.M. hours. The hours between noon and midnight are P.M. hours.

B **Step 1**

Find the starting time.

C **Step 2**

Count the hours.

1 hour

D **Step 3**

Count the minutes.

The walk lasted 4 hours, 10 minutes.

**Convince Me!** **Make Sense and Persevere** After the charity walk, Janey talked with friends from 11:25 A.M. to 11:40 A.M. Then lunch was served from 11:45 A.M. until 2:10 P.M. How long did lunch last?

## Another Example!

You can also use a number line to measure elapsed time.

Janey's charity walk lasted 4 hours, 10 minutes.

The number line shows the number of hours and minutes that elapsed during the walk.

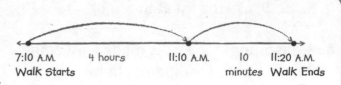

7:10 A.M.    4 hours    11:10 A.M.    10    11:20 A.M.
Walk Starts                          minutes  Walk Ends

## ☆ Guided Practice

### Do You Understand?

**1.** If a start time is 7:15 A.M. and an end time is 7:45 A.M., why do you not have to count hours to find the elapsed time?

**2.** A movie started at 2:30 P.M. and ran for 2 hours, 15 minutes. What time did the movie end?

### Do You Know How?

**3.** Draw a number line to count the hours from 11:00 A.M. to 5:00 P.M. What is the elapsed time?

## Independent Practice ☆

**Leveled Practice** In **4–7**, use clocks or number lines to find the elapsed or end time.

**4.** Start Time: 6:30 P.M.    End Time: 9:50 P.M.

Hours from 6:30 P.M. to 9:30 P.M. _____

Minutes from 9:30 P.M. to 9:50 P.M. _____

The elapsed time is __ hours, ___ minutes.

**5.** Start Time: 10:00 A.M.
End Time: 3:00 P.M.
Elapsed Time:

_____

**6.** Start Time: 9:15 A.M.
End Time: 10:45 A.M.
Elapsed Time:

_____

**7.** Start Time: 11:30 A.M.
Elapsed Time: 5 hours, 25 minutes
End Time:

_____

# Problem Solving

In **8** and **9**, use the list at the right.

8. **Reasoning** Mr. Flores made a list of the times it takes for different items to bake. Which items will take less than $\frac{1}{2}$ hour to bake?

| Item | Baking Time in Minutes |
|------|------------------------|
| Bread | 27 |
| Granola Bars | 21 |
| Pasta Dish | 48 |
| Vegetables | 24 |

9. Which two items, when you add their baking time together, take less time to bake than the pasta dish?

10. Sally finds elapsed time using these clock faces. She counts the hours by 1s, but counts the minutes by 5s. Why does she count the minutes by 5s instead of by 1s?

11. **Higher Order Thinking** A basketball tournament started at 12:15 P.M. and ended at 4:00 P.M. Did the tournament last more than 4 hours? Explain.

12. **Algebra** A farmer is selling 744 pieces of produce. He has 162 watermelons, 345 ears of sweet corn, and some avocados. Write and solve an equation to find how many avocados the farmer is selling. Let *x* stand for the unknown quantity of avocados.

## ✓ Assessment Practice

13. Geo is taking a train from Carlton to Elgin. The train leaves Carlton at 9:25 A.M. and reaches Elgin at 10:55 A.M. How long does the ride last? Use the number line to help.

9:25 A.M. Train Leaves   10:25 A.M.   10:55 A.M. Train Arrives

Ⓐ 30 minutes   Ⓑ 1 hour   Ⓒ 1 hour, 30 minutes   Ⓓ 2 hours

Name _____

## Solve & Share

Madison wants to exercise 30 minutes every day. Before school, she only has enough time to exercise for 10 minutes or less. One day, she exercised for 8 minutes before school and 22 minutes after school. This is one way she can exercise for 30 minutes.

Find two other ways she can exercise before school and after school to reach her goal of exercising for 30 minutes each day.

# Lesson 14-3
## Units of Time: Solve Word Problems

**I can ...**
use representations to solve word problems about time.

© **Content Standards** 3.MD.A.1 Also 3.NBT.A.2
**Mathematical Practices** MP.2, MP.4

Model with math. A number line, bar diagram, or table can be used to show different ways Madison can use her time to exercise 30 minutes each day.

**Look Back!** Do you think there are more than two ways to solve the problem above? Explain.

**Essential Question** # How Can You Add or Subtract Time Intervals?

**A**

*Joaquin made a list of the time he should spend on different activities. Joaquin has practiced playing the piano 35 minutes so far. How much longer does he need to practice?*

A time interval is an amount of time.

After-School Activities

Play with Ron: 50 min
Practice Piano: 45 min
Homework: 60 min

---

**B** **One Way**

You can use a bar diagram to represent the problem and show time intervals.

**45 minutes**

| 35 | ? |
|----|----|

$35 + ? = 45$
$35 + 10 = 45$

What amount of time do you need to add to 35 minutes to equal 45 minutes?

Joaquin has to practice 10 more minutes.

---

**C** **Another Way**

You can use a number line to represent the problem and show time intervals.

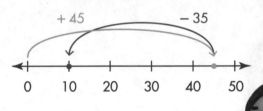

$+45$ $-35$

0  10  20  30  40  50

$45 - 35 = ?$
$45 - 35 = 10$

Joaquin has to practice 10 more minutes.

---

**Convince Me!** **Model with Math** How much longer will it take Joaquin to finish all of his after-school activities? Show one way to represent and solve.

---

Name _____

# ☆ Guided Practice

## Do You Understand?

In **1** and **2**, complete the bar diagram or number line to solve.

**1.** Rhody plans to ride his bicycle for 55 minutes. So far, he has ridden for 29 minutes. How many more minutes does he have to ride?

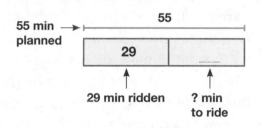

55 min planned →  55

| 29 | _____ |

↑ 29 min ridden      ↑ ? min to ride

## Do You Know How?

**2.** Ms. Darren spends the reading period working with two different reading groups. She meets with the first group for 23 minutes and meets with the second group for 17 minutes. How long is the reading period?

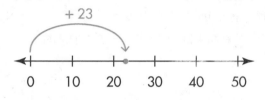

+ 23

0   10   20   30   40   50

# ☆ Independent Practice ☆

**Leveled Practice** In **3–6**, complete or draw a bar diagram or number line to solve.

**3.** Claire and Owen played video games. The first game lasted 24 minutes. After the first game, Claire and Owen had lunch for 30 minutes. The second game lasted 36 minutes. How many minutes did they play the games?

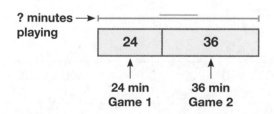

? minutes playing →

| 24 | 36 |

↑ 24 min Game 1      ↑ 36 min Game 2

**4.** Yan jogged for 60 minutes on Friday. Dino jogged 12 fewer minutes than Yan. Both friends swim for 40 minutes each week. How many minutes did Dino jog on Friday?

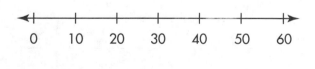

0   10   20   30   40   50   60

**5.** Mr. Hart's class is putting on a play. The play is divided into two acts. Each act lasts 27 minutes. How many minutes long is the play?

**6.** A chef wants to bake a dish for 30 minutes. So far, the dish has been baking for 12 minutes. How many more minutes does the dish need to bake?

# Problem Solving

**7. Reasoning** Ms. Merrill spends 55 minutes washing all the windows in her two-story house. How much time could she have spent on each floor? Complete the chart to show three different ways.

| Time Spent Washing Windows | |
|---|---|
| 1st floor | 2nd floor |
| 25 min | |
| | |
| | |

**8. Number Sense** Harry measures a sticker that is $\frac{4}{2}$ inches. Rhea's sticker is $\frac{6}{2}$ inches. Whose sticker is longer? Explain.

**9. Higher Order Thinking** Mr. Collins is learning to drive a truck. He drives 22 minutes on Monday and 14 minutes on Tuesday. Finally, he drives 6 more minutes on Wednesday than he did on Tuesday. How many total minutes does he practice driving a truck?

## Assessment Practice

**10.** Sonya hikes up a mountain. It takes her 25 minutes to hike to a cliff that is partway up the mountain. After that, she hikes for 17 more minutes to the summit. Use the number line and complete the table to show how many total minutes Sonya spends hiking.

| Destination | Time (min) |
|---|---|
| Hike to Cliff | 25 |
| Hike to Summit | |
| Total | |

**11.** Meg walks a dog named Shep for 12 minutes. Then she walks Sparky. Finally, she walks Brownie for 18 minutes. Meg spends 52 minutes walking all three dogs. Use the number line and complete the table to show how many minutes Meg spends walking each dog.

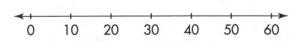

| Dog Walked | Time (min) |
|---|---|
| Shep | |
| Sparky | |
| Brownie | |
| Total | |

Name_____

★ ★
**Solve & Share**

The water bottle below has a capacity of 1 liter. Estimate the capacity of a small bowl, a large bowl, and a pitcher to the nearest half liter. Use an actual 1-liter water bottle, small and large bowls, and a pitcher to solve this problem.

**I can ...**
use a standard unit to estimate liquid volume.

© Content Standard 3.MD.A.2
Mathematical Practices MP.6, MP.8

Be precise. What unit should you use to estimate the capacity of the large bowl?

**Look Back!** After you estimate the capacity of the containers, how can you use a 1-liter water bottle to check that your estimate for each container is reasonable? Check your estimates.

**Essential Question** **How Do You Estimate Capacity?**

**A**

| What is the capacity of the pail? |

 Capacity (liquid volume) is the amount a container can hold measured in liquid units. One metric unit of capacity is the liter (L).

This pail holds about ? liters.

 This water bottle holds about 1 liter.

**B**

Compare the capacity of the water bottle to the capacity of the pail.

The pail appears to be large enough to hold several liters.

Count how many times you can fill a liter container and empty it into the pail.

This pail holds about 8 liters.

You can measure to check that your estimate is reasonable.

**Convince Me!** **Be Precise** Suppose you want to estimate the capacity of the pail to the nearest half liter. How can you check that your estimate is reasonable?

Name_____

# ☆ Guided Practice

## Do You Understand?

**1.** Susie estimates the capacity of a water glass as 3 liters. Hakim estimates the capacity as $\frac{1}{4}$ liter. Is Susie's or Hakim's estimate more reasonable? Explain.

**2.** Find a container that you predict will hold more than a liter and another that you predict will hold less than a liter. Use a liter container to check your predictions by finding the actual capacity of each container.

## Do You Know How?

In **3–6**, circle the better estimate for each.

**3.**

$\frac{1}{4}$ L or 2 L

**4.**

100 L or 1 L

**5.** Bottle of juice

3 L or 1 L

**6.** Cereal bowl

$\frac{1}{4}$ L or 3 L

# ☆ Independent Practice ☆

In **7–14**, circle the better estimate for each.

**7.**

$\frac{1}{4}$ L or 40 L

**8.**

$\frac{1}{8}$ L or 1 L

**9.**

$\frac{1}{2}$ L or 14 L

**10.**

$\frac{1}{4}$ L or 250 L

**11.** Teacup

$\frac{1}{4}$ L or 15 L

**12.** Bathtub

15 L or 115 L

**13.** Soup bowl

$\frac{1}{2}$ L or 3 L

**14.** Teapot

1 L or 10 L

**15.** Write an estimate for the capacity of a dog bowl. _____

**16.** Write an estimate for the capacity of a flower vase. _____

# Problem Solving

**17. Generalize** Which cooler has the greater capacity? Explain your thinking.

Cooler B

Cooler A

**18.** List these containers in order from least capacity to greatest capacity.

Washing machine          Large pot

Soup spoon                    Travel mug

**19.** A basketball team scores 27 points in its first game and 41 points in its second game. After three games, it scores 100 points in all. How many points does the team score in its third game?

**20. Higher Order Thinking** Becky wants to measure the capacity of her brother's baby pool. She has a 1-liter container and a 10-liter container. Which should she use? Explain your reasoning.

**21.** A sandgrouse can soak up water in its fluffy feathers. It can carry the water a long way to its chicks. Does a sandgrouse carry $\frac{1}{10}$ liter of water or 2 liters of water?

A sandgrouse can soak up enough water to fill a perfume bottle.

✓ **Assessment Practice**

**22.** Gary is painting a small storage shed. He estimates that he can do the job with one can of paint. Which of the following is the best estimate of the total liquid volume of a can of paint?

Paint

Ⓐ $\frac{1}{4}$ liter          Ⓑ 4 liters          Ⓒ 40 liters          Ⓓ 400 liters

Name _____

### Solve & Share

Select six different containers. Estimate the capacity of each container. Record your estimates in the table, and arrange the containers in order from least to greatest liquid volume. Then use a marked liter beaker to measure the capacity of each container. Record your measurements in the table. Compare your estimates to your measures. Using your measures, rearrange the containers in order from least to greatest liquid volume.

**I can ...**
use a standard unit to measure liquid volume.

Content Standard 3.MD.A.2
Mathematical Practices MP.3, MP.5, MP.6

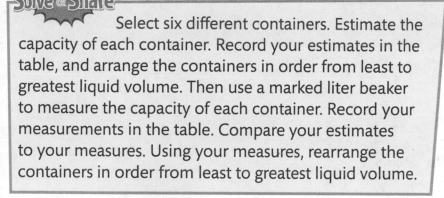

Be precise. When measuring with a 1-liter beaker, you can estimate and measure to $\frac{1}{4}$, $\frac{1}{2}$, or $\frac{3}{4}$ of a liter.

| Container | Estimate | Actual Capacity |
|-----------|----------|-----------------|
|           |          |                 |
|           |          |                 |
|           |          |                 |
|           |          |                 |
|           |          |                 |
|           |          |                 |

**Look Back!** How did you measure the capacity of containers that are less than 1 liter? Is there another way to measure?

**Essential Question** How Do You Measure Capacity?

A

Eric is cleaning his fishbowl and wants to know how much water he needs to refill the fishbowl. How can he find the capacity of the fishbowl?

Eric needs to be precise to measure the capacity of the fishbowl.

B

Pour from the filled fishbowl into the 1-liter container. Empty the container and repeat until the fishbowl is empty.

It is helpful to keep a record of measurements made.

The 1-liter container was filled 5 times.

So, the capacity of the fishbowl is 5 liters.

**Convince Me!** **Critique Reasoning** Jason says, "I think it is better to find the measurement of the fishbowl by filling the fishbowl with liters of water instead of emptying the fishbowl into liter beakers." Is Jason correct?

Practice  Tools  Assessment

## Another Example!

When only part of the 1-liter container is filled, use fractions of liters.

Two 1-liter and one $\frac{1}{2}$-liter containers fill the pot.

The capacity of the pot is $2\frac{1}{2}$ liters.

## ☆ Guided Practice

### Do You Understand?

**1.** What is the capacity of 2 pots like the one shown in the Another Example! above?

**2.** Find a container that you think holds less than a liter. Estimate, and then check your estimate for the capacity of the container.

### Do You Know How?

In **3** and **4**, find the total capacity represented in each picture.

**3.**

**4.**

## ☆ Independent Practice ☆

In **5–7**, find the total capacity represented in each picture.

**5.**

**6.**

**7.**

**8.** Lawrence manufactures jam. He makes 200 liters of grape jam and 350 liters of strawberry jam. He then sells 135 liters of the grape jam. How much jam does Lawrence have left?

**9. Use Appropriate Tools** Find a container that you think holds more than a liter. Estimate, and then check your estimate for the capacity of the container.

**10.** How many 2-liter cartons can be filled with 18 liters of juice?

You can draw a picture to show this problem.

**11.** Which of the following measurements is **NOT** reasonable for the capacity of a full bathroom sink: 15 liters, $\frac{1}{2}$ liter, 10 liters, 9 liters, or 12 liters? Explain.

**12. Higher Order Thinking** Emma prepares 72 liters of punch for an event. She pours all of the punch equally into the pitchers on 9 different tables. If there are 4 pitchers on each table, how many liters of punch are in each pitcher?

You can use bar diagrams to help make sense of and persevere in solving this problem.

### ✅ Assessment Practice

**13.** Use the picture of the water jugs to find the amount of water the team drank during soccer practice.

Ⓐ  6 liters

Ⓑ  7 liters

Ⓒ  8 liters

Ⓓ  23 liters

Before soccer practice

After soccer practice

Name_____

**Activity**

## Solve & Share

Look at the measurements for the mass of the book and the mass of the olive. List 4 items that should be measured using kilograms and 4 items that should be measured using grams. Explain your reasoning.

**I can ...**
use standard units to estimate the masses of solid objects.

© **Content Standard** 3.MD.A.2
**Mathematical Practices** MP.2, MP.3, MP.5

**1 gram**

**1 kilogram**          **1,000 grams = 1 kilogram**

You can use reasoning. How can the mass of a book and the mass of an olive help you make your list?

**Look Back!** How could you use tools to check that the items in part of your list are reasonable choices for measuring mass with grams? Explain.

**Essential Question** **How Can You Use Reasoning to Estimate Mass?**

**A**

*Stephen and Marissa estimated the mass of an apple. Stephen's estimate is 250 grams. Marissa's estimate is 2 kilograms. Which is the better estimate of the mass of an apple?*

Mass is a measure of the amount of matter in an object. Grams and kilograms are two metric units of mass.

1 kilogram (kg)

1 gram (g)

?

**B** **Step 1**

Use known masses and the table to compare grams to kilograms. Select the unit that will give a better estimate.

**Units of Mass**

DATA

1,000 grams = 1 kilogram

The apple is smaller than the cantaloupe. A kilogram is too large of a unit to estimate the mass of the apple.

The grape is smaller than the apple. Grams are smaller units that can be used to estimate the mass of the apple.

**C** **Step 2**

Use a pan balance to find the mass of the apple. Then evaluate Stephen's estimate.

The apple has a mass of 262 grams.

250 grams is close to 262 grams. Stephen's estimate is reasonable.

250 grams is a better estimate than 2 kilograms.

**Convince Me!** **Critique Reasoning** Zoe says two apples would have a mass greater than a kilogram. Do you agree? Explain.

Name_____

## ☆ Guided Practice

### Do You Understand?

**1.** In Step 2 on the previous page, why do you need to find the actual mass of the apple?

**2.** Find an object that you think has a mass more than a kilogram and another that has a mass less than a kilogram. Then determine what tools to use to check your estimate.

### Do You Know How?

In **3–6**, circle the better estimate for each.

**3.**

5 g or 5 kg

**4.**

40 g or 4 kg

**5.** Sunglasses

16 g or 1 kg

**6.** Envelope

1 g or 70 g

## Independent Practice ☆

**Leveled Practice** In **7–18**, circle the better estimate for each.

**7.**

100 g or 10 kg

**8.**

15 g or 15 kg

**9.**

4 g or 400 g

**10.**

200 g or 2 kg

**11.** Bicycle

2 kg or 12 kg

**12.** Feather

1 g or 1 kg

**13.** Horse

5 kg or 550 kg

**14.** Penny

3 g or 300 g

**15.** Dining table

350 g or 35 kg

**16.** Microwave oven

1,500 g or 15 kg

**17.** Kitten

2 kg or 20 kg

**18.** Crayon

20 g or 200 g

# Problem Solving

19. **Use Appropriate Tools** Choose the best tool to measure each item described. Write the correct letter of the tool on the blank.

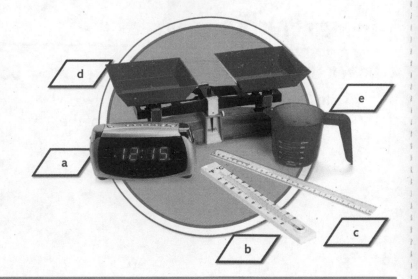

The capacity of a mug ____

The temperature of water ____

The length of a box ____

The mass of a pear ____

The time you finish lunch ____

20. **Number Sense** Ethan will subtract a 3-digit number from 920. He says the difference could be a 1-digit number, a 2-digit number, or a 3-digit number. Write three subtraction equations that show each difference. Be sure you start with 920 and subtract a 3-digit number each time.

> You can use place value and mental math to solve this problem.

21. **enVision® STEM** Clay learned that solids have a definite shape. Now he wants to measure some solids, so he measures the mass of a bead. The bead has a mass of 10 grams. He estimates that 10 beads will have a mass of 1 kilogram. Is he correct? Explain.

22. **Higher Order Thinking** Correct the mistakes in the shopping list below.

Shopping List
2 L of apples
3 kg of milk
5 cm of flour

## Assessment Practice

23. Todd is thinking of an animal with a mass greater than 1 kilogram, but less than 20 kilograms. Which animal could Todd be thinking of?

Ⓐ Horse  Ⓒ Elephant

Ⓑ Cat  Ⓓ Rhinoceros

24. Anna has a bar of soap. She estimates its mass before measuring to find the actual mass. Which units should Anna use for her measure?

Ⓐ Grams  Ⓒ Liters

Ⓑ Kilograms  Ⓓ Inches

☆ Solve & Share ☆

   Work with a group to choose 6 objects whose masses can be measured using a pan balance. Estimate the mass of each object. Then use metric weights to find the actual mass for each in grams (g) or kilograms (kg). Use the table and explain your reasoning.

**I can ...**
use grams and kilograms to measure the mass of objects.

© **Content Standard** 3.MD.A.2
**Mathematical Practices** MP.2, MP.6, MP.7

| Object | Estimate | Actual Mass |
|--------|----------|-------------|
|        |          |             |
|        |          |             |
|        |          |             |
|        |          |             |
|        |          |             |

Look for relationships. Think about how objects are similar or different to help decide whether grams, kilograms, or both are appropriate units for measuring the mass of each object. Show your work!

**Look Back!** How did you decide which metric unit(s) to use when making your estimates? Explain.

**A**

A pan balance with gram and kilogram weights can be used to find the mass of an object. What is the mass of a box of chalk?

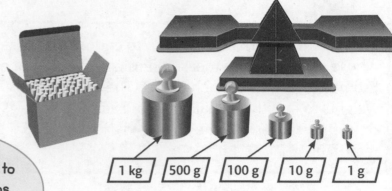

| 1 kg | 500 g | 100 g | 10 g | 1 g |

When measuring mass it is important to be precise. Use grams, kilograms, or both to find an exact measure.

**B**

Place the box on one pan. Place enough gram and kilogram weights on the other pan so the pans balance.

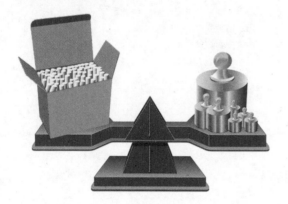

**C**

The box balances with one 1-kilogram weight, two 100-gram weights, and four 10-gram weights.

So, the mass of the box is 1 kilogram 240 grams or 1,240 grams.

Write the larger unit before the smaller unit when recording measurements.

**Convince Me!** **Be Precise** What metric units would you use to estimate the mass of half of a box of chalk? Explain.

Name _____

# ☆ Guided Practice

## Do You Understand?

**1.** Find an object that you think has a mass greater than a kilogram. Find another object that has a mass less than a kilogram. Use a pan balance with gram and kilogram weights to measure the mass of each object.

**2.** If you use a pan balance to measure the mass of a pen, would you use any kilogram weights? Explain.

## Do You Know How?

In **3** and **4**, write the total mass represented in each picture.

**3.**

1 kg      1 kg      1 kg      500 g

**4.**

100 g   100 g      10 g  10 g      1 g  1 g

10 g  10 g   1 g  1 g  1 g

# Independent Practice ☆

In **5–7**, write the total mass represented in each picture.

**5.**

100 g   100 g

500 g   100 g   100 g

10 g   10 g   10 g   1 g

**6.**

1 kg      1 kg      1 kg

1 kg      1 kg      1 kg

**7.**

1 kg      1 kg      100 g

1 g  1 g  1 g  1 g  1 g  1 g

# Problem Solving

8. **Algebra** Olivia put 220 grams of nuts in a bag. Then she added more nuts to the bag. The total mass of Olivia's bag of nuts was 850 grams. Use the equation $220 + a = 850$ to find the mass in grams of the nuts Olivia added to her bag.

9. An adult manatee has a mass of about 450 kilograms. What is the mass of 2 adult manatees?

450 kg

10. **Reasoning** Sophie used a pan balance to measure the mass of a pineapple. The pans balanced when she used one 500-gram weight and three 100-gram weights. Zach measured the same pineapple but used eight 100-gram weights. Did someone make a mistake? Explain.

11. **Higher Order Thinking** Lawrence bought some red potatoes with a mass of 410 grams. He also bought white potatoes with a mass of 655 grams. Did he buy more or less than 1 kilogram of potatoes? Explain how you know.

12. Meg uses 16 kilograms of butter to make 8 large batches of cookies. She uses an equal amount of butter for each batch. How many kilograms of butter are used for each batch?

13. Kalista has 154 grams of glitter. She uses 97 grams to sprinkle the tops of the tables. How many grams of glitter remain?

☑ **Assessment Practice**

14. Evan used a pan balance and metric weights to measure the total mass of 3 bricks. What is the mass of the 3 bricks?

Ⓐ 6 kilograms

Ⓑ 5 kilograms

Ⓒ 4 kilograms

Ⓓ 3 kilograms

**560**    **Topic 14** | Lesson 14-7

Name _____

## Solve & Share

The animals at a pet store eat 80 kilograms of vegetables each day. How many kilograms of vegetables do they eat in one week?

Drawing bar diagrams and writing equations help you model with math.

80 kilograms

# Lesson 14-8
## Solve Word Problems Involving Mass and Liquid Volume

**I can ...**
solve problems about mass and liquid volume.

Ⓒ **Content Standards** 3.MD.A.2 Also 3.OA.A.3, 3.OA.C.7
**Mathematical Practices** MP.1, MP.4

**Look Back!** Describe the plan you used to solve the problem.

**How Can You Solve Problems Involving Mass and Liquid Volume?**

**A**

In a juice factory, one 50-liter container had 28 liters of juice in it. An hour later, it had 45 liters of juice. How many liters of juice were added?

You can use reasoning to figure out the meaning of the numbers. The drawing shows how the amount changed.

28 liters to start

45 liters an hour later

**B** Use a bar diagram.

45 liters in all

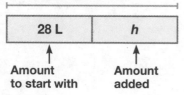

| 28 L | h |

↑ Amount to start with    ↑ Amount added

You know the total and one part.

Bar diagrams can help you understand what operation to use.

**C** Write and solve equations.

Pictures can help you understand what operation to use.

$28 + h = 45$
$45 - 28 = h$

Subtract to solve the problem.

$$\begin{array}{r} 45 \\ -28 \\ \hline 17 \end{array}$$

17 liters of juice were added to the container.

**Convince Me!** **Make Sense and Persevere** In the example above, another beaker had 33 liters of juice. How many total liters of juice were there in all? How can you solve this problem?

# ☆ Guided Practice

## Do You Understand?

**1.** Suppose 42 liters of juice were evenly divided into 6 batches. How many liters of juice are in each batch? Write and solve an equation.

## Do You Know How?

**2.** Alex buys a box of pudding mix and a box of cocoa. The mass of the box of pudding mix is 100 grams. The total mass of the 2 boxes is 550 grams. What is the mass of the box of cocoa?

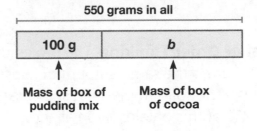

550 grams in all

| 100 g | b |
|-------|---|

Mass of box of pudding mix    Mass of box of cocoa

# ☆ Independent Practice ☆

**Leveled Practice** In **3–6**, use bar diagrams or equations to help solve.

**3.** Peter divided 120 liters of water equally into 3 containers. How many liters did Peter pour into each container?

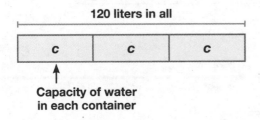

120 liters in all

| c | c | c |
|---|---|---|

Capacity of water in each container

**4.** Adeela pours 235 liters of milk into a blue vat and 497 liters of milk into a red vat. How many liters of milk does she pour in all? Write and solve an equation.

**5.** Samantha bought 523 grams of grapes. After eating some grapes, she had 458 grams. How many grams did she eat?

**6.** Omar is shipping 3 boxes. Each has a mass of 8 kilograms. What is the total mass of all of the boxes?

# Problem Solving

In **7** and **8**, use the table. In **8**, use the bar diagram.

**7.** Professor Newman has collected a soil sample from the forest preserve in her town. What is the total mass of the 3 minerals in the soil sample?

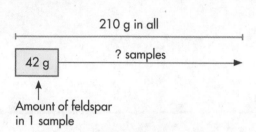

| Soil Sample | |
| --- | --- |
| **Component** | **Quantity** |
| Quartz | 141 g |
| Calcite | 96 g |
| Feldspar | 42 g |

**8. Higher Order Thinking** The professor finds that there is the same amount of feldspar in each of the soil samples that she takes. If there are 210 grams of feldspar in all, how many soil samples does she collect?

210 g in all

42 g   ? samples

Amount of feldspar in 1 sample

**9.** Elijah has 2 hours before dinner. He spends the first 37 minutes practicing his guitar and the next 48 minutes doing his homework. How much time is left until dinner?

**10. Make Sense and Persevere** Write and solve a word problem about the bar diagram.

678 g

| 239 g | $a$ |
| --- | --- |

## Assessment Practice

**11.** Eric filled a container to the 18-liter mark with juice an hour ago. The juice is now at the 15-liter mark. Mark the amount of juice Eric had on the beakers. Then find how many liters of juice have been poured out.

Ⓐ 3 liters

Ⓑ 4 liters

Ⓒ 5 liters

Ⓓ 6 liters

Amount of juice one hour ago

Amount of juice now

Name_____

★ ☆ ★
**Solve & Share**

Nina wants to arrive at the community center at 9:30 A.M. for an art class. It takes her 15 minutes to walk to the center, 30 minutes to make and eat breakfast, and 15 minutes to get ready after eating. What time should Nina start making breakfast? Use reasoning to decide.

**I can ...**
make sense of quantities and relationships in problem situations.

Ⓒ **Mathematical Practices** MP.2 Also MP.3, MP.6
**Content Standard** 3.MD.A.1

**Arrive at the Community Center**

**Thinking Habits**

*Be a good thinker!*
*These questions can help you.*

• What do the numbers and symbols in the problem mean?

• How are the numbers or quantities related?

• How can I represent a word problem using pictures, numbers, or equations?

**Look Back!** **Reasoning** Does it make sense to use "minutes" as the unit for the answer to this problem? Explain.

**Essential Question**

# How Can You Use Reasoning to Solve Problems?

**A**

*Eric's family wants to arrive at a movie theater at 2:30 P.M. It takes them 30 minutes to eat lunch, 15 minutes to get ready after eating, and 30 minutes to travel to the theater.*

*What time should the family start eating lunch? Use reasoning to decide.*

You can draw a picture to help with your reasoning.

**Arrive at Theater**

### What do I need to do to solve this problem?

I need to start with the end time. Then I need to use the time lengths given and work backward to find the starting time.

**B**

### How can I use reasoning to solve this problem?

**I can**

- identify the quantities I know.

- draw a number line to show relationships.

- give the answer using the correct unit.

**C**

Here's my thinking...

I used a number line to show the quantities and my reasoning.

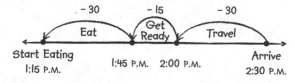

30 minutes before 2:30 P.M. is 2:00 P.M.
15 minutes before 2:00 P.M. is 1:45 P.M.
30 minutes before 1:45 P.M. is 1:15 P.M.

Eric's family should start eating lunch at 1:15 P.M.

**Convince Me!** **Reasoning** How can you check that the solution given above makes sense?

Practice  Tools  Assessment

# ☆ Guided Practice

**Reasoning**

Kevin's doctor appointment is at 10:30 A.M. It takes Kevin 30 minutes to clean his room, 20 minutes to get ready after he cleans, and 20 minutes to walk to the doctor's office. What time should Kevin start cleaning his room? Use reasoning to decide.

> Use reasoning to show how quantities in a problem are related.

**1.** Describe the quantities you know.

**2.** Solve the problem and explain your reasoning. You can use a picture to help.

# ☆ Independent Practice ☆

**Reasoning**

Doreen's favorite television show begins at 5:30 P.M. She will get her hair cut before the show. It takes Doreen 10 minutes to walk to the hair salon and 10 minutes to walk home. Her haircut takes 25 minutes. What time should Doreen leave home so that she will get back in time for her show? Use reasoning to decide.

**3.** Describe the quantities you know.

**4.** Solve the problem and explain your reasoning. You can use a picture to help.

**5.** How did you know whether to use A.M. or P.M. in your answer to Exercise **4** above?

**School Talent Show**

Karina is planning a talent show for 28 students. The table below tells how long each act lasts. Karina needs 5 minutes to introduce each act. She also needs to allow a 20-minute break. The break does not need to be introduced. The show must end at 9:00 P.M.

| Acts Before Break | Length in Minutes | Acts After Break | Length in Minutes |
|---|---|---|---|
| 3rd grade dancers | 10 | 5th grade singers | 10 |
| 3rd grade singers | 10 | 5th grade magic act | 10 |
| 4th grade singers | 10 | 5th grade dancers | 10 |
| 4th grade magic act | 15 | Finale | 30 |

6. **Be Precise** What is the total time needed for all the acts before the break? Explain your thinking.

7. **Critique Reasoning** Sachi says that the 5th grade singers should begin at 7:40 P.M. Phil says that the 5th grade singers should begin at 8:00 P.M. Who is correct?

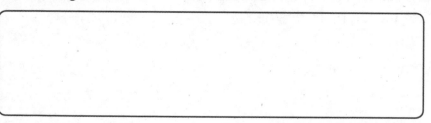

Use reasoning. Think about the meaning of each of the numbers.

8. **Reasoning** What time should the talent show begin? Explain your reasoning. You can draw a picture to help.

Name_____

Find a partner. Get paper and a pencil. Each partner chooses a different color: light blue or dark blue.

Partner 1 and Partner 2 each point to a black number at the same time. Both partners subtract the lesser number from the greater number.

If the answer is on your color, you get a tally mark. Work until one partner has seven tally marks.

While playing the game, partners can use addition to check their subtraction.

**I can ...**
add and subtract within 1,000.

 **Content Standard** 3.NBT.A.2
**Mathematical Practices** MP.3, MP.6, MP.7, MP.8

| Partner 1 | | | | | Partner 2 |
|---|---|---|---|---|---|
| **790** | 139 | 283 | 430 | 84 | **243** |
| **382** | 228 | 95 | 542 | 235 | **610** |
| **180** | 180 | 375 | 173 | 164 | **555** |
| **327** | 249 | 547 | 150 | 47 | **133** |
| **705** | 572 | 194 | 657 | 462 | **869** |
| | 79 | 487 | 689 | 63 | |

| Tally Marks for Partner 1 |
|---|
| ﾌﾞﾙ1 |

| Tally Marks for Partner 2 |
|---|
| ﾞﾞﾞﾞﾙ/1 |

## Understand Vocabulary

1. Cross out any units below that are **NOT** measurement units of *capacity*.

   gram          inch          kilogram     hour          liter

2. Cross out any units below that are **NOT** measurement units of *mass*.

   kilogram     minute       hour          gram          liter

3. Cross out any amounts below that are shown in *grams* or *kilograms*.

   5 kg          2 L          80 in.          250 g          12 kg

Choose the right term from the box. Write it in the blank.

4. The hours between midnight and noon are _____ hours.

5. An amount of time is a _____.

6. The hours between noon and midnight are _____ hours.

7. 1 _____ equals 1,000 grams.

8. The total amount of time that passes from the beginning time to the ending time is called the _____.

## Use Vocabulary in Writing

9. Maggie wants to measure this container. Use at least 3 terms from the Word List to explain how Maggie can measure the container in different ways.

Name _____

## Set A — pages 533–536

**What is the time to the nearest minute?**

The hour hand is between 10 and 11. The time is after 10:00.

Count by 5s from the 12 to the 5.
5, 10, 15, 20, 25 minutes.

After counting by 5s, count the marks by 1.
5, 10, 15, 20, 25, 26, 27 minutes.

The digital time is 10:27.
It is 27 minutes after 10 o'clock or 33 minutes before 11 o'clock.

**Reteaching**

**Remember** that, for minutes, count numbers on the clock by 5s, then count marks by 1.

Write the time shown on each clock in two ways.

1.

2.

## Set B — pages 537–540

Tomaz starts practicing his viola at 4:25 P.M. He practices until 5:05 P.M. How much time does he practice?

The amount of time is under 1 hour, so count the minutes from the start time to the end time, by 5s.

There are 40 minutes between 4:25 P.M. and 5:05 P.M. So, Tomaz practices for 40 minutes.

**Remember** that you can use a clock face to find elapsed time.

In **1–3**, find the elapsed time.

1. Basketball practice begins at 6:30 P.M. and lasts until 8:15 P.M. How much time does practice last?

2. Mr. Walters starts preparing breakfast at 6:45 A.M. He finishes at 7:50 A.M. How long does it take for him to prepare breakfast?

3. Jean goes for a horseback ride. She leaves the barn on her horse at 2:10 P.M., and comes back at 2:50 P.M. How long was her ride?

**Set C** pages 541–544

You can show addition and subtraction of time intervals on a number line.

In the morning, Xavier runs for 19 minutes. In the evening, he runs for 27 minutes. How much time does he spend running in all?

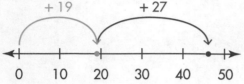

$19 + 27 = ?$

$19 + 27 = 46$    So, Xavier runs for 46 minutes.

**Remember** to decide whether you need to add or subtract.

In **1**, solve by drawing a number line or a bar diagram.

1. It takes Don 52 minutes to drive to work. He has already driven for 16 minutes. How many more minutes will it take Don to drive to work?

**Set D** pages 545–548

Estimate the capacity of a pitcher.

Think about what you already know. A liter is about the same size as a large water bottle. A pitcher usually holds more liquid than a water bottle. So, 2 liters seems like a good estimate.

**Remember** that capacity can be measured using liters.

In **1–4**, circle the better estimate.

1.

   1 L or 10 L

2. 

   $\frac{1}{4}$ L or 8 L

3. Drinking glass
   5 L or $\frac{1}{2}$ L

4. Washing machine
   40 L or 4 L

**Set E** pages 549–552

How much water is in this beaker?

Use the scale to determine how full the beaker is. Think of the scale as a number line. Each mark represents 1 liter. The water is 3 marks above 5 liters.

There are 8 liters in the beaker.

**Remember** to use the correct units when measuring capacity.

In **1** and **2**, find the total capacity.

1.

2.

Name_____

### Set F  pages 553–556

Estimate the mass of a battery.

A kilogram is too heavy, so estimate using grams.

Think about what you already know. A gram is about the same weight as a grape. A battery weighs about as much as a bunch of grapes. So 30 grams seems like a good estimate.

**Remember** that mass can be measured using grams and kilograms.

In **1–6**, circle the better estimate for the mass.

**1.**

15 g or 15 kg

**2.**

500 g or 500 kg

**3.** One sheep

800 g or 80 kg

**4.** Bag of flour

2 g or 2 kg

**5.** Notebook computer

3 g or 3 kg

**6.** Quarter

5 g or 500 g

### Set G  pages 557–560

What is the mass of this bar of soap?

When a pan balance is even, the mass on the left side equals the mass on the right side.

Find the total of the weights on the left side. Use mental math and place value to help add.

$100 + 10 + 5 + 1 + 1 + 1 = 118$

The bar of soap has a mass of 118 grams.

**Remember** to use the correct units when measuring mass.

In **1** and **2**, find the total mass.

**1.**

500 g    100 g    100 g    1 g

**2.**

1 kg        1 kg      100 g    100 g    5 g    5 g

**Set H** | pages 561–564

There are 7 people bowling together. Each owns their own bowling ball. The mass of each bowling ball is 5 kilograms. What is the total mass of the team's bowling balls?

? kg in all

| 5 kg | 5 kg | 5 kg | 5 kg | 5 kg | 5 kg | 5 kg |

$7 \times 5 = $ ▪

$7 \times 5 = 35$

**The total mass of the the team's bowling balls is 35 kg.**

**Remember** that you can use bar diagrams or equations to represent problems.

In **1** and **2**, use bar diagrams or equations to help solve.

1. The water tank in Mary's yard holds 60 liters of water. She used 13 liters to water her plants. How many liters of water remain in the water tank?

2. Eric has 3 dogs that each have a mass of 8 kilograms. What is the total mass of all of Eric's dogs?

**Set I** | pages 565–568

Think about these questions to help you **reason abstractly and quantitatively**.

**Thinking Habits**

- What do the numbers and symbols in the problem mean?

- How are the numbers or quantities related?

- How can I represent a word problem using pictures, numbers, or equations?

**Remember** to consider the units in the information you are given.

At 1:00 P.M., Ted will meet a friend in the park. Ted needs 30 minutes to walk to the park. Ted needs 15 minutes to eat lunch and 10 minutes to prepare lunch. When must Ted start to prepare lunch?

1. Describe the quantities you know.

2. How can you show the relationships in this problem?

3. When must Ted start to prepare lunch?

**574**     **Topic 14** | Reteaching    

Name_____

**1.** Draw hands on the clock to show 8:36. What time will it be in 2 hours and 6 minutes?

```
[                              ]
[                              ]
[                              ]
```

**2.** Jessica and Cody ran a long-distance race during an afternoon. The start times were different so that all the runners did not start at the same time. Who finished faster, and by how many minutes?

**Jessica**

Start       End

**Cody**

Start       End

Ⓐ Jessica; 5 minutes faster than Cody

Ⓑ Cody; 5 minutes faster than Jessica

Ⓒ Jessica; 10 minutes faster than Cody

Ⓓ They finished in the same amount of time.

**3.** Two stores in a small town sell bags of apples. At Store A, each bag weighs 2 kilograms. At Store B, each bag weighs 4 kilograms. If you buy 6 bags at each store, how many more kilograms of apples will you buy from Store B?

```
[                              ]
[                              ]
[                              ]
```

**4.** Name the metric unit that could be used to measure the capacity of a kitchen sink. Then, using that unit, write a reasonable estimate for the capacity of a kitchen sink.

```
[                              ]
[                              ]
[                              ]
```

**5. A.** Mason is looking for a tool to measure the mass of an apple. Which tool should he use?

Ⓐ Pan balance   Ⓒ 1-cup container

Ⓑ Ruler           Ⓓ Clock

**B.** Using the tool identified in **Part A**, what unit will Mason use to measure the mass of the apple?

Ⓐ Grams          Ⓒ Cups

Ⓑ Minutes        Ⓓ Inches

**6.** Dale's school bus picks him up at 7:45 A.M. To get ready for school, Dale needs 15 minutes to eat breakfast, 10 minutes to make lunch, and 10 minutes to get dressed. What time does Dale need to begin getting ready for school?

**A.** Describe the quantities you know.

**B.** Solve the problem. Explain your reasoning. You can use a picture to help.

**7.** Mary has a total of 18 liters of water in 6 bottles. Jess has a total of 15 liters in 3 bottles. If the bottles are equally filled, how much more water is in each of Jess's bottles than in Mary's bottles?

**8.** Eric played the guitar for 33 minutes on Monday and 19 minutes on Tuesday. Write and solve an equation to find how many more minutes Eric played the guitar on Monday.

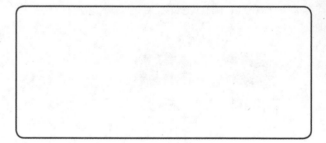

**9.** Mrs. Griggs writes a shopping list saying she needs to buy 1 gram of apples. Is this reasonable? Explain.

Name_____

**10.** Irene measured the mass of a bag of apples using kilograms. Forest measured the same bag using grams. How did the measurements compare? Select all the sentences that are true.

☐ There were more grams than kilograms.

☐ There were more kilograms than grams.

☐ There was an equal number of grams and kilograms.

☐ There were fewer grams than kilograms.

☐ There were fewer kilograms than grams.

**11.** Jason said the mass of his book is about 1 kilogram. Julie said it is 1 liter. Who is correct? Select the best answer.

Ⓐ Jason is correct because kilograms are units of mass, and liters are units of capacity.

Ⓑ Julie is correct because liters are metric units.

Ⓒ They are both correct because kilograms and liters are units of mass.

Ⓓ Neither is correct because their estimates are not reasonable.

**12.** Explain why it would be better to use grams rather than kilograms to measure the mass of a crayon.

**13.** It took Wallace 45 minutes to read part of a chapter of his science book. He finished reading the rest of the chapter in 17 minutes. Write and solve an equation to find how much time Wallace spent reading the chapter.

**14.** Four brothers, Raphael, Don, Leo, and Mike, went to the gym to exercise. Don and Mike both started at 2:21 P.M. and exercised for 33 minutes. Raphael and Leo both started when Don and Mike finished and exercised until 3:36 P.M. For how many minutes did the brothers exercise in total?

**15.** Mark used a pan balance to find the mass of his basketball. He said it was 580 kilograms. Is his answer reasonable? Explain.

**16.** Look at the time on the clock below.

**A.** Select all of the ways to write this time.

☐ 3:46

☐ 14 minutes before 4 o'clock

☐ 46 minutes after 3 o'clock

☐ 9 minutes before 4 o'clock

☐ 4:14

**B.** What time was it 2 hours, 45 minutes ago?

**17.** Maryann went to the grocery store at 3:10 P.M. She arrived home 1 hour, 15 minutes later.

**A.** What time did she arrive home?

**B.** Her neighbor Betty Sue got to the grocery store at the same time as Maryann and got home at 4:02 P.M. How much less time did Betty Sue spend shopping?

**18.** Ricardo used 337 grams of flour to bake in the afternoon. He had already used 284 grams of flour to bake in the morning. Write and solve an equation to find how many grams of flour Ricardo used in all.

**19.** A tank contained 750 liters of water. After some water drained out, the tank had 250 liters of water. Write and solve an equation to find how many liters of water drained out.

Name_____

**Family Reunion**

Anita and her brother Logan make plans for a family reunion.

1. Use the **Fruit Bought** table to answer the question. Logan estimated the mass of the fruit. He forgot to include the unit of mass. For each item, explain if he used a gram or kilogram.

| Fruit Bought | |
| --- | --- |
| **Item** | **Estimated Mass** |
| Bag of grapefruit | 4 |
| One lemon | 90 |
| One watermelon | 3 |

2. Use the **Mass of One Lime** picture to answer the questions.

**Part A**

Each lime has the mass shown at the right. What is the mass of one lime?

Mass of One Lime

10 g   10 g   10 g

**Part B**

Logan needs to buy at least 200 grams of limes. He plans to buy 7 limes. Will he buy enough? Use your response to Part A to explain.

3. Use the **Liquids Needed** table to answer the question.

Logan measures the liquids they need. Complete the table to show if the capacity of each container will likely be less than or greater than 1 liter.

| Ingredient | Container Capacity |
| --- | --- |
| Vinegar | |
| Milk | |
| Water | |

| Liquids Needed | |
| --- | --- |
| **Ingredient** | **Container** |
| Vinegar | Spoon |
| Milk | Measuring cup |
| Water | Large pot |

The **Broth Used** picture shows the amount of broth that Anita started with and the amount she had left after she poured some into two different soups.

4. Use the **Broth Used** picture to answer the questions.

   **Part A**

   How much broth did Anita use?

   **Part B**

   Anita poured an equal amount of broth into 2 pots. How much did she pour into 1 pot?

5. Logan's recipe says it takes 50 minutes to cook chicken. After 22 minutes pass, Logan flips the chicken. How many more minutes does the chicken have to bake after Logan flips it? Show your work on a number line.

6. Use the **Before Reunion** table to answer the question.

   Anita and Logan want to be at the reunion at 1:45 P.M. They need to clean, pack, and drive to the reunion. What time should they start? Explain.

| Before Reunion | |
| --- | --- |
| **Activity** | **Time in Minutes** |
| Clean | 20 |
| Pack | 15 |
| Drive | 55 |

# TOPIC 15

## Attributes of Two-Dimensional Shapes

**Essential Question:** How can two-dimensional shapes be described, analyzed, and classified?

**Digital Resources**

Interactive Student Edition · Activity · Visual Learning · Video · Practice

Assessment · Games · Tools · Glossary

*Even though a ball is not moving yet, there are still forces acting on it.*

*The force of a kick will change the motion of the ball.*

*I did not know that! Here is a project on forces and motion.*

---

**enVision STEM Project: Forces and Motion**

**Do Research** Use the Internet or other sources to find information about forces and the motion of an object. What does a balanced force mean? What happens when forces are unbalanced?

**Journal: Write a Report** Include what you found. Also in your report:

- Give examples of balanced and unbalanced forces on objects.

- Draw a picture that shows force acting on an object and the result.

- Describe the shapes in your drawing.

Name_____

# Review What You Know

**A-Z Vocabulary**

Choose the best term from the box.
Write it on the line.

| | |
|---|---|
| • circle | • pentagon |
| • hexagon | • triangle |

1. A shape with exactly 6 sides is called a _____.

2. A shape with exactly 3 sides is called a _____.

3. A shape with exactly 5 sides is called a _____.

## Name Shapes

Write the name of each figure.

4.

5.

6.

7.

## Shapes

In **8–11** write the number of vertices each figure has.

8.

9.

10.

11.

12. How many faces does a cube have?

　Ⓐ 3　　　　Ⓑ 4　　　　Ⓒ 5　　　　Ⓓ 6

13. How are squares and triangles the same? How are they different?

**Pick a Project**

**PROJECT 15A**

## Where do professional baseball players play their games?

**Project:** Create Quadrilateral Riddles

**PROJECT 15B**

## How are books measured?

**Project:** Collect Data about the Shapes of Books

**PROJECT 15C**

## Where are quadrilaterals around us in everyday life?

**Project:** Build a Quadrilateral Model

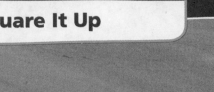

## Math Modeling
## Square It Up

Video

Before watching the video, think:

It takes a long time to make a design like this in the sand or snow. And that reminds me—if snowshoes let you walk on snow, why don't water shoes let you walk on water?

**I can ...**
model with math to solve a problem that involves using attributes of 2-D shapes to compare weights.

© **Mathematical Practices** MP.4 Also MP.6, MP.8
**Content Standards** 3.MD.A.2 Also 3.G.A.1

Name _____

**Solve & Share**

Fold a square piece of paper to make the fold lines as shown below. Find as many different quadrilaterals as you can using the fold lines and the edges of the square paper. Sketch each quadrilateral you find and describe it.

The area of each small triangle on the paper represents a unit fraction. Write the unit fraction, and then find what fraction of the whole square each of your quadrilaterals represents.

**I can ...**
identify quadrilaterals and use attributes to describe them.

© **Content Standards** 3.G.A.1 Also 3.NF.A.1, 3.G.A.2
**Mathematical Practices** MP.1, MP.4, MP.7

You can look for relationships. What attributes of the quadrilaterals can help you identify each by name?

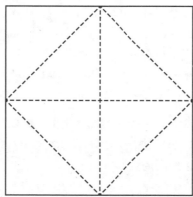

**Look Back!** Describe how you used what you know about quadrilaterals to identify the shapes.

Essential Question

# What Are Some Attributes of Quadrilaterals?

**A**

*The welcome to Florida sign is a quadrilateral. How can you describe quadrilaterals?*

Remember, a polygon is a closed shape that has only straight sides. A quadrilateral is a polygon with four sides and four angles.

An angle is formed when two sides of a polygon meet.

The point where two sides meet is a vertex.

side →

right angle

vertex

**B** Some quadrilaterals have special names.

   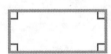 

| Trapezoid | Parallelogram | Rectangle | Rhombus | Square |
|---|---|---|---|---|
| Exactly one pair of sides on lines that never cross | Opposite sides are the same length. Opposite angles are the same size. | Four right angles, or square corners. *A rectangle is a special parallelogram.* | All sides the same length *A rhombus is a special parallelogram.* | Four right angles and all sides the same length *A square is a special parallelogram.* |

**Convince Me!** **Make Sense and Persevere** Draw a quadrilateral that is an example of one of the shapes listed in Box B. Name the shape. Then draw a quadrilateral that is **NOT** an example of a shape listed in Box B.

Name _____

## Another Example!

These are convex polygons. All angles point outward.

These are concave polygons. One or more angles point inward.

## ☆ Guided Practice

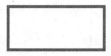

### Do You Understand?

1. This figure is a rectangle, but it is **NOT** a square. Why?

2. Draw two different quadrilaterals that are **NOT** rectangles, squares, or rhombuses.

### Do You Know How?

In **3–6**, write as many special names as possible for each quadrilateral.

3.    4.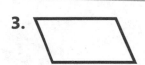

5.    6.

## Independent Practice ☆

In **7–9**, write as many special names as possible for each quadrilateral.

7.    8. _____   9.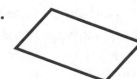

In **10**, name all the possible quadrilaterals that fit the rule.

10. Has 2 pairs of opposite sides that are equal _____

# Problem Solving

In **11** and **12**, write the name that best describes the quadrilateral. Draw a picture to help.

**11.** **A-Z** **Vocabulary** A rectangle with all sides the same length is a _____ .

**12.** **A-Z** **Vocabulary** A parallelogram with four right angles is a _____ .

**13.** I am a quadrilateral with opposite sides the same length. Which quadrilaterals could I be?

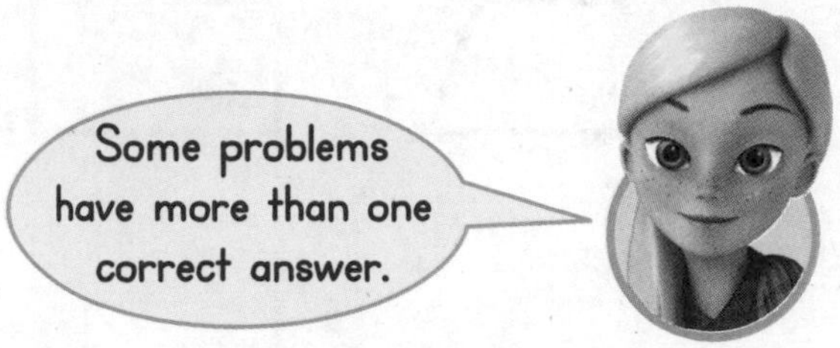

*Some problems have more than one correct answer.*

**14.** **Higher Order Thinking** Jae says that the figure on the left is a trapezoid. Carmen says that the figure on the right is a trapezoid. Who is correct? Explain.

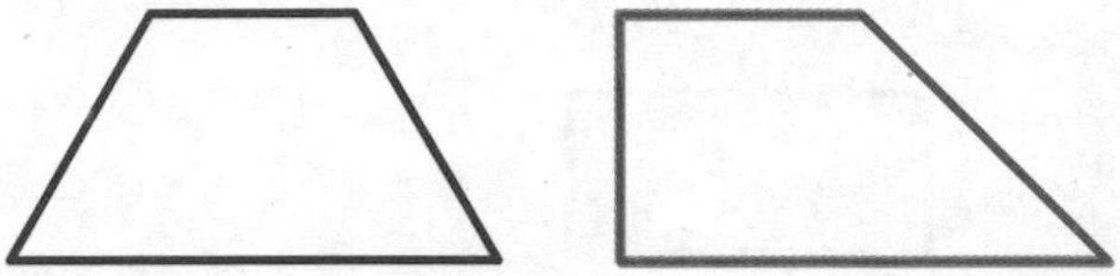

**15.** **Model with Math** Sue bought a book for $12, two maps for $7 each, and a pack of postcards for $4. Use math you know, bar diagrams, equations, or properties of operations, to find Sue's total cost.

**16.** **Algebra** Angela drew 9 rhombuses and 6 trapezoids. She wants to find $b$, the total number of angles in her quadrilaterals. Explain how Angela can find $b$.

## ✓ Assessment Practice

**17.** A square and a rhombus are shown at the right. Which attributes do these shapes always have in common? Select all that apply.

- ☐ Number of sides
- ☐ Side lengths
- ☐ Angle measures
- ☐ Right angles
- ☐ Number of angles

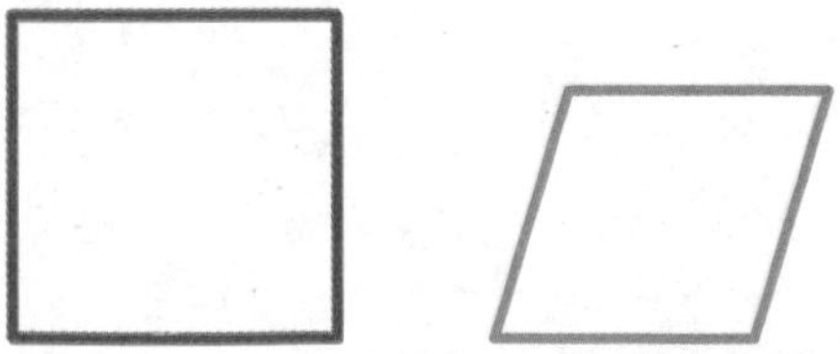

☆ ☆
**Solve & Share**

Sort the shapes below into two groups. Use colored pencils or crayons to color each group a different color. How did you sort the shapes? How are the shapes in both of your groups alike?

**I can ...**
classify shapes in several ways based on how they are alike and how they are different.

© **Content Standards** 3.G.A.1 Also 3.NF.A.1, 3.G.A.2
**Mathematical Practices** MP.3, MP.5, MP.8

You can use what you know to generalize. What attributes are the same in the shapes?

A

B

C

D

E

F

G

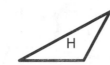
H

I

J

K

L

**Look Back!** What fraction of the triangles above have each attribute: all sides equal in length, no sides equal in length, exactly two equal angles, or one right angle?

**Essential Question** **How Can You Describe Different Groups of Shapes?**

**A**

Ethan made two groups of polygons. How are the groups different? How are the groups alike?

When you classify groups of shapes, you identify the attributes of each and then compare them with other shapes.

Group 1: Rhombuses

Group 2: Trapezoids

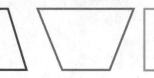

**B**

Here is one way the two groups are different.

In Group 1, each polygon has sides that all are the same length.

In Group 2, each polygon has sides that are not all the same length.

**C**

Here are some ways the two groups are alike.

In Group 1 and Group 2, all of the polygons have 4 sides.

In Group 1 and Group 2, all of the polygons have 4 angles.

In Group 1 and Group 2, all of the polygons are quadrilaterals.

**Convince Me!** **Construct Arguments** Draw a quadrilateral that does not belong to either Group 1 or Group 2. Explain why it does not belong to either group.

Name _____

# ☆ Guided Practice

## Do You Understand?

1. Nellie drew a group of rectangles and a group of trapezoids. How are the shapes in each group different?

2. How are rectangles and trapezoids alike?

3. What larger group of polygons do all of Nellie's shapes belong to?

## Do You Know How?

In **4–6**, use the groups on the previous page.

4. Draw a shape that belongs to Ethan's Group 1.

5. Draw a shape that belongs to Ethan's Group 2.

6. Why is there a square in Group 1?

# Independent Practice ☆

In **7–11**, use the groups below.

**Group 1**

**Group 2**

7. How are the shapes in Group 1 different from the shapes in Group 2?

8. How are the two groups alike?

9. What larger group do all the shapes belong to?

10. Draw a shape that could go in Group 2 but not Group 1.

11. Draw a shape that could go in Group 1 but not Group 2.

# Problem Solving

In **12-14**, use the picture at the right.

**12.** How are the yellow shapes and the blue shapes different? How are they alike?

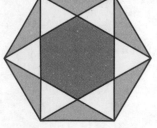

**13.** Which larger group of polygons do the yellow and blue shapes belong to?

**14.** Does the pink shape belong to the group identified in Exercise **13**? Explain.

**15.** Draw a quadrilateral that is **NOT** a rectangle, a rhombus, or a square.

**16.** Todd bought a jacket for $57 and two maps for $9 each. What was the total cost?

**17. Use Appropriate Tools** Victoria wants to make two same-sized rhombuses. What tool can she use? Explain.

**18. Higher Order Thinking** Jessalyn needs to find $3 \times 3$, $4 \times 6$, and $7 \times 2$. She draws area models to solve the problem. What polygon group do her area models all belong to? Explain.

## Assessment Practice

**19.** What is the name of a shape that is **NOT** always a rectangle, but is a quadrilateral?

    Ⓐ Square

    Ⓑ Triangle

    Ⓒ Hexagon

    Ⓓ Parallelogram

**20.** Which shape could be sorted into a group of parallelograms or a group of rhombuses?

    Ⓐ Square

    Ⓑ Rectangle

    Ⓒ Trapezoid

    Ⓓ Hexagon

Name _____

☆ **Solve & Share** ☆

Describe at least two attributes that are the same in all or some of these shapes. Describe two attributes that are different.

**I can ...**
analyze and compare quadrilaterals and group them by attributes.

© **Content Standards** 3.G.A.1 Also 3.MD.C.5b
**Mathematical Practices** MP.2, MP.7

You can use structure. Look for common attributes, such as lengths of sides or sizes of angles.

A   B   C   D   E

**Look Back!** Draw a quadrilateral that is different from all the quadrilaterals above. Tell how it is different.

**Essential Question**

# How Can You Analyze and Compare Shapes?

**A**

*What are different ways you can classify the quadrilaterals shown below?*

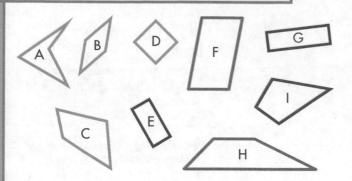

Quadrilaterals have 4 sides. They also have differences, so you can classify them into smaller groups.

**B** Shapes B, D, E, F, and G are also parallelograms. Each has two pairs of sides that have the same length.

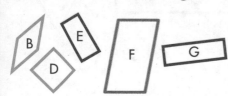

**C** Shapes D, E, and G are also rectangles. Each has 4 right angles.

**D** Shapes B and D are parallelograms that are also rhombuses. Each has 4 equal-length sides.

Shape D is a square and is in every group. It is a quadrilateral, a parallelogram, a rectangle, and a rhombus.

**Convince Me!** **Reasoning** Which of the shapes above can you cover with whole unit squares and not have any gaps or overlaps? What attributes do these shapes have in common?

# ☆ Guided Practice

## Do You Understand?

**1.** Which shape on the previous page is a rhombus but not a rectangle? Explain.

**2.** Can you have a square trapezoid? Explain.

## Do You Know How?

**3.** Which shapes on the previous page are not a parallelogram, rectangle, rhombus, or square?

**4.** What attributes does a square have because it is always a rectangle?

# ☆ Independent Practice ☆

In **5–9**, list all the polygons shown at the right that fit each description. If there could be no such polygon, tell why.

**5.** Is not a parallelogram

**6.** Is a quadrilateral but not a parallelogram or trapezoid

**7.** Is a square and not a parallelogram

**8.** Is a rhombus and not a rectangle

**9.** Is a parallelogram and not a rhombus

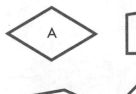
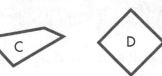

# Problem Solving

**10.** Cy put blocks 1 and 2 together to make a new shape. How are the blocks he used alike? How are they different?

---

**11. Reasoning** Explain which of the shapes at the right you can cover with whole unit squares and not have any gaps or overlaps.

---

**12. Higher Order Thinking** Draw a quadrilateral with no sides the same length. Tell why it is not a parallelogram.

Use definitions to support your answer.

**13.** Sam needs 25 minutes to get ready and 15 minutes to bike to swim practice. Practice starts at 4:00 P.M. What time should Sam start getting ready?

---

☑ **Assessment Practice**

**14.** Look at these polygons.

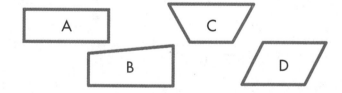

**Part A**

Name one attribute that all 4 polygons have.

**Part B**

Name an attribute that both A and D have that B and C do not.

Name_____

## Solve & Share

Draw shapes that match all of these clues. Use math words and numbers correctly to name each shape and explain how your shapes match the clues.

**Clue 1:** *I am a polygon with 4 sides.*

**Clue 2:** *I am a polygon with 4 right angles.*

**Clue 3:** *My area is 12 square units.*

**I can ...**
be precise when solving math problems.

© **Mathematical Practices** MP.6 Also MP.1, MP.3, MP.5
**Content Standards** 3.G.A.1 Also 3.MD.C.7b

## Thinking Habits

*Be a good thinker! These questions can help you.*

- Am I using numbers, units, and symbols appropriately?

- Am I using the correct definitions?

- Am I calculating accurately?

- Is my answer clear?

**Look Back!** **Be Precise** How did you use math terms or numbers to make your explanation clear?

**A**

*What shapes can you draw for this riddle?*

*I am a polygon with 4 sides.*
*I have 4 right angles.*
*My opposite sides are equal in length.*

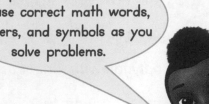

Be precise means that you use correct math words, numbers, and symbols as you solve problems.

**What do I need to do to solve this problem?**

I will read the given information and use it to draw shapes that match the description.

**B** **How can I be precise in solving this problem?**

**I can**

- correctly use the information given.

- use pictures or objects to identify possible answers.

- decide if my answer is clear and appropriate.

**C**

Here's my thinking...

I know that the shape is a 4-sided polygon with 4 right angles and opposite sides that are equal in length.

I can draw shapes that match all of the clues. Then I can name each shape.

Square    Rectangle

Each of the shapes has 4 sides, 4 right angles, and opposite sides that are equal in length.

**Convince Me!** **Be Precise** Draw a shape for this riddle. Explain how it matches the clues.

I am a polygon with 4 sides.
None of my angles are right angles.
None of my sides are the same length.

Practice   Tools   Assessment

# ☆ Guided Practice

**Be Precise**

Students in Mr. Tesla's class drew pictures of their favorite shapes. Jackie made a polygon with 4 sides. It has 4 right angles, but not all of the shape's sides are the same length.

Be precise. Carefully consider and use the information you are given to solve problems.

1. What math words and numbers are important in this problem?

2. Draw and name the type of polygon Jackie made.

3. How can you check to make sure your answer is clear and correct?

# ☆ Independent Practice ☆

**Be Precise**

Students in Mrs. Edison's class designed a mural to show what they have learned about quadrilaterals. Ethan made a shape with opposite sides that are the same length.

4. What math words and numbers are important in this problem?

5. Draw a possible polygon that Ethan could have made. Is there more than one type of quadrilateral that would correctly match the description? Explain.

6. How can you check to make sure your answer is clear and correct?

# Problem Solving

**Crazy Quilts**

Each student in Ms. Beardon's art class is designing a panel for a crazy quilt. Students can use different colors, but each panel will be the same shape. The attributes of the panel design are as shown at the right.

> • 4 equal sides
>
> • 4 right angles

Draw and name a shape to match this description. Answer Exercises **7-10** to solve the problem.

**7. Make Sense and Persevere** What do you know? What are you asked to do?

**8. Be Precise** What math terms and numbers can help you solve the problem?

**9. Use Appropriate Tools** Choose tools to help you solve this problem. Then draw and name a possible panel design.

> Make sure to use correct definitions so your answers can be precise.

**10. Critique Reasoning** Tabby followed Ms. Beardon's directions and made a quilt panel with the shape shown below. Did she follow directions correctly? Explain.

Name_____

**Follow the Path**

Shade a path from **START** to **FINISH**. Follow the products and quotients that are even numbers. You can only move up, down, right, or left.

**I can ...**
multiply and divide within 100.

 **Content Standard** 3.OA.C.7
**Mathematical Practices** MP.2, MP.6, MP.7

| Start | | | | | | | |
|---|---|---|---|---|---|---|---|
| 6 × 2 | 9 ÷ 1 | 9 × 5 | 24 ÷ 4 | 10 × 0 | 56 ÷ 7 | 3 × 8 | 35 ÷ 5 |
| 20 ÷ 5 | 5 × 8 | 8 × 2 | 36 ÷ 6 | 54 ÷ 6 | 3 × 5 | 2 × 3 | 27 ÷ 3 |
| 3 × 7 | 15 ÷ 3 | 5 × 7 | 5 ÷ 1 | 25 ÷ 5 | 6 ÷ 6 | 9 × 8 | 21 ÷ 7 |
| 48 ÷ 8 | 2 × 9 | 42 ÷ 7 | 3 × 5 | 8 ÷ 2 | 5 × 4 | 30 ÷ 5 | 9 × 9 |
| 3 × 6 | 5 × 1 | 6 × 10 | 0 ÷ 6 | 4 × 6 | 7 × 1 | 9 × 1 | 45 ÷ 9 |
| 9 × 6 | 4 × 8 | 72 ÷ 8 | 9 × 3 | 9 ÷ 3 | 4 × 4 | 18 ÷ 9 | 16 ÷ 2 |
| 5 × 5 | 2 × 7 | 81 ÷ 9 | 6 ÷ 2 | 4 × 7 | 80 ÷ 8 | 3 × 9 | 9 × 4 |
| 63 ÷ 9 | 4 × 3 | 7 × 8 | 8 × 9 | 10 ÷ 5 | 24 ÷ 8 | 9 × 7 | 40 ÷ 5 |
| | | | | | | | Finish |

**A-Z**
Glossary

**Word List**

- angle
- parallelogram
- polygon
- quadrilateral
- rectangle
- rhombus
- right angle
- square
- trapezoid

## Understand Vocabulary

Circle all the terms that match each description.

1. A quadrilateral

   square      rhombus      trapezoid      polygon

2. A polygon

   angle      quadrilateral      rectangle      square

3. A polygon with 4 right angles

   square      trapezoid      rhombus      rectangle

4. A parallelogram

   rhombus      triangle      rectangle      trapezoid

For each term, draw an example and a nonexample.

|  | Example | Non-example |
|---|---|---|
| **5.** Right angle |  |  |
| **6.** Rectangle |  |  |
| **7.** Trapezoid |  |  |

## Use Vocabulary in Writing

8. Use at least 3 terms from the Word List to explain why a *square* is a *rectangle*.

**TOPIC 15**

**Set A** pages 585–588

You can draw quadrilaterals and describe them by their attributes.

**Name:** Parallelogram
**Attribute:** 2 pairs of opposite sides the same length

**Name:** Quadrilateral
**Attributes:** 2 pairs of sides the same length

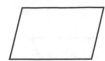

**Name:** Rectangle
**Attributes:** 2 pairs of opposite sides the same length, 4 right angles

**Remember** that a polygon with 4 sides is a quadrilateral.

In **1–3**, draw the shapes named or described below and describe their attributes.

1. Trapezoid          2. Rhombus

3. A quadrilateral that is **NOT** a trapezoid, parallelogram, rectangle, rhombus, or square.

**Set B** pages 589–592

How are the shapes in Groups 1 and 2 different? How are they alike?

**Group 1**

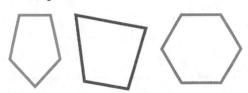

**Group 2**

The shapes in the groups are different because in Group 1, all shapes are convex. In Group 2, all shapes are concave.

The shapes in both groups are alike because they all have straight lines and are closed. Therefore, they all are polygons.

**Remember** that all of the shapes in these groups have something in common.

In **1** and **2**, use the groups below.

**Group 1**

**Group 2**

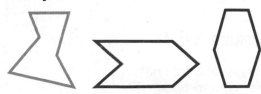

1. How are the shapes in Groups 1 and 2 different?

2. How are the shapes in Groups 1 and 2 alike?

All of the shapes below have 4 sides, so they are quadrilaterals. Some quadrilaterals can be classified into multiple groups.

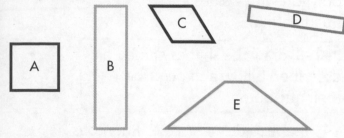

Parallelograms have 2 pairs of sides that have the same length. Shapes A, B, C, and D are parallelograms.

Rhombuses have 4 equal-length sides. Shapes A and C are rhombuses.

Rectangles have 2 pairs of sides that have the same length and 4 right angles. Shapes A, B, and D are rectangles.

Squares have 4 equal-length sides and 4 right angles. Shape A is a square.

Trapezoids have 1 pair of sides on lines that do not cross. Shape E is a trapezoid.

**Remember** that quadrilaterals with different names can have some of the same attributes.

In **1–4**, list all the polygons that fit the given attributes.

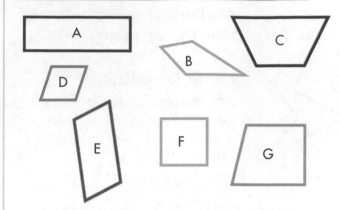

1. Has at least 2 right angles but is not a rectangle

2. Has pairs of sides the same length but is not a rectangle

3. Is a quadrilateral with no right angles

4. Has 4 sides the same length but is not a square

Think about these questions to help you **attend to precision**.

**Thinking Habits**

- Am I using numbers, units, and symbols appropriately?
- Am I using the correct definitions?
- Am I calculating accurately?
- Is my answer clear?

**Remember** to consider all parts of the question.

Anton drew a quadrilateral with 4 sides the same length and 4 right angles.

1. What quadrilateral did he draw?

2. Is there any other shape that he could have drawn? Explain.

Name_____

**1.** What other category does a parallelogram fall under?

Ⓐ Quadrilateral; because it has 4 right angles

Ⓑ Square; because it has 4 sides

Ⓒ Quadrilateral; because it has 4 sides

Ⓓ Rhombus; because all 4 sides are the same length

**2.** Use the words in the box below. Write the names for the shapes in the correct columns.

| Quadrilateral | Parallelogram |
|---|---|
|  |  |
|  |  |
|  |  |

rectangle  rhombus  square  trapezoid

**3.** Name and draw a picture of a concave polygon with 4 sides.

**4.** What are the possible shapes a parallelogram with 4 right angles could be?

**5.** The shapes are sorted into two groups—circled and not circled. How are the shapes in the two groups different?

**6.** Select all true statements.

☐ A trapezoid is a parallelogram.

☐ A parallelogram is a quadrilateral.

☐ A square is a rhombus.

☐ A triangle is a quadrilateral.

☐ A square is a rectangle.

**7.** What two quadrilaterals did Kim use to make the rug design? What do the shapes have in common?

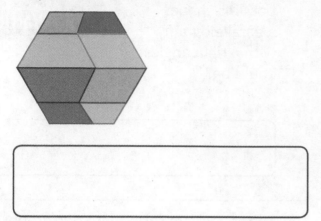

**8.** Look at each group.

Group 1          Group 2

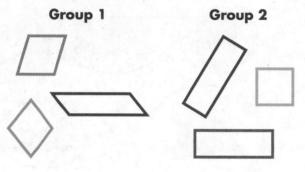

**A.** How are the two groups alike?

**B.** How are the two groups different?

**9.** Which statement must be true about a rectangle?

Ⓐ It is a parallelogram.

Ⓑ It is a square.

Ⓒ It is a trapezoid.

Ⓓ It is a rhombus.

**10.** Is a square always a rhombus? Explain.

**11.** Name and draw a quadrilateral that is **NOT** a rectangle or rhombus. Is there another shape you could have drawn? Explain.

Name_____

## Pet Tags

Amelia and Bryce work at a pet store that sells pet identification tags in many shapes. The **Pet Tags** diagram shows the different shapes available.

Use the **Pet Tags** art to answer Questions **1–4**.

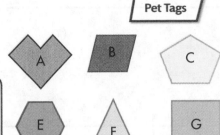

1. A customer asks Amelia if the store has any pet tags that are concave. How should Amelia respond?

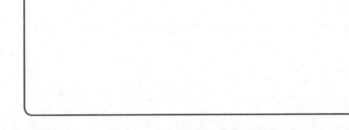

2. Another customer asks Bryce which pet tags have 2 pairs of equal-length sides and are quadrilaterals. Which tags have these attributes? Include the common name of each shape.

3. The store owner wants to mark for sale any pet tags that are not rectangles. Which tags should she mark for sale, and what shapes are they?

4. The owner asks Bryce to group the tags to show which ones have at least 1 pair of equal-length sides. Complete the table with the pet tag labels.

| Equal Sides | No Equal Sides |
|---|---|
|  |  |

5. Use the **Pet Tags** diagram and the **Tag Sort** table to answer the questions in Part A and Part B.

Amelia sorts some of the pet tags into two different groups.

| Tag Sort | |
| --- | --- |
| **Group 1** | **Group 2** |
| B, G, D, H | A, C, E, F |

**Part A**

How are the groups different?

**Part B**

How are the groups alike?

Use the **Pet Tags** diagram to answer Questions **6** and **7**.

6. A customer says she wants to buy the pet tag that is a rhombus and a rectangle. What tag does she want? Explain.

7. Design a new pet tag that has 2 pairs of sides the same length, but that is not a rectangle or a rhombus. Explain the shape you drew.

# Solve Perimeter Problems

**Essential Question:** How can perimeter be measured and found?

Digital Resources

Interactive Student Edition · Activity · Visual Learning · Video · Practice

Assessment · Games · Tools · Glossary

Animals live in a habitat.

Some animals can only live in certain habitats.

Lots of animals live here! Here is a project on habitats and perimeter.

## enVision STEM Project: What Lives Here?

**Do Research** Use the Internet or other sources to research habitats. Include a list of animals that can survive in a certain habitat and some that could not survive there.

**Journal: Write a Report** Include what you found. Also in your report:

- Draw a picture on grid paper to represent one of the habitats you researched. Label the habitat to show what you might find there. Count the number of square units or the area the habitat measures.

- Find the perimeter of the habitat. Then find another possible perimeter with the same area.

Name_____

# Review What You Know

## Area of Figures

Find the area for each figure. Use grid paper to help.

4.
4 in.
7 in.

5.
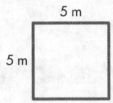
5 m
5 m

6. The area of a rectangle is 32 square centimeters. The rectangle is 4 centimeters wide. How long is the rectangle?

Ⓐ 4 centimeters   Ⓑ 8 centimeters   Ⓒ 16 centimeters   Ⓓ 32 centimeters

## Area of Irregular Shapes

7. What is the area of the figure at the right? Explain how you solved this problem.

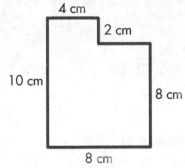
4 cm
2 cm
10 cm
8 cm
8 cm

## Dividing Regions into Equal Parts

8. Circle the shapes that show equal parts. For those shapes, label one of the parts using a unit fraction.

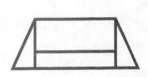

Name_____

**PROJECT 16A**

### Where is sugar cane grown?

**Project:** Design a Sugarcane Field

**PROJECT 16B**

### What does an interior designer do?

**Project:** Collect Data on Common Objects

## PROJECT 16C

### What does a builder actually build?

**Project:** Create a Perimeter Game

## PROJECT 16D

### Why is it helpful to have a reservation at a restaurant?

**Project:** Create a Poster for a Restaurant Seating Chart

Name_____

## Solve & Share

Troy made a drawing of his garden. Each square in the grid below has a side length of 1 foot. Find the distance around Troy's garden. Then use grid paper to draw a different garden shape that has the same distance around.

**I can ...**
find the perimeter of different polygons.

ⓒ **Content Standard** 3.MD.D.8
**Mathematical Practices** MP.2, MP.4, MP.6

Be precise when finding the total distance. You know the length of each side of the garden.

**Look Back!** Use words, numbers, and symbols to explain how you found the distance around Troy's garden.

**A**

Gus wants to put up a fence to make a dog park. He made two different designs. What is the perimeter of each dog park design? Which design should Gus use?

scale: ⊢ = 1 ft

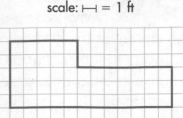

The distance around a figure is its perimeter.

3 ft · 6 ft · 7 ft · 9 ft · 3 ft

The perimeter of the dog park needs to be at least 30 feet.

**B** **One Way**

You can find the perimeter by counting unit segments.

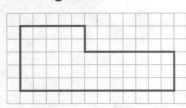

scale: ⊢ = 1 ft

The perimeter is 34 feet.
34 > 30. Gus could use this design.

**C** **Another Way**

Add the lengths of the sides to find the perimeter.

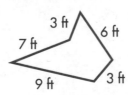

3 ft · 6 ft · 7 ft · 9 ft · 3 ft

3 + 9 + 7 + 3 + 6 = 28
The perimeter is 28 feet.
28 < 30. Gus could not use this design.

**Convince Me!** **Model with Math** Draw a different dog park design that Gus could use. Find the perimeter of your design.

Name_____

# ☆Guided Practice

## Do You Understand?

**1.** What is the perimeter of the garden shown in the diagram below?

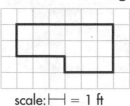

scale: ⊢⊣ = 1 ft

**2.** In Exercise **1**, how do you know what unit to use for the perimeter?

## Do You Know How?

In **3** and **4**, find the perimeter.

**3.**

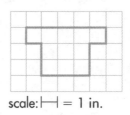

scale: ⊢⊣ = 1 in.

**4.**

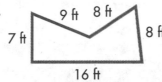

9 ft   8 ft
7 ft              8 ft
16 ft

# Independent Practice ☆

**Leveled Practice** In **5–7**, find the perimeter of each polygon.

**5.**

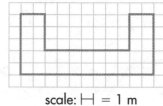

scale: ⊢⊣ = 1 m

**6.**

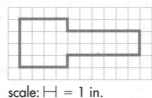

scale: ⊢⊣ = 1 in.

**7.**

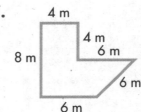

4 m
4 m
8 m      6 m
         6 m
6 m

**8.** On the grid below, draw a figure with a perimeter of 20 units.

You can draw many different shapes that have the same perimeter.

# Problem Solving

**9.** Niko makes beaded necklaces in three different sizes. How many more beads does it take to make 2 medium necklaces than 1 large necklace? Write equations to solve.

| Size of Necklace | Number of Beads |
|---|---|
| Small | 68 |
| Medium | 129 |
| Large | 212 |

**10.** Jani put this sticker on his notebook. What is the perimeter of the sticker?

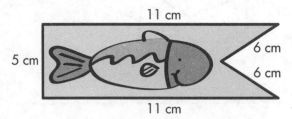

11 cm

5 cm

6 cm

6 cm

11 cm

**11. Reasoning** What is the perimeter of the shape below?

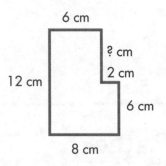

6 cm

? cm

2 cm

12 cm

6 cm

8 cm

**12. Number Sense** Jenny needs 425 cubes. There are 275 cubes in a large bag. There are 175 cubes in a small bag. Will one large bag and one small bag together have enough cubes? Explain.

**13. Higher Order Thinking** The perimeter of this trapezoid is 40 inches. What is the length of the missing side?

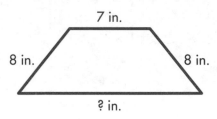

7 in.

8 in.        8 in.

? in.

**14.** Mr. Karas needs to find the perimeter of the patio shown at the right. What is the perimeter of the patio?

Ⓐ   48 yards

Ⓑ   50 yards

Ⓒ   52 yards

Ⓓ   54 yards

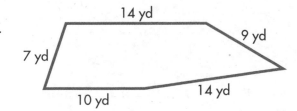

14 yd

9 yd

7 yd

10 yd

14 yd

Activity

## Solve & Share

What is the perimeter of the rectangle below? Show two ways to find the perimeter, other than measuring.

**I can ...**
find the perimeter of polygons with common shapes.

© **Content Standards** 3.MD.D.8 Also 3.OA.A.3, 3.OA.C.7
**Mathematical Practices** MP.1, MP.3, MP.7

You can use structure. How could what you know about the attributes of common shapes help you find the perimeter?

5 in.

3 in.

**Look Back!** How could you use addition and multiplication to find the perimeter?

Visual Learning  A-Z Glossary

**Essential Question** **How Can You Find the Perimeters of Common Shapes?**

Visual Learning Bridge

**A**

*Mr. Coe needs to find the perimeter of two swimming pool designs. One pool shape is a rectangle. The other pool shape is a square. What is the perimeter of each pool?*

6 m

10 m

9 m

---

**B** Find the perimeter of the pool that has a rectangular shape.

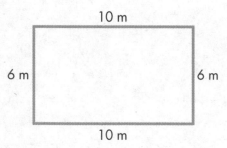
10 m
6 m        6 m
10 m

$10 + 6 + 10 + 6 = 32$ or
$(10 \times 2) + (6 \times 2) = 32$
The perimeter of this pool is 32 meters.

 Remember, opposite sides of a rectangle are the same length.

**C** Find the perimeter of the pool that has a square shape.

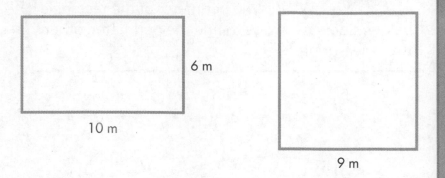 Remember, all four sides of a square are the same length.

9 m
9 m        9 m
9 m

$9 + 9 + 9 + 9 = 36$ or $4 \times 9 = 36$
The perimeter of this pool is 36 meters.

---

**Convince Me!** **Make Sense and Persevere** Darla drew the parallelogram at the right. Write equations that show how to find the perimeter.

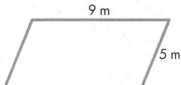
9 m
5 m

---

**Another Example!**

An **equilateral triangle** has 3 sides that are the same length.

$4 + 4 + 4 = 12$ or $3 \times 4 = 12$.

So, the perimeter of this equilateral triangle is 12 inches.

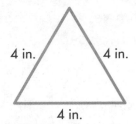

4 in.        4 in.

4 in.

## ☆Guided Practice

### Do You Understand?

1. How can you use multiplication and addition to find the perimeter of a rectangle with a length of 6 feet and width of 4 feet?

2. Explain how you can find the perimeter of a square with a side length of 7 cm.

### Do You Know How?

For **3** and **4**, find the perimeter.

3. Rectangle

4 ft

8 ft

4. Square

5 cm

## Independent Practice ☆

In **5–7**, find the perimeter of each polygon.

5. Square

6 in.

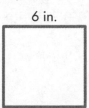

6. Rectangle

12 cm

6 cm

7. Equilateral triangle

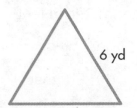

6 yd

# Problem Solving

In **8** and **9**, use the picture at the right.

8. The base of the glass house to the right is a rectangle. What is the perimeter of the base of the house?

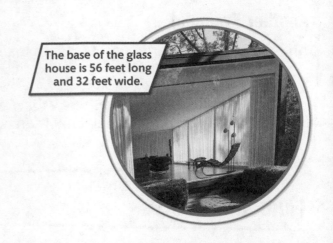

The base of the glass house is 56 feet long and 32 feet wide.

9. The owner of the house decides to build an extension. The new base is 112 feet long and 64 feet wide. What is the new perimeter?

---

10. Identify the number of sides and vertices in the hexagon below.

11. **Critique Reasoning** Mark says he can find the perimeter of a square zoo enclosure by multiplying the length of one side by 4. Is Mark correct? Why or why not?

---

12. **Higher Order Thinking** Dan drew the trapezoid at the right. The top is 3 inches long. The bottom is twice as long as the top. The length of each side is 5 inches. How can you find the perimeter of the trapezoid? Label the lengths of the sides.

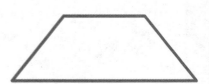

---

13. Mikayla draws a rectangle with side lengths of 4 feet and 8 feet. What is the perimeter, in feet, of Mikayla's rectangle?

Ⓐ 12 feet

Ⓑ 16 feet

Ⓒ 20 feet

Ⓓ 24 feet

14. Emma draws an equilateral triangle with side lengths of 5 inches each. What is the perimeter, in inches, of Emma's triangle?

Ⓐ 5 inches

Ⓑ 10 inches

Ⓒ 15 inches

Ⓓ 20 inches

Name_____

☆ ☆
**Solve & Share**

Jon has 16 feet of wood that he uses to make a sandbox that has 4 sides. He makes sides with lengths of 6 feet, 5 feet, and 3 feet. What length should he make the fourth side to use all 16 feet of the wood?

**I can ...**
find the unknown length of a polygon by using a known perimeter.

© **Content Standards** 3.MD.D.8 Also 3.OA.D.8, 3.NBT.A.2
**Mathematical Practices** MP.1, MP.2, MP.7

Use reasoning to show how the perimeter and given side lengths are related.

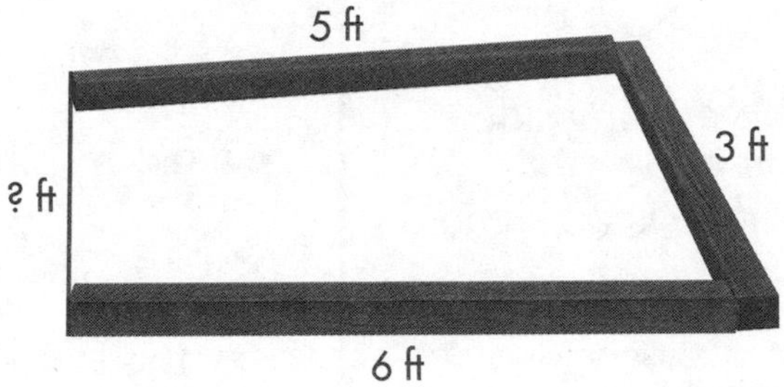

5 ft

3 ft

? ft

6 ft

**Look Back!** Describe the plan you used to solve the problem.

**Essential Question**

# How Can You Find an Unknown Side Length from the Perimeter?

**A**

Lilia is making a decoration out of straws and cloth, with lace around the outside. How long should she cut the fourth straw to use all of the lace?

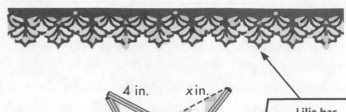

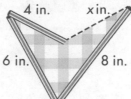

4 in.  x in.

6 in.  8 in.

Lilia has 22 inches of lace

Lilia needs to find the length that will give the shape a perimeter of 22 inches.

**B**

Draw a bar diagram and write an equation.

Let $x$ = the length of the missing side.

The perimeter of the shape is 22 inches.

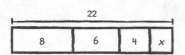

| | 22 | | |
|---|---|---|---|
| 8 | 6 | 4 | x |

$8 + 6 + 4 + x = 22$

$18 + x = 22$

**C**

Solve.

$18 + x = 22$

Think: 18 plus what equals 22?

$18 + 4 = 22$, so $x = 4$.

So, the fourth side should be 4 inches long.

You can also use subtraction to find $22 - 18 = 4$.

---

**Convince Me!** **Look for Relationships** If Lilia had 25 inches of lace, how would the length of the fourth straw change? Explain how to solve.

##  Guided Practice

### Do You Understand?

**1.** In the problem on the previous page, why does $x + 8 + 6 + 4$ equal the perimeter, 22 inches?

**2.** Write an equation you could use to find the length of the missing side of this triangle with a perimeter of 23 cm. Then solve.

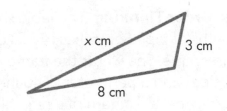

x cm

3 cm

8 cm

### Do You Know How?

In **3** and **4**, find the length of the missing side for each polygon so it has the perimeter given.

**3.** perimeter = 30 cm

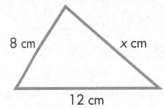

8 cm          x cm

12 cm

**4.** perimeter = 25 ft

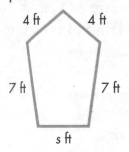

4 ft     4 ft

7 ft          7 ft

s ft

##  Independent Practice

In **5–10**, find the length of the missing side for each polygon so it has the perimeter given.

**5.** perimeter = 24 in.

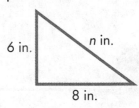

6 in.     n in.

8 in.

**6.** perimeter = 30 m

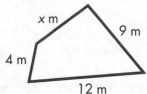

x m

9 m

4 m

12 m

**7.** perimeter = 37 yd

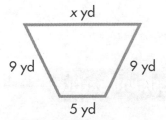

x yd

9 yd          9 yd

5 yd

**8.** perimeter = 37 cm

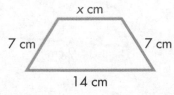

x cm

7 cm          7 cm

14 cm

**9.** perimeter = 18 ft

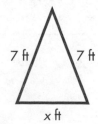

7 ft     7 ft

x ft

**10.** perimeter = 32 in.

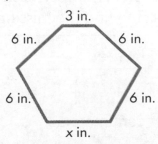

3 in.

6 in.          6 in.

6 in.          6 in.

x in.

# Problem Solving

11. These plane figures each have equal sides that are whole numbers. One figure has a perimeter of 25 inches. Which could it be? Explain.

12. **enVision® STEM** Letitia gave one garden 40 liters of water each day. She gave another garden 80 liters of water each day. How much more water did the second garden get in one week?

13. **Make Sense and Persevere** Mason has 18 feet of wood to frame a rectangular window. He wants the window to be 3 feet wide. What should be the length? Show how you know your answer is correct.

14. The floor of Novak's room is shown below. It has a perimeter of 52 feet. Write an equation to find the missing side length in Novak's room.

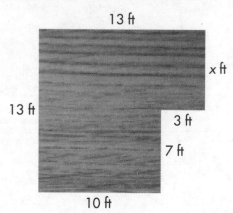

13 ft

x ft

13 ft

3 ft

7 ft

10 ft

15. **Higher Order Thinking** The table shows the lengths of pipe Sonya has to make a picture frame. She wants the frame to have 5 sides and a perimeter of 40 inches. Draw and label a diagram of a possible picture frame Sonya could make.

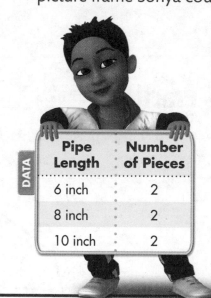

| | Pipe Length | Number of Pieces |
|---|---|---|
| DATA | 6 inch | 2 |
| | 8 inch | 2 |
| | 10 inch | 2 |

✓ **Assessment Practice**

16. Mark draws the quadrilateral at the right with a perimeter of 28 cm. Select numbers from the box to write and solve an equation to find the missing side length.

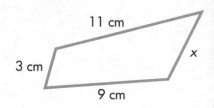

11 cm

3 cm

x

9 cm

| 0 | 1 | 2 | 3 | 4 | 5 | 6 | 7 | 8 | 9 |

$x + \boxed{\phantom{0}}\boxed{\phantom{0}} + \boxed{\phantom{0}} + \boxed{\phantom{0}} = \boxed{\phantom{0}}\boxed{\phantom{0}}$

$x = \boxed{\phantom{0}}$ centimeters

Name _____

☆ ☆
**Solve & Share**

Draw 2 different rectangles with a perimeter of 10 units. Find the area of each rectangle. Compare the areas.

**I can ...**
understand the relationship of shapes with the same perimeter and different areas.

Be precise when drawing and finding the perimeter and area. Think about how perimeter and area are measured and recorded.

© **Content Standards** 3.MD.D.8 Also 3.OA.C.7, 3.MD.C.7b
**Mathematical Practices** MP.6, MP.8

**Look Back!** Explain why the rectangles have different areas.

**Essential Question** **Can Rectangles Have Different Areas but the Same Perimeter?**

**A**

Beth, Nancy, and Marcia build rectangular pens for their rabbits. Each pen has a perimeter of 12 feet. Which rectangular pen has the greatest area?

*Drawings help you see how the rectangles are similar and different.*

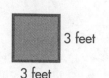 1 foot / 5 feet

 2 feet / 4 feet

3 feet / 3 feet

**B** **Beth's Plan**

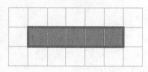

Find the perimeter:
$P = 5 + 1 + 5 + 1 = 12$ feet

To find the area, multiply the number of rows by the number of square units in each row.

$A = 1 \times 5 = 5$ square feet

Beth's pen has an area of 5 square feet.

**C** **Nancy's Plan**

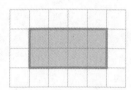

Find the perimeter:
$P = 4 + 2 + 4 + 2 = 12$ feet

Find the area:
$A = 2 \times 4 = 8$ square feet

Nancy's pen has an area of 8 square feet.

**D** **Marcia's Plan**

Find the perimeter:
$P = 3 + 3 + 3 + 3 = 12$ feet

Find the area:
$A = 3 \times 3 = 9$ square feet

Marcia's pen has an area of 9 square feet.

Marcia's pen has the greatest area.

**Convince Me!** **Generalize** Find possible rectangular pens that have a perimeter of 14 feet. Do they have the same area? What can you generalize from this information?

Name _____

# ☆ Guided Practice

## Do You Understand?

**1.** In the plans on the previous page, what do you notice about the area of the rectangles as the shape becomes more like a square?

**2.** Austin is building a rabbit pen with 25 feet of fence. What are the dimensions of the rectangle he should build to have the greatest possible area?

## Do You Know How?

In **3–6**, use grid paper to draw two different rectangles with the given perimeter. Write the dimensions and area of each rectangle. Circle the rectangle that has the greater area.

**3.** 16 feet

**4.** 20 centimeters

**5.** 24 inches

**6.** 40 meters

# ☆ Independent Practice ☆

In **7–10**, use grid paper to draw two different rectangles with the given perimeter. Write the dimensions and area of each rectangle. Circle the rectangle that has the greater area.

**7.** 10 inches

**8.** 22 centimeters

**9.** 26 yards

**10.** 32 feet

**Leveled Practice**  In **11–14**, write the dimensions of a different rectangle with the same perimeter as the rectangle shown. Then tell which rectangle has the greater area.

**11.**
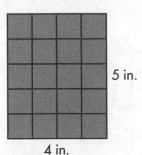
5 in.

4 in.

**12.**
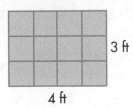
3 ft

4 ft

**13.**
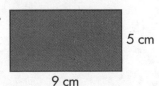
5 cm

9 cm

**14.**
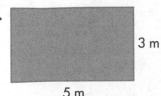
3 m

5 m

# Problem Solving

**15. Generalize** Trish is breaking ground for a rose garden in her backyard. The garden will be a square with a side of 7 meters. What will be the area of the rose garden?

**16.** Karen drew a rectangle with a perimeter of 20 inches. The smaller side measured 3 inches. Karen said the longer side of the rectangle had to be 7 inches. Is she correct?

**17. Higher Order Thinking** Rectangles X and Y have the same perimeter. Without measuring or multiplying, how can you know which rectangle has the greater area?

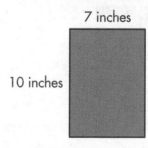

**18. Algebra** Marcus made the same number of free throws in each of 4 basketball games. Each free throw is worth 1 point. If he made a total of 24 free throws, how many did he make in each game? How many free throw points did he score in each game?

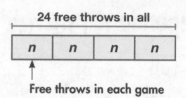
24 free throws in all

Free throws in each game

## Assessment Practice

**19.** Bella draws two rectangles. Select all the statements that are true about Bella's rectangles.

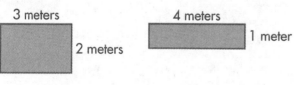
3 meters
2 meters

4 meters
1 meter

☐ They have the same side lengths.

☐ They have different side lengths.

☐ They have the same perimeter.

☐ They have a different area.

☐ They have the same area.

**20.** Select all the equations that can be used to find the area of the rectangle.

7 inches
10 inches

☐ $10 \times 7 = a$

☐ $(5 \times 7) + (5 \times 7) = a$

☐ $a = 10 \times 7$

☐ $7 \times 7 = a$

☐ $10 \times 10 = a$

Name _____

Activity

☆ **Solve & Share** ☆

Jessica has 12 square tiles that she wants to use to make rectangles. Find 3 different rectangles she can make using all 12 square tiles in each of the rectangles. Include the area and perimeter of each rectangle. Then compare the areas and perimeters.

**I can ...**
understand the relationship of shapes with the same area and different perimeters.

© **Content Standards** 3.MD.D.8 Also 3.OA.C.7, 3.MD.C.7b
**Mathematical Practices** MP.2, MP.3, MP.5

You can select appropriate tools, such as grid paper or cut-out squares, and use them to help solve the problem.

**Look Back!** How does the shape of each of the rectangles affect the perimeter?

**Essential Question** **Can Rectangles Have the Same Areas but Different Perimeters?**

**A**

In a video game, you have 16 castle tiles to make a rectangular castle, and 16 water tiles for a moat. How can you completely surround the castle with water?

16 castle tiles

Make rectangles that have an area of 16 square units. Find the perimeter of each rectangle.

16 water tiles

The castle tiles represent the area and the water tiles represent the perimeter.

**B**

Find the area:
$A = 1 \times 16$
$= 16$ square units

Find the perimeter:
$P = (2 \times 16) + (2 \times 1)$
$= 32 + 2$
$= 34$ units

**C**

Find the area:
$A = 2 \times 8$
$= 16$ square units

Find the perimeter:
$P = (2 \times 8) + (2 \times 2)$
$= 16 + 4$
$= 20$ units

**D**

Find the area:
$A = 4 \times 4$
$= 16$ square units

Find the perimeter:
$P = (2 \times 4) + (2 \times 4)$
$= 8 + 8$
$= 16$ units

Only the $4 \times 4$ castle can be surrounded by 16 water tiles.

**Convince Me!** **Critique Reasoning** Izzie says that if the number of castle tiles increases to 25, it is possible to use exactly 25 water tiles to surround the castle. Do you agree or disagree? Why?

☆ **Guided Practice**

**Do You Understand?**

1. In the example on the previous page, what do you notice about the perimeter of the rectangles as the shape becomes more like a square?

2. In Round 2 of the video puzzle game, you have 24 castle tiles. What is the least number of water tiles you will need to surround your castle?

**Do You Know How?**

In **3–6**, use grid paper to draw two different rectangles with the given area. Write the dimensions and perimeter of each rectangle, and tell which rectangle has the smaller perimeter.

3. 6 square feet

4. 36 square yards

5. 64 square meters

6. 80 square inches

☆ **Independent Practice** ☆

In **7–10**, use grid paper to draw two different rectangles with the given area. Write the dimensions and perimeter of each rectangle. Circle the rectangle that has the smaller perimeter.

7. 9 square inches

8. 18 square feet

9. 30 square meters

10. 32 square centimeters

**Leveled Practice** In **11–14**, write the dimensions of a different rectangle with the same area as the rectangle shown. Then tell which rectangle has the smaller perimeter.

11.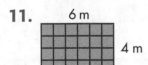
6 m
4 m

12.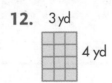
3 yd
4 yd

13.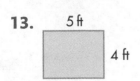
5 ft
4 ft

14.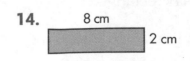
8 cm
2 cm

# Problem Solving

**15.** Sue bought 2 sweaters for $18 each and a pair of mittens for $11. About how much money did she spend? About how much did she get in change if she paid with 3 twenty-dollar bills?

**16. Reasoning** The perimeter of a rectangle is 12 feet. The perimeter of another rectangle is 18 feet. Both rectangles have the same area. Find the area and the dimensions of each rectangle.

**17. Higher Order Thinking** Park School and North School cover the same area. In physical education classes, each student runs one lap around the school. At which school do the students have to run farther? How do you know?

Park School    North School

**18.** Ms. Fisher is using 64 carpet squares to make a reading area in her classroom. Each square measures 1 foot by 1 foot. She wants to arrange the 64 squares in a rectangular shape with the smallest possible perimeter. What dimensions should she use for her reading area?

**19.** Bella is putting down patches of sod to start a new lawn. She has 20 square yards of sod. Give the dimensions of two different rectangular regions that she can cover with the sod. What is the perimeter of each region?

## ✓ Assessment Practice

**20.** Lakisha draws two rectangles. Which statement is true about Lakisha's rectangles?

Ⓐ They have the same dimensions.

Ⓑ They have the same shape.

Ⓒ They have the same perimeter.

Ⓓ They have the same area.

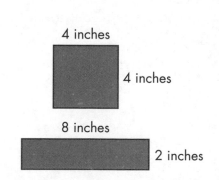

4 inches

4 inches

8 inches

2 inches

Name _____

☆ ☆
**Solve & Share**

Suppose you want to cut a piece of webbing to make a strap to wrap around your math book. Measure the width and height of your book, then use those dimensions to find a possible length for the strap. Be sure to include extra webbing for a buckle. Use reasoning to decide.

**I can ...**
understand the relationship between numbers to simplify and solve problems involving perimeter.

© **Mathematical Practices** MP.2 Also MP.1, MP.3, MP.6
**Content Standard** 3.MD.D.8

### Thinking Habits

*Be a good thinker!*
*These questions can help you.*

• What do the numbers and symbols in the problem mean?

• How are the numbers or quantities related?

• How can I represent a word problem using pictures, numbers, or equations?

**Look Back!** **Reasoning** Explain how to solve the problem using a different unit. Does the length you found need to change?

**Essential Question**

# How Can You Use Reasoning to Solve Problems?

**A**

*Anna is setting up 3 of these tables end-to-end in a long row for a party. Each person sitting at a table needs a space that is 2 feet wide.*

*How can Anna find out how many people can be seated at the tables? Use reasoning to decide.*

You can draw a picture to help with your reasoning.

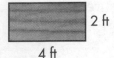
4 ft | 2 ft

**What do I need to do to solve this problem?**

I need to use the information I know to find the number of people that can sit at 3 tables.

**B** **How can I use reasoning to solve this problem?**

**I can**

- identify the quantities I know.

- draw a picture to show relationships.

- give the answer using the correct unit.

**C**

Here's my thinking...

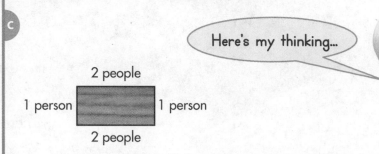

2 + 1 + 2 + 1 = 6. I know 6 people can sit at 1 table.

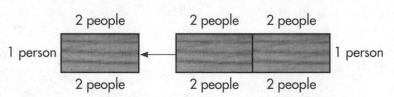

For 3 tables, the number of people at the ends stays the same. There are 4 more people at each side. 6 + 1 + 6 + 1 = 14. I know 14 people can sit at 3 tables.

**Convince Me!** **Reasoning** Anna decides to turn the tables sideways. Now they are joined along the longer sides. How does this change the number of people who can be seated? You can use a picture to help.

Name _____

# ☆ Guided Practice

**Reasoning**

Corrine has 3 triangular tables with sides that are the same length. She wants to know how many people she can seat if she puts the tables together side to side in a row. Each person needs a space of 2 feet. How many people can be seated?

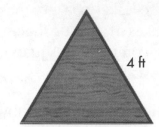

4 ft

**1.** Describe the quantities given.

**2.** Solve the problem and explain your reasoning. You can use a picture to help.

# ☆ Independent Practice ☆

**Reasoning**

Tito has 3 trapezoid blocks. He wants to find the perimeter of the blocks when he places them together side to side in a row.

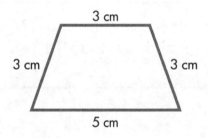
3 cm
3 cm     3 cm
5 cm

Use reasoning by thinking about how the numbers in the problem change.

**3.** Describe the quantities given.

**4.** Solve the problem and explain your reasoning. You can use a picture to help.

# Problem Solving

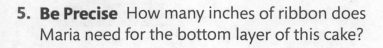

**A Wedding Cake**
The Cakery Bakery makes tiered wedding cakes in various shapes. Maria buys ribbon to decorate three squares of a cake. The ribbon costs 50¢ a foot.

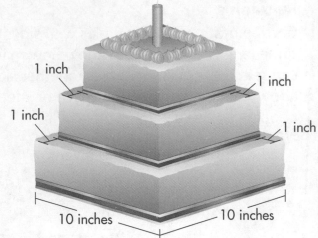

1 inch
1 inch
1 inch
1 inch
10 inches
10 inches

5. **Be Precise** How many inches of ribbon does Maria need for the bottom layer of this cake?

6. **Make Sense and Persevere** How long is a side of the middle layer? Explain how you know your answer makes sense.

7. **Reasoning** How many inches of ribbon does Maria need for the middle layer and top layer? Use reasoning to decide.

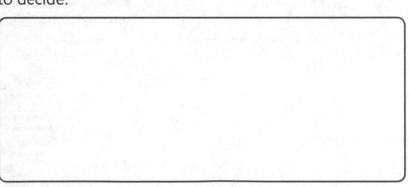

Drawing a diagram can help your reasoning when solving a problem.

8. **Critique Reasoning** Maria says that if she buys 100 inches of ribbon she will have enough ribbon for all 3 layers. Grace says Maria needs more than 100 inches of ribbon. Who is correct? Explain.

**Find a Match**

Work with a partner. Point to a clue. Read the clue.

Look below the clues to find a match. Write the clue letter in the box next to the match.

Find a match for every clue.

**Fluency Practice Activity**

**I can ...**
add and subtract within 1,000.

**Content Standard** 3.NBT.A.2
**Mathematical Practices** MP.3, MP.6, MP.7, MP.8

**Clues**

**A** The missing number is 725.

**E** The missing number is 381.

**B** The missing number is 898.

**F** The missing number is 83.

**C** The missing number is 580.

**G** The missing number is 750.

**D** The missing number is 419.

**H** The missing number is 546.

|  |  | (B) |  |
|---|---|---|---|
| $\_\_ + 219 = 969$ | $529 - 148 = \_\_$ | $642 + 256 = \_\_$ | $878 - \_\_ = 332$ |
|  |  |  |  |
| $850 - \_\_ = 125$ | $\_\_ + 511 = 930$ | $910 - 827 = \_\_$ | $399 + 181 = \_\_$ |

# Vocabulary Review

Glossary

## Word List

- area
- equation
- multiplication
- perimeter
- rectangle
- square
- square unit

## Understand Vocabulary

Write T for *true* or F for *false*.

**1.** _____ To find the *area* of a *square*, you can multiply the side length by 4.

**2.** _____ *Perimeter* is measured in *square units*.

**3.** _____ You can use a subtraction or a *multiplication equation* to find the *area* of a *rectangle*.

**4.** _____ A *rectangle* with a width of 6 inches and a length of 8 inches has a *perimeter* of 28 inches.

**5.** _____ A *square* with a side length of 5 meters has an *area* of 20 square meters.

In **6–8**, tell if each equation shows a way to find the *area* or *perimeter* of the shape.

**6.**

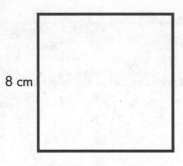

8 cm

$8 \times 4 = ?$

_____

**7.**

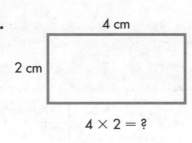

4 cm

2 cm

$4 \times 2 = ?$

_____

**8.**

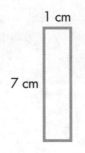

1 cm

7 cm

$7 + 7 + 1 + 1 = ?$

_____

## Use Vocabulary in Writing

**9.** Compare the perimeter and area of each figure. Use at least 2 terms from the Word List in your answer.

**Figure A**      **Figure B**

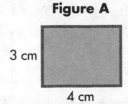

3 cm

4 cm

1 cm

6 cm

Name _____

**Set A** | pages 613–620

You can find the perimeter by counting unit segments.

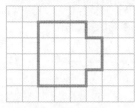

⊢⊣ = 1 cm

The perimeter of this shape is 16 centimeters.

You can find the perimeter of a shape by adding the lengths of the sides.

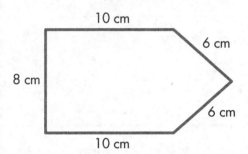

10 cm
6 cm
8 cm
6 cm
10 cm

$10 + 10 + 8 + 6 + 6 = 40$
The perimeter of this shape is 40 centimeters.

**Reteaching**

**Remember** that the distance around a figure is its perimeter.

In **1–3**, find the perimeter of each figure.

**1.**

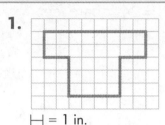

⊢⊣ = 1 in.

**2.**

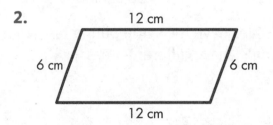

12 cm
6 cm        6 cm
12 cm

**3.**

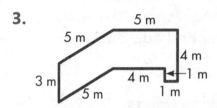

5 m
5 m          4 m
3 m      4 m  ⊢1 m
5 m      1 m

**Set B** | pages 621–624

If you know the perimeter, you can find the length of a missing side. What is the missing side length of this polygon?

perimeter = 21 yd

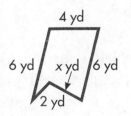

4 yd
6 yd  x yd  6 yd
2 yd

$x + 2 + 6 + 4 + 6 = 21$

$x + 18 = 21$

$3 + 18 = 21$ so $x = 3$

The missing side is 3 yards long.

**Remember** that to find the missing side length, you need to find the sum of the known sides.

Find the missing side length.

**1.** perimeter = 35 cm

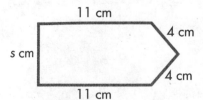

11 cm
4 cm
s cm
4 cm
11 cm

Find the perimeter and area of these rectangles.

8 ft

3 ft

$P = (2 \times 3) + (2 \times 8)$    $A = 8 \times 3$
   $= 22$ feet            $= 24$ square feet

7 ft

4 ft

$P = (2 \times 4) + (2 \times 7)$    $A = 7 \times 4$
   $= 22$ feet            $= 28$ square feet

The rectangles have the same perimeter. The rectangles have different areas.

**Remember** that two rectangles can have the same perimeter but different areas, or the same area but different perimeters.

Draw two different rectangles with the perimeter listed. Find the area of each rectangle.

**1.** $P = 24$ feet

Draw two different rectangles with the area listed. Find the perimeter of each rectangle.

**2.** $A = 64$ square inches

Think about these questions to help you **reason abstractly and quantitatively**.

**Thinking Habits**

- What do the numbers and symbols in the problem mean?

- How are the numbers or quantities related?

- How can I represent a word problem using pictures, numbers, or equations?

**Remember** to think about how the quantities in the problem are related. You can use a picture to show relationships.

Julian has 5 triangle blocks with sides that are the same length. What is the perimeter of the blocks if Julian places them together side to side?

2 in.

**1.** Describe the quantities given.

**2.** Solve the problem and explain your reasoning. You can use a picture to help.

**1.** Tori is making a square table. Each side is 6 feet long. Is the perimeter of the table the same as the area of the table? Explain.

**2.** Robert's tile design is shown below.

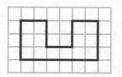

Draw another tile design that has the same area but a different perimeter from Robert's design.

**3.** Della drew a rectangle with a perimeter of 34 centimeters. She labeled one side 7 centimeters, but she forgot to label the other side. Write the missing side length in the box.

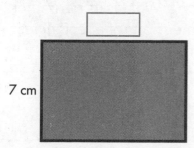

7 cm

**4.** Mrs. Gee has 24 carpet squares. How should she arrange them so that she has the smallest perimeter?

Ⓐ 12 by 2 rectangle

Ⓑ 1 by 24 rectangle

Ⓒ 8 by 3 rectangle

Ⓓ 4 by 6 rectangle

**5.** Al's playground design is below.

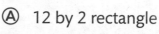

Which of the following shapes has a different area but the same perimeter as Al's design?

Ⓐ
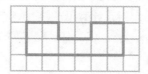

Ⓑ

Ⓒ

Ⓓ

**6.** The perimeter of the sign is 24 feet. What is the missing side length?

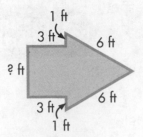

1 ft
3 ft
6 ft
? ft
3 ft
6 ft
1 ft

Ⓐ 4 feet     Ⓒ 6 feet

Ⓑ 5 feet     Ⓓ 7 feet

**7.** Ms. Kent measures the perimeter of a common shape. One of the sides is 7 centimeters, and the perimeter is 21 centimeters. If all of the sides are the same length, what shape does Ms. Kent measure? Explain.

**8.** Kyle drew two shapes. Select all of the statements that are true about the shapes.

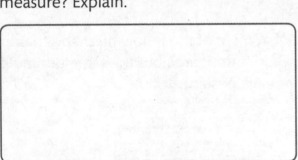

4 cm        8 cm    2 cm

☐ The shapes have different perimeters.

☐ The shapes have the same perimeter.

☐ The shapes have different areas.

☐ The shapes have the same area.

☐ The square has a greater area than the rectangle.

**9.** Mandy's trapezoid-shaped garden has a perimeter of 42 feet. She knows the length of three sides: 8 feet, 8 feet, and 16 feet. What is the length of the fourth side?

**10.** Pepper's dog pen is shown below.

6 m

4 m

**A.** Find the perimeter and area of the dog pen.

**B.** Could a square with whole-number side lengths have the same perimeter as the dog pen? The same area? Explain.

**11.** A square picture frame has sides 24 inches long. What is its perimeter? Find the dimensions of a rectangle whose perimeter is less.

Name_____

## Park Planning

Mrs. Martinez is planning a new park. Three possible designs are shown below. There will be a path along each side of the park.

**Design A**

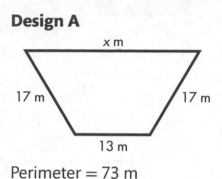

Perimeter = 73 m

**Design B**

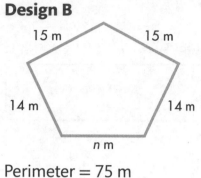

Perimeter = 75 m

**Design C**

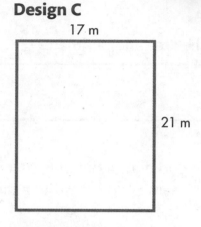

Use **Design A**, **Design B**, and **Design C** figures to answer Questions **1–3**.

1. For Design A, how long will the path be for the missing side length?

2. For Design B, how long will the path be for the missing side length?

3. Mrs. Martinez chooses the design with the greatest perimeter.

   **Part A**

   What is the perimeter of Design C? Explain.

   **Part B**

   Which design did Mrs. Martinez choose?

Use the **Sandbox Design** figure to answer Question **4**.

**Sandbox Design**

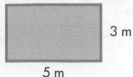

3 m

5 m

4. The park will have a sandbox.
   One design is shown at the right.

   **Part A**

   Find the area and perimeter of the sandbox design.

   ┌─────────────────────────────────────────────┐
   │                                             │
   │                                             │
   └─────────────────────────────────────────────┘

   **Part B**

   On the grid draw a different rectangular sandbox design
   with the same perimeter but a different area. Circle the figure
   that has the greater area.

Use the **South Pond** figure to answer Question **5**.

**South Pond**

4 m

3 m

5. There will be two ponds in the park.
   Each pond will be a rectangle.

   **Part A**

   Find the area and perimeter of the south pond.

   ┌─────────────────────────────────────────────┐
   │                                             │
   │                                             │
   │                                             │
   └─────────────────────────────────────────────┘

   **Part B**

   The north pond has the same area but a different perimeter.
   Draw a figure for the north pond.
   Circle the figure that has the greater perimeter.

**North Pond**

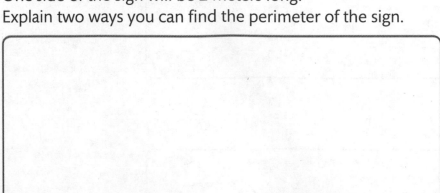

6. The park will have a sign in the shape of a square.
   One side of the sign will be 2 meters long.
   Explain two ways you can find the perimeter of the sign.

   ┌─────────────────────────────────────────────┐
   │                                             │
   │                                             │
   │                                             │
   │                                             │
   │                                             │
   │                                             │
   └─────────────────────────────────────────────┘

# enVision® Mathematics
## Common Core

## Photographs

Every effort has been made to secure permission and provide appropriate credit for photographic material. The publisher deeply regrets any omission and pledges to correct errors called to its attention in subsequent editions.

Unless otherwise acknowledged, all photographs are the property of Savvas Learning Company LLC.

Photo locators denoted as follows: Top (T), Center (C), Bottom (B), Left (L), Right (R), Background (Bkgd)

**1** Gemenacom/Shutterstock; **3** (T) Pisaphotography/ Shutterstock, (C) NASA images/Shutterstock, (B) Tetra Images/Alamy Stock Photo; **4** (Bkgrd) Boris Bulychev/ Shutterstock, ArtCookStudio/Shutterstock **37** Jacek Chabraszewski/Fotolia; **39** (T) Harry B. Lamb/ Shutterstock, (B) John Green/Cal Sport Media/Alamy Stock Photo; **40** (T) John Green/Cal Sport Media/ Alamy Stock Photo, (B) Monkey Business Images/ Shutterstock **73** Pk7comcastnet/Fotolia; **75** (T) Monkey Business Images/Shutterstock, (C) David M. Schrader/Shutterstock, (B) Jeff Kinsey/Shutterstock; **76** (Bkgrd) NavinTar/Shutterstock, MO_SES Premium/ Shutterstock, MO_SES Premium/Shutterstock **113** Christopher Dodge /Shutterstock; **115** (T) Joe Petro/Icon Sportswire/Getty Images, (B) Olekcii Mach/ Alamy Stock Photo; **116** (T) Image Source/REX/ Shutterstock, (B) Stockbroker/123RF **165** Ann Worthy/ Shutterstock; **167** (T) STLJB/Shutterstock, (C) Bmcent1/iStock/Getty Images, (B) Monkey Business Images/Shutterstock; **168** (Bkgrd) Ewastudio/123RF, Versus Studio/Shutterstock; **180** Ian Scott/Fotolia **205** Marques/Shutterstock; **207** (T) Stephanie Starr/ Alamy Stock Photo, (B) Hero Images Inc./Alamy Stock Photo; **208** (T) Compassionate Eye Foundation/ DigitalVision/Getty Images, (B) Spass/Shutterstock **249** Barbara Helgason/Fotolia; **251** (T) Africa Studio/ Shutterstock, (C) Tonyz20/Shutterstock, (B) Ermolaev Alexander/Shutterstock; **252** (Bkgrd) Oleg Mayorov/ Shutterstock, LightSecond/Shutterstock **285** Erni/ Shutterstock; **287** (T) Richard Thornton/Shutterstock,

(B) Hxdyl/Shutterstock; **288** (T) The Linke/E+/Getty Images, (B) David Grossman/Alamy Stock Photo; **308** Goodshoot/Getty Images; **310** Keren Su/Corbis/ Getty Images; **320** Rabbit75_fot/Fotolia **333** Arnold John Labrentz/ShutterStock; **335** (T) Judy Kennamer/ Shutterstock, (C) ESB Professional/Shutterstock, (B) Zuma Press, Inc./Alamy Stock Photo; **336** (Bkgrd) Monkey Business Images/Shutterstock, Faberr Ink/ Shutterstock, **346** (L) hotshotsworldwide/Fotolia, (C) Imagebroker/Alamy, (R) Imagebroker/Alamy; **348** John Luke/Index open; **356** David R. Frazier Photolibrary, Inc/Alamy **377** Sam D'Cruz/Fotolia; **379** (T) Stephen Van Horn/Shutterstock, (B) FS11/ Shutterstock; **380** (T) Shafera photo/Shutterstock, (B) Impact Photography/Shutterstock; **384** Palou/ Fotolia **405** Nancy Gill/ShutterStock; **407** (T) 123RF, (C) Light field studios/123RF, (B) Hurst Photo/ Shutterstock; **408** (Bkgrd) Igor Bulgarin/Shutterstock, Bartolomiej Pietrzyk/Shutterstock, Ianinas/ Shutterstock **433** B.G. Smith/Shutterstock; **435** (T) Andy Deitsch/Shutterstock, (B) Liunian/ Shutterstock; **436** (T) Holbox/Shutterstock, (B) Hannamariah/Shutterstock; **481** Cathy Keifer/ ShutterStock **483** (T) Cheryl Ann Quigley/ Shutterstock, (C) Niko Nomad/Shutterstock, (B) Mavadee/Shutterstock; **484** (Bkgrd) Photo.ua/ Shutterstock, India Picture/Shutterstock **531** (T) Iassedesignen/Shutterstock, (B) Rawpixel/ Shutterstock; **532** (T) 581356/Shutterstock, (B) S_oleg/Shutterstock; **547** (T) Photolibrary/Photos to go, (B) Simple Stock Shot; **548** (L) Ecopic/iStock/ Getty Images, (R) Simple Stock Shot; **555** (T) Stockdisc/Punch Stock, (C) Jupiter Images, (B) Getty Images **581** Amy Myers/Shutterstock; **583** (T) Rhona Wise/Epa/REX/Shutterstock, (C) Giocalde/ Shutterstock, (B) Anmbph/Shutterstock; **584** (Bkgrd) Peter Turner Photography/Shutterstock, (T) Peyker/ Shutterstock, (B) Michael Leslie/Shutterstock **609** Photocreo Bednarek/Fotolia; **611** (T) Margouillat Photo/Shutterstock, (B) Ksenia Palimski/Shutterstock; **612** (T) Topten22photo/Shutterstock, (B) Hola Images/Alamy Stock Photo